Youth Ministry That Transforms

A comprehensive analysis of the hopes, frustrations, and effectiveness of today's youth workers

Youth Ministry That Transforms

A comprehensive analysis of the hopes, frustrations, and effectiveness of today's youth workers

YOUTH
SPECIALTIES
ACADEMIC

A DIVISION OF HARPERCOLLINS*PUBLISHERS*

Merton Strommen

Karen E. Jones

Dave Rahn

Youth Ministry That Transforms: A comprehensive analysis of the hopes, frustrations, and effectiveness of today's youth workers

Copyright ©2001 by Karen E. Jones and Dave Rahn

Youth Specialties Books, 300 S. Pierce St., El Cajon, CA 92020, are published by Zondervan Publishing House, 5300 Patterson Ave. S.E., Grand Rapids, MI 49530.

Library of Congress Cataloging-in-Publication Data

Strommen, Merton P.
  Youth ministry that transforms: a comprehensive analysis of the hopes, frustrations, and effectiveness of today's youth workers / Merton P. Strommen, Karen Jones, David Rahn.
     p. cm.
  Includes bibliographical references and index.
  ISBN 0-310-23820-X
  1. Church work with youth. I. Jones, Karen, 1956- II. Rahn, Dave, 1954- III. Title.

BV4447 .S727 2001
259'.2—dc21

2001017723

Edited by Lorna McFarland Hartman and Tim McLaughlin
Cover and interior design by Razdezignz
Design of figures by Mary Fletcher and Paz Design Group

Printed in the United States of America

01 02 03 04 05 06 07 / / 10 9 8 7 6 5 4 3 2 1

Contents

Acknowledgements

Many people have been involved in this expansive project, without whom the research reported here and this book would not have been possible. To each of them we express our deepest gratitude.

We thank Lilly Endowment for their vision and generous funding of the *Study of Protestant Youth Ministers in America.* This book is the result of Lilly's decision to say yes to our request for money.

While we're speaking of money, we also thank The Huston Foundation. Late in the project they came through with additional funding so that we could employ the sophisticated statistical analyses that were needed to go beyond a polling effort.

A substantial amount of underwriting was also done by Huntington College through the Link Institute. We appreciate deeply Huntington's commitment to youth ministry excellence.

The study represented in this book was the initial brainchild of our former colleague, Mark Lamport. We are glad that he was able to launch this project, and sorry that he was not able to participate with us until it was completed.

We were blessed by the conscientious and gifted efforts of John Smith, an undergraduate student without whose administrative contributions this project would have been lost many times over. Thanks also to Carma Cummins, who preceded John in the capacity of research assistant.

A number of denominational and parachurch leaders helped us formulate our study in the earliest stages, including Kenneth Hill (African Methodist Episcopal), Doug Clay (Assembly of God), Sheryl Kujawa (Episcopal), Chuck Wysong (Evangelical Covenant), Steve Hudson (Evangelical Free), Kelly Chapman (Evangelical Lutheran), Edith Colden (National Baptist Convention), Gina Yeager (Presbyterian Church/USA), Richard Ross (Southern Baptist Convention), Steve Games (United Methodist), Bob Lonac (Young Life), Bill Muir (Youth for Christ), and Matt Nocas (Youth With a Mission). While a number of these persons are no longer serving their churches and organizations in a youth ministry capacity, their contribution to this project while still in office was essential.

Milo and Mark Brekke of Brekke Associates, Inc., combine a passion for matters of faith with a passion for analytical integrity. As our statistical consultants, they were with us throughout the project, and we are proud to have had the benefits of their analytic expertise. We thank them for their genuine partnership and patient coaching.

We also express our appreciation to the many people whose review of the manuscript helped make something so important more readable and meaningful. These persons include these grad students in the youth ministry program at Huntington College: Alan Mercer, Heather Heidelman, Patrick Rowland, Brian Kramer, Kent Yost, Shane Smith, and Mark Werner. They are each youth ministry veterans in some capacity, and we are grateful for their thoughtful interaction with the content in its formative stage. Others who have provided helpful feedback include Gary Newton (our Huntington College colleague and professor of educational ministries), Peter Strommen (Lutheran Bishop/ELCA), Monty Hipp (former national youth director, Assembly of God), Wes Black (professor, youth education, Southwestern Baptist Theological Seminary), Paul Hill (director, Center for Youth Ministries, Wartburg Seminary), Dick Hardel (director, Youth and Family Institute, Augsburg College), Richard Ross (youth consultant, LifeWay Ministries, Southern Baptist Convention), Mark H. Senter III (professor, Trinity Evangelical Divinity School), Bryce Smith (pastor, youth and family, Oak Grove Church), Richard Bimler (former national youth director, Lutheran Church/Missouri Synod), and Milo and Mark Brekke (research scientists, Brekke Associates, Inc.).

Merton Strommen

In 1996 a total of 7,500 youth ministers from all over the country assembled in Atlanta's Georgia Dome for the largest gathering of youth ministers to date. A sample of 2,130 was secured that represented full-time youth ministers from dozens of denominations and parachurch organizations. These people reflected a wide range of age, geography, and experience.

They were asked to tell, among other things—

- What they liked best about youth ministry.
- What particularly pleased them in their work with youth.
- What they found most encouraging or discouraging.
- Their biggest obstacle to an effective youth ministry.
- Their biggest present concern in youth ministry.

The answers they gave to 20 such questions identified them as a dedicated group, concerned about their youth, but troubled with a variety of perplexing issues. We took their responses and made them the primary source of items used in the study reported in this book—the first national sample survey of Protestant youth ministers ever carried out.

A research base for a new profession

The purpose of this study is to provide a research base for a budding profession...to present a conceptual model that describes a transformational youth ministry...to provide a basic text in youth ministry that supplies needed guidelines.

The title of this book—*Youth Ministry That Transforms*—expresses our threefold purpose:

- To transform youth ministries that have been heading in the wrong direction.
- To help youth ministries become more effective in transforming youths.
- To provide the basis for transforming the training and preparation of youth ministers.

This overall purpose is a serious one, and for good reason. Youth ministers today are being asked to carry out one of the most important ministries in the church: the task of being Godbearers to an age group that is struggling to establish a Christian identity. Parents and congregational leaders expect them to bring most of their youth into a living fellowship with Jesus Christ.

This ministry of high expectations is made more difficult because it is being carried out in a rapidly changing world—a world, furthermore, that is neither kind to youths nor gracious to youth ministers. Youth ministry is very difficult work, far more difficult than parents and congregational leaders realize. The pressures on a youth minister are enormous, and these pressures are ones for which few have been adequately prepared.

This book's subject is serious for another reason: the church *must* give special attention to the health of this profession. If young people are not being helped into a living and serving relationship with Jesus Christ, what future does the church have? That is why the authors are convinced that an effective youth ministry is one of the most important endeavors of the church, outranked only by the ministry of transferring back to parents the responsibility for passing on the faith.

God's call to all of us is that we become a missional church—a church that seeks to reach all youth in a community, including those whose values are cluttered and twisted by media and their peer group. Conscious of this call, youth ministers find themselves wrestling with this question: *How as God's partner do I reach these young people with the gospel?* It's not an easy question. Ministries that reached youth in previous years may not be effective today.

The authors have a special interest in seeing that these findings are used to increase the effectiveness of the youth ministry profession—an interest that grows out of a special sense of call that we have for service in this strategic ministry. For each of us, youth ministry has become more than a profession—it has become a lifetime addiction. And because we are deeply involved in this work, we deeply desire that the findings of this study be thoughtfully studied, discussed, and implemented.

Why this is a critical study

Why is this study an important one for pastors, professional youth leaders, professors of youth ministry, youth ministers, and volunteer youth leaders?

- Because it alerts us to the concerns of youth ministers—concerns that cause many leave to leave this profession during their early years of service.
- Because it draws attention to the difficulties faced by youth min-

isters serving in small congregations.

- Because it identifies the pervasive influence of factors like the following on a youth minister's effectiveness: denominational affiliation, size of youth group, theological stance, approach to youth work, extent of training, and years spent as a youth minister.
- Because it shows the kind of academic preparation and in-service training that is especially needed for success and professional growth.
- Because it identifies areas of notable strengths and weaknesses that would not be recognized except through the kind of comparisons made in this study.
- Because it identifies the important role of a congregation in sponsoring an effective youth ministry—support a congregation must give, ownership it must take.
- Because it presents the elements needed for a youth ministry that transforms.

Background to the study: Understanding our sample, research, and model

Familiarity with three aspects of the study is critical to fully understanding it: the uniqueness of our *sample*, the kind of *research* that we have used to make analyses and report findings, and the conceptual *model* that provides the outline for this book and gives an overview of what you will find.

The sample that supplied the information

The information in this book is based on the responses of 2,416 youth ministers to a 260-item paper-and-pencil survey. The respondents were drawn randomly in 1998 from lists of full-time youth ministers supplied by 11 denominational offices and two parachurch youth groups. Figure I.1 depicts nine categories of respondents who participated in the study.

Due to several small samples (a couple of them *very* small) and due to similarity in mission or religious culture, certain groups were combined for analytic purposes: Assembly of God and Youth With a Mission; Presbyterian Church (U.S.A.) and National Baptist Convention (U.S.A.); Evangelical Covenant, Evangelical Free, and Independent Fundamentalist Churches of America; and Young Life and Youth for Christ. These combinations yielded nine "denominational families," which are used for *denominational group comparisons* throughout the book.

The groups depicted in Figure I.1 represent various religious cultures. Each has been uniquely shaped by its history and theology. But

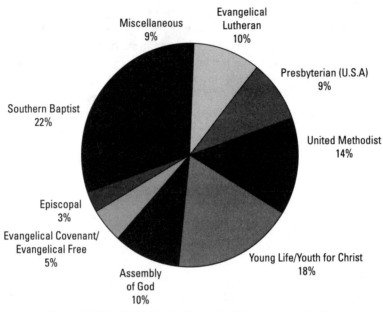

Figure I.1 Participants by denomination or organization

when these denominational groups are combined into a composite sample, we arrive at a fairly accurate picture of the variety of U.S. youth ministers.

In the chapters that follow, you will see findings organized by the same denominations or national youth organizations listed in figure I.1. As you will discover, these comparisons result in some provocative findings—comparisons that will disappoint some and encourage others. They serve to convincingly demonstrate that a religious culture does indeed have a shaping influence on how its youth ministers live out their sense of call.

There is another way to describe our sample—by classifying participants on the basis of their tenure, or the number of years they have served as youth ministers. Figure I.2 illustrates that our sample ranges from novitiates—those that have been serving for three years or less (14 percent)—to tried-and-true veterans—youth ministers who have served for 16 years or more (22 percent).

It is clear from figure I.2 that the youth ministers in our sample represent a wide range of experience—a very significant point, because the longer one serves in this position, the more one has probably learned, the more effective one's youth leadership has likely become, and the more valuable one's opinion about youth ministry is.

As documented in chapter nine, those who have served for 16 years or more perceive themselves as the most competent in job performance, in confident leadership, in effective relationships with youth, in theo-

Figure I.2 How five items focus on time conflict

logical grounding, in developing adult volunteers, in being motivated by God's calling, and in a creative response to the youth culture. Conclusion? Years of service make a great deal of difference. The longer-serving youth workers also tend to be serving in the largest churches and with the largest youth groups

Those who perceive themselves to have the least competence in the qualities identified above are youth ministers who have served three years or less. Tenure makes a big difference not only in what is learned over the years, but in a natural screening process: that is, those less effective drop out, leaving more able persons to continue serving in the profession.

It is possible that our sample is slanted towards *career* youth ministers—those with considerable experience and presumably some success. We say *success* because these respondents would not have remained in this stressful profession for over 16 years if they had not been seeing the lives of their youths transformed by the power of the Holy Spirit. So if this sample *is* slanted towards career youth ministers, we believe that is good—for it means that these better informed and more knowledgeable youth ministers have given us information that is especially worth noting.

It needs to be stated that the percentages given in figure I.2 may not describe the number of youth ministers currently serving in each category of experience—for some chosen in our random sample did not participate in the study. These nonrespondents may well have included those youth ministers who were struggling, frustrated, or otherwise overwhelmed by the demands of their job—and who consequently viewed our invitation to fill out the survey as simply another distraction. Hence they did not participate.

By refusing to participate, nonrespondents may have reduced the percentage of those serving less than three years. We can venture this hypothesis because our data show that this less-than-three-years tenure group is the most stressed by their job, the ones experiencing the greatest difficulty, and the ones most tempted to leave the profession.

Tenure is not the only variable associated with striking differences between youth ministers. Attendance at their youth meetings makes a big difference, as does Sunday morning worship service attendance, the educational level of the youth minister, and whether or not one is seminary trained. It makes a difference, too, if one's theological orientation is conservative or liberal, one's community large or small, or one's approach to youths is primarily entertainment or missional.

Comparisons will be made between youth ministers grouped according to these variables, then we will explore the findings—many of which are provocative and even disturbing.

The type of research used in this study

Two different kinds of research can be used in carrying out a study such as this. One is polling, well known because of its use in estimating the percentage of people who will vote for a certain presidential candidate, or in determining how people feel about specific issues.

If the sample used in polling efforts is truly random and large enough (e.g., 2,000), a fairly accurate estimate can be gained of how many would vote for a certain person in a national election. But the information remains valid only for a short time; it can change markedly within months.

If a poll is to be accurate, it must have the participation of *all* the people drawn into the random sample. If only a low percentage of the sample participates, the results of such a poll when generalized to a national population can be very misleading.

The second kind of research—namely, the kind used in this study (and also the kind used in my book *Five Cries of Youth*)—goes a step beyond polling. Like polling, it gains its survey information from a national random sample. But it goes an important step further in how the data are analyzed and reported: rather than reporting data based on single items of unknown and usually low reliability, clusters of intercorrelated items are derived that can provide scores with a known and much higher reliability. This approach makes it possible to identify the conceptual structure underlying the survey answers of respondents and to make fairly precise comparisons between groups.

Here is what this means:

Searching for the underlying structure
When the 2,416 youth ministers thoughtfully responded to 243 items (17 of the 260 were demographic and biographical items), they responded to scattered but conceptually related sets of items in the same way.

For example, those who gave a high rating to one item in a scattered set of five or six items tended to give a high rating to *all* the items in the set. Simultaneously, those who gave a low rating to one item also tended to give a low rating to the other items constituting the same set. They did this because certain concepts of youth ministry are ingrained in their thinking; hence, they answered the items in ways that reflected their thinking. This means there were patterns of response as a result of the way they answered the 243 items.

We did not form clusters of items on the basis of item content, or any other item characteristic, such as logical interrelatedness. Rather we used three standard mathematical procedures for identifying interrelated items—based on patterns in the way the youth ministers responded to items in the survey (see Appendix A for details). These analyses identified 48 such patterns or clusters of items. (See Link Institute's Web site—www.linkinstitute.com—for tables supplying the technical information about each of these 48 clusters.)

When we looked at each of these 48 clusters, we could easily identify the concept that served as a skewer for the items—that is, the concept of ministry being held by the 2,416 youth ministers. These resulting clusters of items serve as building blocks for the structure that underlies the entire book. An example of a cluster is illustrated in figure I.3 (the items in this example are described in chapter two, which considers the first cluster).

Figure I.3—Elements in a transformational youth ministry

We scored each cluster of items by assigning a value to each of its item responses, then averaging them. The resulting scores serve as measures of the concept described by the items. As measures, these cluster scores are far superior in reliability to single items, such as those that are used in typical polling efforts.

Then our analytic specialists, Mark and Milo Brekke of Brekke Associates, Inc., subjected these cluster scores to what is known as *second-order factor analysis*, which grouped the cluster scores into families that made eminent sense.

True, the analysis was guided by *type* of item (e.g., items assessing the respondents' concerns, items assessing what training the respondents desired), but the analysis was also guided by how youth ministers organize their thinking about ministry: they unconsciously reflected their frame of reference in the consistency with which they answered certain sets or clusters of items. *By detecting these unconsciously communicated dimensions of the respondents' thinking, the second-order factor analysis was able to establish seven distinct families that form the structure of this study and provide the outline for this book.*

We believe these families of item clusters describe the thinking of today's youth ministers. Furthermore, it is a structure that is not likely to change for many years. When I carried out trend analyses on the structure underlying my *Five Cries of Youth,* I found no change after 15 years in four of the five cries, and only a slight change in the fifth cry. (The structure underlying this study will be identified later in this introduction.)

Using cluster scores to make group comparisons

As you might assume, the cluster scores (based on the responses of the 2,416 youth ministers), range from low to high—and in so doing, usually form distributions of scores that variously approximate a normal distribution.

Because we wanted to make group comparisons that are precise, we decided to adopt the use of standard scores. Standard scores are far superior to percentiles, which, like rubber bands, vary in size of interval according to where they appear in a distribution.

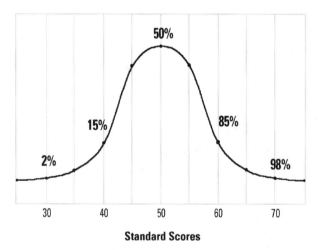

Standard Scores

Figure I.4—How a distribution of cluster scores is measured

In this method of scoring, 50 is always the average score, and the distance between scores (such as between 40 and 45, or between 50 and

55) is always the same (see Appendix A for further explanation). Because standard scores are precise, we can make precise comparisons. In this study, we limited our consideration to those differences that could have occurred by chance only once in a hundred times. Such differences between groups are three standard scores or more. With this as a high standard, differences between groups can be regarded not only as having statistical significance, but also practical significance.

In the chapters that follow, we will compare groups to see if their score distributions vary significantly from each other. For example, and as you will note in figure I.5, a certain group (such as a denomination) may have many higher scores and fewer lower scores than typifies the rest. As a result its overall average score may be 54. That means it is four standard scores above the mean of 50—a very significant difference.

Another group (again, a denomination) may have more who scored lower on the same measure and fewer who achieved higher scores. As a result this denomination may have an average score of not more than 46. The difference between the two denominations is actually 8 standard scores—again, a highly significant difference.

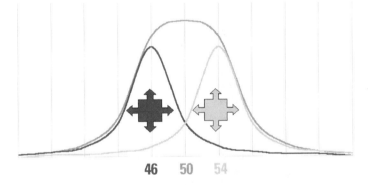

Average Score for Each Distribution

Figure I.5—How comparisons are made between groups

Unlike typical polling, this kind of research supplies information that is not as dependent upon a 100 percent response from those chosen in the sample as is information from single items alone. The cluster structure—that is, the underlying conceptual structure—is likely to be the same even when all do not choose to participate.

It is well to recognize, however, that the findings of research presented in this book are no more than an approximation of reality. We do not present the results, however carefully secured they are, as representing ultimate truth. Research findings in the social sciences never are. They are nothing more than an extension of our senses—a way to see more clearly what we intuit or observe in real life.

The value of this study is that it provides an enormous amount of never-before-available information about youth ministers. This information can provide the grist for animated discussions and, ultimately, the basis for taking youth ministry in new and needful directions.

A conceptual model for youth ministry that transforms

The information emerging from this study has much to say about a transformational youth ministry. Because the rich resource of documentation tends to be overwhelming in its quantity, we have organized the data using a conceptual model.

The model is based on how cluster and factor analyses organized the data. We don't give these statistical techniques credit for what you see, however—the techniques were able to identify only what respondents had in their minds and made evident when answering the items in the survey.

The survey they answered was entitled "A Study of Protestant Youth Ministers in America," which asked respondents to give answers to 243 items in six sections:

- Youth Ministry Concerns
- Evaluating Your Youths
- Evaluating Your Youth Ministry
- How I View My Leadership
- Organizational Issues
- Desired Professional Growth

Respondents were also asked to respond to 17 demographic and biographic items—important details that made it possible to compare groups by variables such as denomination, youth group size, seminary training, church attendance, years of service, community size, and the like.

As described earlier, the statistical analyses of answers given by these 2,416 youth ministers to 243 items showed that there was an underlying structure of factors to the answers they gave. These factors became the building blocks for our conceptual model. When put together to form the model reflected in figure I.6, you will see that it represents the wisdom of our respondents. It gives a good description of the important elements in a transformational youth ministry.

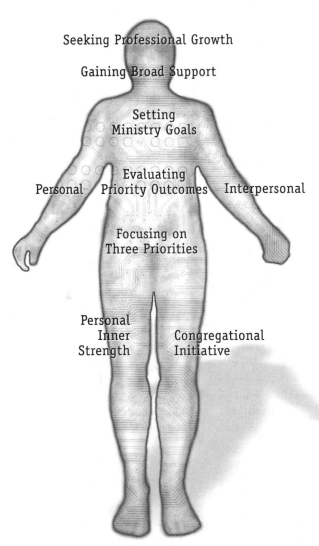

Seeking Professional Growth

Gaining Broad Support

Setting
Ministry Goals

Evaluating
Personal   Priority Outcomes   Interpersonal

Focusing on
Three Priorities

Personal
Inner   Congregational
Strength   Initiative

Figure I.6—The conceptual model with no highlighting

At the beginning of each chapter, you will see this conceptual model drawn as a youth worker with the element highlighted that is discussed in that chapter. Here's a brief overview of what these chapters contain.

CHAPTER 1
A Recent Invention: The Profession of Youth Ministry identifies the foundation for today's youth ministry by briefly tracing the history of how the profession got started...how youth work began under the leadership of men serving in national offices...and how it was not until 1937 that we have the first record of a youth minister being hired to serve a local congregation.

Congregational Initiative: To Erase Six Concerns Troubling Youth Ministers tells why congregational initiative is an absolute must for a transformational youth ministry. It is foundational that congregational leaders assume responsibility for mitigating or eliminating six concerns that have sufficient power to pressure a youth minister out of the profession. Taking initiative in ways described by this chapter helps create a healthier congregation.

Here are the six concerns that emerged in the research:
- Time conflict between job demands and personal needs.
- Time conflict between administrative duties and the need for youth contact.
- A prevailing disconnect between youth and the church to which they belong.
- A disinterested and apathetic youth group.
- A salary inadequate to support a family plus a youth budget too spare for needed program activities.
- A subtle lack of respect or personal support for the position of youth minister.

Of the six concerns, the most pervasive and widely felt is the first—a continuing struggle for youth ministers to balance their youth ministry job with their personal life. Few people in a congregation understand the unique demands that are placed on a conscientious youth minister. Few realize that the job demands more than time allows. Therefore thoughtful assistance from the congregation is required.

Descriptions identifying the extent to which these six are troubling concerns can be found in this chapter, along with suggestions as to what congregations can do to address each concern.

Personal Inner Strength: To Offset Six Concerns Debilitating Youth Ministers. A youth ministry needs two muscular legs to get off to a running start: *congregational initiative* and the youth minister's *personal inner strength*. This chapter deals with the personal inner strength that youth ministers must bring to the task, another foundational aspect of a transformational youth ministry.

Youth ministers must assume responsibility for undergirding all that they do with the resources of God. Unless this foundational action is observed, a spiritual fatigue can overwhelm youth ministers, making them vulnerable to self-destruction. This fatigue is expressed in a variety of ways and shows its effects in personal feelings identified in the study.

Through their pattern of responses, youth ministers identified six such personal concerns—six perils that can sink a career. Furthermore, they are problems that few ministers are likely to admit in public.

- Feelings of personal inadequacy
- Strained family relationships
- A growing loss of confidence
- Feeling unqualified for the job
- Disorganized in one's work habits
- Burnout

At the top of the list are feelings of personal inadequacy. The second most intense worry is strained family relations: four out of five in the study are married, and of these a significant number feel their family gets only the leftovers of a youth minister's time. This precipitates tension and creates a troublesome issue for both youth minister and spouse.

The chapter discusses these issues in detail and identifies what a youth minister might do when seeking to cope with them. It also shows that youth ministers serving youth groups that number less than 40 and those serving for less than three years are most vulnerable to the concerns discussed in this chapter.

CHAPTER 4

Focusing on Three Top Ministry Priorities identifies three commanding priorities that are considered to be the most important aspects of a transformational youth ministry. These three priorities form the basic agenda for a youth minister:

- A clearly stated mission statement
- The training of volunteer leaders
- The spiritual development of youth

Youth ministers deemed this last priority—the spiritual development of youth—as the most compelling of the three, the top priority of the 2,416 respondents. (It is also the top priority in a parallel Delphi National Study that involved college professors of youth ministry.) Considerable (and provocative) variation occurs among youth ministers when they are grouped according to denomination. Youth ministers of some denominations accord greater importance to the spiritual development of their youth than others. The same is true for youth ministers grouped on the basis of theological orientation or approach to youth work.

Seventy percent of respondents consider the training of volunteer leaders to be of high importance, yet sadly admit to a marked discrepancy between declared importance and their degree of accomplishment.

This chapter presents the evidence and discusses the differences among ministry priorities that appear when comparisons are made on the basis of denomination, theological orientation, and approach to youth work.

Evaluating Priority Outcomes: An Example. At appropriate times one must ask evaluative questions: "What are we achieving?...What changes do we see in the spiritual development of our youths, their sense of ownership, and the health of family relationships?...What changes are we seeing in the attitudes of youths, their interest, their service involvement, and their public witness?"

So chapters five, six, and seven focus on determining how well the three priorities explained in chapter four are being achieved, a task basic in a transformational youth ministry.

Chapter five presents an example of evaluation by reviewing a 1980 study, from which we can see how the objectives of denominational leaders can mute the command of Christ to "go and make disciples." The year 1980 marks a low and discouraging point in the history of youth work, due largely to the dismantling of national youth organizations and, in some denominations, to the clouding of what had been the historic Christian mission of youth organizations.

Evaluating Priority Outcomes: What Is Youth Ministry Achieving Today? focuses on what youth ministry is achieving today. Fortunately, the findings show that more is being achieved today than was reported for 1980. Progress is seen in the evaluations that the youth ministers give for these three coveted outcomes:

- The spiritual development of youth
- Youth coming to own their ministry
- Strengthened family relationships

Marked differences appear, however, in how well these outcomes are perceived as being achieved. These differences appear when youth ministers are grouped on the basis of denomination, size youth group, size of congregation, theological orientation, and approach to youth work.

An emerging frontier in youth ministry is family ministry. While ranking it high in importance, few youth ministers evaluate themselves as having done well in strengthening family relationships. But here again the respondents' denominational affiliation and years of experience in the field make a difference in their success at family ministry.

CHAPTER 7

Evaluating Priority Outcomes: Youth Response and Witness focuses on youth's responses:

- Their joyous attitudes of respect and love
- Their demonstration of interest

- Their involvement in serving church and community
- Their public witness and ministry

In this evaluation notable differences appear on the basis of denomination, years in the ministry, size of youth group, size of congregation, theological orientation, and approach to youth work. There is no question but that an evaluation of youth's responses by their youth minister is colored by their setting and affiliation. That is, it makes a difference *where* one works.

CHAPTER 8

Setting Ministry Goals: Personal and Interpersonal describes ten different aspects of youth ministry leadership, or ministry goals, that contribute to a minister's sense of satisfaction in the profession. These ten fall into two natural categories: *personal growth* and *interpersonal relationships*.

Personal-growth goals relate to job performance, leadership, cultural sensitivity, theological grounding, and commitment to specialized training. This chapter identifies the importance youth ministers place on each of these personal goals.

Interpersonal-relationship goals determine the degree to which professional youth ministers enjoy the rewards of relational ministry. This chapter reveals the degree to which youth ministers serve out of a sense of calling and live out that calling in a relationship with youth, parents, volunteer leaders, and ministry peers.

CHAPTER 9

Setting Ministry Goals: Significant Goal Modifiers explores the astounding differences between groups of youth ministers when it comes to achieving the professional ministry goals identified in chapter eight. Especially significant are the differences that appear—
- Between youth ministers who serve large youth groups and those who serve small ones.
- Between those who have received seminary training and those who have received none at all.
- Between those serving in churches where Sunday morning audiences are large, and those in churches whose worship services are small.

Chapter nine focuses on these significant goal modifiers and tries to understand why there are such differences in the extent to which goals are being achieved in personal growth and interpersonal relationships.

CHAPTER 10

Gaining Broad Support: Organizational Climate. Because youth ministry does not happen in a vacuum, the youth minister's sense of personal fulfillment and perception of effectiveness are greatly affected by the quality of support and the amount of affirmation given by a church's leadership and congregation.

Do youth ministers receive the support they need? Do they feel valued and respected? Are their churches vibrant communities of faith which welcome innovation and respect divergent thinking? Are their ministries free from conflict and tension?

Chapter ten gives answers to these and other questions about organizational climate. As might be expected, the responses are not uniform for all groups; significant differences appear between groups of youth ministers in the degree to which they perceive support.

CHAPTER 11

Gaining Broad Support: Shared Ownership. To the question *Whose responsibility is it to minister to the young people in this community?* our study replies with this conclusion: the church must own the task. Chapter eleven identifies three important aspects of shared ownership:

- Strong congregational support
- Helping parents minister to their teenage children
- Giving youth ownership of the ministry

These three clusters emerged from the apparent desire of youth ministers to see these facets of ownership manifested in their youth ministry. Youth ministers from mainline denominations give these items the highest ratings of importance, indicating their perception that shared ownership is an absolute imperative—and in so doing, reflect an appreciation for a congregationally oriented faith (as opposed to an individualistic faith).

CHAPTER 12

Seeking Professional Growth: Desired Training focuses on the issue of training for professional growth. In a day when there are several emerging approaches to training youth ministers, this report by 2,416 youth ministers identifies what they feel is needed.

Youth ministers are aware of the fact that their task exceeds their capabilities. This chapter identifies eight aspects of training deemed necessary to meet developmental needs:

- Training in communicating biblical and life-changing truth
- Understanding adolescent development leading to effective counseling
- Arriving at effective and personally fulfilling ministry strategies
- Gaining Biblical knowledge and pastoral ministry skills
- Gaining knowledge of family development and parental training skills

- Training in administration and management
- Having specific opportunities to gain new ideas
- Having opportunities for mentoring relationships and peers

It is apparent that among these youth ministers, *practical* knowledge is valued more than *cognitive* knowledge. Furthermore, those most hungry for professional growth are the least experienced and those with the least education.

The three most universally agreed-upon training needs are—

- Gaining new ideas
- Learning how to nurture youth in their spiritual development
- Enjoying close and challenging staff relationships

The chapter ends with a focus on developing a professional development plan—one that we hope will be genuinely transformational for the practice of youth ministry.

Seeking Professional Growth

Gaining Broad Support

Setting
Ministry Goals

Evaluating
Personal   Priority Outcomes   Interpersonal

Focusing on
Three Priorities

Personal
Inner   Congregational
Strength   Initiative

Chapter 1

A Recent Invention: The Profession of Youth Ministry
Merton Strommen

It may seem strange to call youth ministry a recent invention. After all, efforts to serve youth have been with us for a long time.

One can go back to 1524 and hear Martin Luther addressing the civil magistrates of all the cities of Germany, saying, "I pray all of you for the sake of God and of youth, not to think slightingly of educational problems. For it is a serious and great matter, at the heart of Christ and all mankind, that we help and advise the young people."[1]

The roots of American youth work

Within our own country we can go back to 1724 when the devout and zealous Cotton Mather, pastor to colonial Americans, organized societies to sustain the faith of young people. It was a time, according to historian Frank Otis, when impurity, infidelity, and intemperance were rife. At the funeral of pastor's widow Mrs. Mary Norton, for instance, mourners consumed 51 gallons of wine.

Another case in point: in his Fast Day sermon, a colonial pastor lamented, "Vast numbers, young and old, male and female, are given to intemperance, so it is a common thing to see drunken women as well as drunken men."[2]

In such a setting Cotton Mather published the pamphlet "Proposals for the Revival of Dying Religion," whose preamble included—

> **We, whose names are underwritten, having by the grace of God been awakened in our youths to a serious concern about the things of our everlasting peace, and to an earnest desire suitably and religiously 'to remember our Creator in the days of our youth" and to give our hearts into the service of God through our Lord Jesus Christ, do covenant and agree together.**[3]

Societies that formed as a result of Mather's proposals met weekly for prayer, Bible study, and singing. Mather noted that these societies "proved to be strong engines to uphold godliness." He also observed, however, that these societies "were frowned on by the Puritan fathers, who viewed them as a dangerous innovation."[4]

In September 1860 an incident of historical importance in the development of youth societies occurred: a young people's prayer meeting was formed in Brooklyn's Lafayette Avenue Presbyterian Church. Its format, according to its pastor, Theodore Cuyler, was the highly successful prayer-meeting approach of the YMCA—the example and model Cuyler needed for his congregation. When 40 youth and young adults signed the constitution he had developed, they agreed that the purpose of their society should be the conversion of souls, the development of Christian character, and the training of new converts in religious work. Significantly, this statement of purpose later found its way into the constitutions of youth societies organized by most of the principal denominations.[5]

Other congregations soon imitated Lafayette Avenue Presbyterian Church's weekly-prayer-meeting approach. It was not long until a Young People's Association had been formed, which linked these congregational youth organizations together.

The legacy of Christian Endeavor

This same prayer-meeting approach powerfully influenced Dr. Francis Clark when he established his Christian Endeavor society in 1881.[6] Clark developed an organizational model for the youth of his congregation—one that was both highly structured and demanding. This model proved to be so successful in gaining members and developing intense loyalties that most church bodies soon adopted it. Central to his organizational plan was a Christian Endeavor Society pledge that was to be taken by all members (although some denominations chose not to adopt it):

> **Trusting in the Lord Jesus Christ for strength, I promise Him that I will strive to do whatever He would like to have me do; that I will make it a rule of my life to pray, and to read the Bible every day, and to support my own church in every way, especially by attending all her regular Sunday and midweek services, unless prevented by some reason which I can conscientiously give to my Savior, and that, just so far as I know how, throughout my whole life, I will endeavor to lead a Christian life.**
>
> **As an active member, I promise to be true to all my duties, to be present at, and to take part, aside from singing, in every Christian Endeavor prayer meeting, unless hindered by some reason which I**

can conscientiously give to my Lord and Master. If obliged to be absent from the monthly consecration meeting of the society I will, if possible, send at least a verse of scripture to be read in response to my name at the roll-call.[7]

It is amazing that this pledge, required in all Christian Endeavor Societies, did not deter but rather contributed to the organization's attractiveness. Clark's Societies sprang up all over the U.S. Endeavor societies were established in the Navy, in prisons, in schools, in police stations, and on mission fields.[8]

It is difficult to overstate how popular the Christian Endeavor approach made youth work. During the 1890s national conventions were held in Boston, Cleveland, Chattanooga, Toronto, and Indianapolis. The largest Christian Endeavor convention was held in Boston in 1895, when 56,000 people attended.[9] These conventions became the model for ones held later by denominational youth organizations.

Although the youth groups in most of the Protestant denominations became affiliated with the Society of Christian Endeavor and as affiliates adopted its general format, some denominations eventually organized their *own* youth organizations: the Epworth League, the Walther League, and the Luther League, to name a few.

Southern Baptists, for example, were unsatisfied with the Christian Endeavor approach, citing its failure to link young people with the church. They feared a loss of loyalty among their own youth and a lack of affiliation with the denomination. So they organized and sponsored their own youth groups. The first to be formed in 1884 was called the "Baptist Young People's Union," a youth organization that was officially recognized and established as a denominational organization in 1893.[10]

Another group that chose not to affiliate with the Society of Christian Endeavor was the Lutherans. Their first successful attempt to organize young people's work in any Lutheran congregation was in 1851, when 70 young men in a Lutheran congregation formed a society that became a model for other groups. These societies officially organized in 1893 as the Walther League, for the declared purpose of "keeping young people in the true Lutheran Church."[11] The Luther League and Epworth Leagues were similarly formed.

Separate and deeply denominational though these organizations were, it was Christian Endeavor that had inspired their creation.

The first professional youth leaders

It is difficult to nail down exactly when professionals emerged on the scene to give full-time attention to youth work. We do know that in 1915 a Protestant church body employed a worker to devote full time to youth work on a denominational level—and the hiring of other professional leaders on a denominational level soon followed.[12] The Young People's Luther League hired its first full-time field secretary in 1919, and the Walther League hired its first full-time executive secretary in 1920.[13]

Denominational professionals

Professional leaders on the denominational level preceded the advent of youth ministers serving congregations. Some of these professionals were hired by a department of religious education, others by the denomination's youth organization, and some by their denomination's youth department. In many cases these leaders (almost always men) were financed by "Youth Sunday" offerings and contributions made by the youth themselves.

Any help a congregation needed for its youth program came from the denomination's headquarters in the form of services provided by the professional executives and their staff. These people supplied program materials, resources, and training in conducting meetings and running a youth organization. These extensive services were highly appreciated by churches.

Youth functioning as members of a league or society assumed the responsibility of electing their own officers and secretaries. The ones they elected were given several days of training at denominational workshops on how to carry out their role and promote the purposes of their youth organization. These youth, ranging in age from 13 to 22, owned their youth organization—it was theirs, and they ran it with the assistance of adult advisers.

I joined a professional staff of denominational youth leaders in 1944 and came to know the unique camaraderie that characterized these leaders. We felt part of history in launching a much-needed frontier activity. I found these leaders to be bright, articulate, creative, and dedicated churchmen eager to serve their Lord and church. We sought to learn from each other, keenly aware of the fact that we were blazing new trails and writing the books on youth work.

The golden years

By the 1950s professional staffs in most denominations had expanded considerably, and their services to congregations were now enjoying both a welcome and wide commendation. These were the golden years in congregational youth work. The Evangelical Lutheran Church in America (one of seven different Lutheran bodies) during the 1950s, for example, had six professional staff in its home office and seven regional youth directors out in the field assisting congregations.

Other denominations had as many as 15 professionals, and most had at least five to ten such people. The most impressive array of such specialists were found in the Southern Baptist Convention, whose national youth ministry staff early totaled 50 professionals.[14] These professional youth directors came to be viewed quite favorably in their respective denominations.

When the Lutheran World Federation held its assembly in Minneapolis in 1957, a parade of church leaders was held down Nicollet Avenue, the principal avenue that wound its way through the business district. The significance that youth work held in that denomination was demonstrated in the parade: among the assembly's notables waving to the crowd that filled the sidewalks were seven convertibles with seven Lutheran youth directors. This would not be likely to happen today.

A milestone of Protestant youth work was the youth ministry evaluation in 1955, conducted by the Committee on Youth Work of the National Council of Churches. Under the leadership of Helen Spaulding, director of Christian Education Research, this national survey identified how youth of seventeen participating denominations felt about their youth program. Randomly selected youth and young adults in 188 congregations were interviewed by denominational youth directors and professors of church colleges and seminaries.

It is interesting how apparently positively the respondents were about church at a time when there were hardly any paid congregational youth ministers. When asked "Is the church a really vital factor in your life?" 93 percent of the active youth and 73 percent of the inactive youth said yes—this, when no main-line congregations reported having a youth minister. The only professional youth leaders (aside from pastors) found in these 188 randomly selected congregations were directors of Christian education—and only 3 percent of the congregations were found to have had such professional help.[15]

Parachurch professionals

During this same period—the 1940s and '50s—leaders of parachurch groups began appearing on the scene.

- **Young Life**. Jim Rayburn launched Young Life in 1941 as a leader-centered and evangelism-focused youth approach. Having just graduated from seminary, Rayburn shaped his approach to young people while serving as a seminarian youth minister at Gainesville (Texas) Presbyterian Church from 1938 until 1941. As youth evangelist he had become chiefly interested in reaching those untouched by any knowledge of Christ—"those youth that stayed carefully and stubbornly away from churches."[16] By 1964 there were over 400 of his Young Life clubs in existence.[17]

- **Youth for Christ.** Jack Hamilton was this organization's first full-time leader of club-oriented youth ministry. Starting in 1946, the high-energy Hamilton reported 700 clubs that had been established by 1951.[18] When a study's disconcerting results showed that the very people the organization claimed to reach were remaining outside the program's influence, a shift in philosophy of ministry was introduced and with it a change in name: Campus Life.

- **Youth With a Mission.** Founded by Loren Cunningham in 1960, YWAM soon had 5,000 short-term missionaries and 887 North American full-time personnel overseas, operating out of 90 centers established as separate corporations. Young people were not the target of this mission, but its evangelists.[19]

These and other parachurch clubs—such as Fellowship of Christian Athletes—differed radically from church-oriented groups in the nature of their leadership: instead of being served by pastors and congregational lay adults, the parachurch organizations or clubs depended on leaders whom the organization itself trained and sent out.

The exact figures of those who served in the early years as full-time workers with youth are not available because careful records were not kept. But we do know that by 1970 Youth for Christ and Young Life organizations each employed over 1,000 staff members.[20] When staffs of several other parachurch organizations are added, one finds the numbers mounting impressively.

The beginnings of a struggling youth profession

The Third Baptist Church of St. Louis gives us the earliest record of a full-time youth minister. In 1937 this church had decided they needed a youth worker to serve them full-time.[21]

From the mid-1950s to around 1970, the position of "youth pastor" was becoming established as an important member of the pastoral staff in evangelical churches. Churches typically employed laypersons to work with groups of high school students. And since no real training was available, many of these youth leaders simply imitated what they had seen happening in parachurch club programs.[22]

By 1980 there were around a thousand ministers of youth serving in Southern Baptist congregations. When other professional church staff members who had youth ministry assignments in their job description were included, the figure swelled to over 8,000 men and women in youth ministry-related staff positions by 1980. No other denomination came close in terms of numbers involved in youth ministry.[23]

Within the Roman Catholic Church the position of youth ministry represents the newest professional ministry. When a national study was made in 1990 of parishes randomly selected from all 13 National Catholic Conference Bishops regions, a small but significant sample of youth ministers appeared in the sample:

- Half were young men whose future in the ministry seemed to be very limited.
- Nearly half were thirty years old or younger.
- Nearly 85 percent were under forty years old.
- Nearly two-thirds were single.
- 85 percent were college graduates; a third had master's degrees.[24]

With the blossoming of youth ministry as a profession from the 1960s through the 1990s, colleges and seminaries encouraged the trend with course offerings. (The first known full-time "professor of youth education" was Phillip Harris, hired in 1949 at Southwestern Baptist Theological Seminary.[25]) Yet it's been only during the last two decades that most church colleges and seminaries have become serious about equipping these youth workers for their daunting task. Most have had to learn through trial and error. Veteran and highly successful youth minister Doug Fields remembers well how unprepared he was for his first years as a youth minister.

> **During my first years in youth ministry, I remember standing in front of junior high students and basking in their looks of anticipation. I was young, fun, energetic, and well liked. The faces said, *This is going to be good.***
>
> **But only a few years later, when things weren't going as well, I saw a different look—one that said, *This better be good.* Because I lacked knowledge and skills, I thought the students didn't like me anymore. Their enthusiasm waned, attendance dropped, volunteers found other church ministries to which they could devote their time, and our programs changed every time I spied on another youth ministry. Parents as well as church elders questioned what was happening, and I accepted all the problems as my fault.**
>
> **I constantly looked over my shoulder to see if other people were thinking what I was thinking—**

that maybe I wasn't the right person for youth ministry despite my having the necessary goods.

Even though I worked exhausting hours, the job wasn't getting done the way everyone seemed to want. Previously unspoken expectations surfaced, and they fueled my workaholic personality to fix everything, even though I couldn't specifically identify the problems. My desire for doing ministry had long moved from pleasing God to appeasing people. I wanted to be liked by everyone.[26]

Discontent, rapid turnover, and this study

Fields makes it abundantly clear how easily youth workers, untrained and discouraged, would find the task too demanding and leave the profession. This oft observed fact has led to a much quoted but unsubstantiated statistic: the tenure of the average youth minister on a particular job is a year and a half or less. I know of no study that establishes that statistic. Someone must have made an estimate based on personal observation—and being a person of some authority, has been quoted ad infinitum.

A similar concern—about church pastors who leave the ministry—caused the United Church for Homeland Ministries in 1970 to commission a national study of ex-pastors. Its purpose was to determine why these pastors left the ministry. Their large and careful study found that no more that one percent of their clergy drops out each year. In other words, their denomination was not facing a dropout crisis. Instead of a runaway epidemic, they were facing a persistent low-grade infection.[27]

Yet there are distinct differences between the pressures faced by senior ministers and youth ministers. The pressure to succeed is especially acute for youth ministers, who—despite their lack of knowledge, skills, and experience—are expected to attract young adolescents to a life of commitment to Christ and the church. It is a daunting task made increasingly difficult by the expectations of adults and a notable lack of congregational support.

Such differences in the natures of parish ministers (or senior pastors) and youth ministers result in widely contrasting perceptions of their work, made particularly evident in a national study conducted by Murnion for the National Catholic Conference of Bishops in 1992. This report shows that the vast majority of parish ministers find their ministry very satisfying (93 percent), that it gives them a sense of accomplishment (92 percent), and that it is spiritually rewarding (91 percent).[28] These high percentages indicate an overwhelming affirmation of pleasure in serving as parish ministers.

The same report, however, tells a very different story about how *youth ministers* in the same church evaluate their work. Here is a summary of what the researchers found to be true for this newest profession in the Roman Catholic Church.

> **Of the various ministry positions, youth ministers seem to derive the least satisfaction and support. The full-time youth ministers find ministry the least affirming, their coworkers the least affirming, their supervisors the least satisfied, parishioners the least satisfied, and youth ministers the least likely to encourage others to enter parish ministry.**[29]

How many flee the ministry?
Turnover among youth ministers

If every denomination had a similar report of its professional youth ministries, one would have to say that the profession is in trouble. At this time, however, far too little is known about basic career issues; factors such as job satisfaction, effectiveness, and longevity beg for information in order to alter the perceived high turnover in personnel.

What is the turnover rate now among youth ministers? We do not really know. But our sample of 2,416 youth ministers shows that there is a much longer tenure for the average youth minister than has been assumed (see figure 1.1).

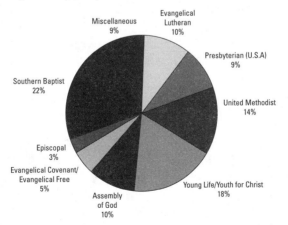

Figure 1.1—Number of years in youth ministry

What we don't know is how these percentages would change if the 48 percent from our study who were nonrespondents had participated in our study. It is reasonable to suppose that a disproportionate number of these also would be disconcerted and discouraged. Indeed, the fact they did not participate in our survey may well reinforce the fact that they were feeling overwhelmed by their jobs and consequently were not ready customers for a survey requiring another hour of their time.

Still, we have before us a fairly stable picture of tenure for youth ministers in eight denominations and two parachurch groups. Most have weathered the initial storm of learning how to conduct a youth ministry and are making a career for themselves.

Troubling concerns of youth ministers

Yet what are the pressures inherent in this career? What troubles or concerns do youth ministers face that can eventually drive them out of the profession? These are the questions that fueled this study, which gave considerable attention to professional dilemmas faced by youth ministers. As explained in the previous chapter, our study was conducted in 1996 at the Youth Leadership Conference in Atlanta ("Atlanta 96: Youth Leaders United for Spiritual Awakening"), where 7,500 youth ministers from all over the country assembled at the Georgia Dome for the largest gathering of youth ministers to date. A sample of these was secured—2,130 full-time youth ministers from dozens of denominations and parachurch organizations representing a wide range of age, geography, and experience filled out a sentence-completion questionnaire consisting of 20 item stems. An item stem, in this case, is the supplied part of an open-ended research question, like the examples listed below. These are five of the 20 items included in the questionnaire—

- What I like best about youth ministry is...
- My biggest obstacle to an effective youth ministry is...
- My biggest concern today in youth ministry is...
- It pleases me in youth ministry when...
- What discourages me most about my youth ministry is...

Their 20 fill-in answers were carefully tabulated to gain significant information from youth ministers serving in all parts of the country. Their written comments identified concerns such as the following:

- Administration allows me too little time to be with my youth.
- I am bothered by the lack of respect given me in my job.
- My lack of training in counseling limits my effectiveness.
- It's a struggle to balance my youth ministry job and personal life.
- My biggest obstacle to effective youth ministry is myself.

These responses gave us a good idea of the concerns most troubling to youth ministers today. They identified the range and universe of gritty issues that characterize this profession. The written responses supplied the grist we needed for developing the items needed in our national study. (Note: A summary report of the Sentence Completion responses can be found at Link Institute's Web site, www.linkinstitute.com.)

With the participants' responses in hand, it became our purpose to discover how extensive these concerns are and to identify the people particularly troubled by each major concern. Our study revealed 12 distinct concerns that pressure today's youth ministers. Six of these (discussed in Chapter 2) are created by adults and youth in congregations they serve. The other six concerns—(discussed in chapter 3) possible outcomes of the first six that relate to the personal life of the youth minister—are inner feelings that eventually lead to burnout.

THINK IT OVER, TALK IT THROUGH

1. What are the features in the history of youth ministry that have contributed to its present state?

2. If you were to contribute a sidebar to this chapter offering your own experiences in youth ministry as a "slice of history," what would you highlight?

3. What do *you* think the greatest concerns are troubling youth ministers today? (Don't peek ahead!)

4. What's been most influential in the historical development of youth ministry for your particular denomination/organization?

Notes 1

1. G.H. Trabert, *Church History for the People* (Columbus: Lutheran Book Concern, 1923), 227-228.

2. Frank Otis, *The Development of the Young People's Movement* (Chicago: University of Chicago Press, 1917), 3.

3. Otis, 23.

4. F.G. Cressey, *The Church and Young Men* (Chicago: Fleming H. Revell, 1903), 85.

5. Otis, 37.

6. Otis, 37.

7. Charles Courtoy, "A Historical Analysis of Three Eras in Mainline Protestant Youth Work in America as a Basis for Clues for the Future of Youth Work," dissertation (Divinity School of Vanderbilt University: 1976), 45.

8. Otis, 62.

9. Courtoy, 46.

10. Karen Jones, "A Study of the Difference Between Faith Maturity Scale and Multidimensional Self-Concept Scale Scores for Youth Participating in Two Denominational Ministry Projects," dissertation (Southern Baptist Theological Seminary: 1998), 2, 3.

11. Clarence Peters, "Developments of the Youth Programs of the Lutheran Churches in America," dissertation (Concordia Seminary: 1951), 85, 89.

12. Peters, 29.

13. Peters, 93.

14. Bob R. Taylor, *The Work of the Minister of Youth* (Nashville: Convention Press, 1982), 5.

15. Helen Spaulding and Olga Haley, "A Study of Youth Work in Protestant Churches," report (National Council of Churches in the U.S.A.: 1955), 84.

16. Emile Cailliet, *Young Life* (New York: Harper and Row, 1963), 15, 18.

17. Mark Senter III, *The Coming Revolution in Youth Ministry: And Its Radical Impact on the Church* (Wheaton: Victor Books, 1992), 125-127.

18. Senter, 129.

19. Senter, 28.

20. Senter, 141.

21. Jones, 4.

22. Senter, 142.

23. Taylor, 5.

24. Philip Murnion, *Parish Ministers: Laity and Religious on Parish Staffs* (New York: National Pastoral Life Center, 1992), 54.

25. Jones, 4.

26. Doug Fields, "The Power of God," *Youthworker* 14, 6 (July/August, 1998), 49.

27. Gerald Jud, et al, *Ex-Pastors: Why Men Leave the Parish Ministry* (Boston: Pilgrim Press, 1970), 59.

28. Murnion, 54.

29. Murnion, 54.

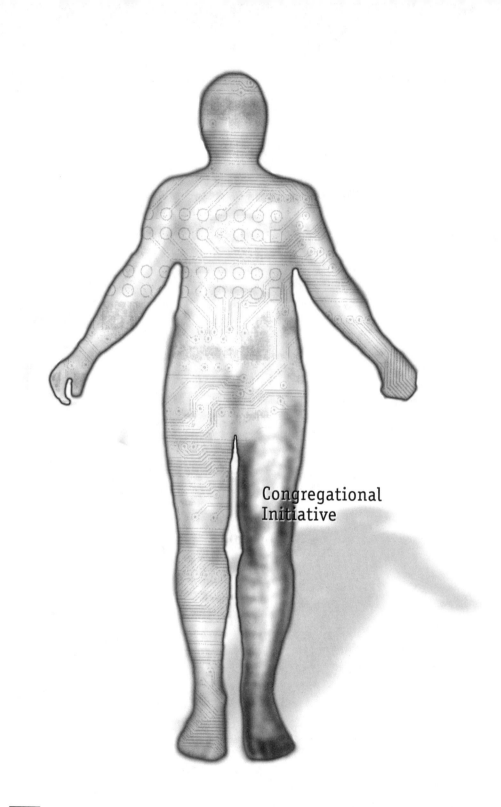

Congregational
Initiative

Chapter 2

Congregational Initiative: To Erase Six Concerns Troubling Youth Ministers
Merton Strommen

The first building block in the conceptual model deals with initiatives that a congregation needs to take in preparing the way for a youth minister—initiatives that can mitigate or eliminate six concerns, or roadblocks to an effective youth ministry.

These six concerns are usually precipitated by such things as—

- A congregation's tendency to load extra tasks and expectations on a youth minister.
- A congregation's providing too little help with administrative details.
- A disconnect between youth and the church.
- Disinterested and apathetic youth.
- An inadequate salary and youth budget.
- Low perceptions of the job's importance among the congregation, and even outright disrespect toward the youth minister.

Triggered by any of these problems, the six concerns we'll be discussing in this chapter can have a devastating effect on the morale and spirit of a youth minister. For that reason it is foundational that congregational leaders assume responsibility for addressing these issues. The concerns they create have the power to gradually push a youth minister out of the profession. Suggestions will be given as to what a congregation can do—suggestions that will make for healthier congregations.

Concerns that undermine effectiveness and confidence of youth workers

These six concerns were compiled from how respondents completed item stems, the supplied part of an open-ended research question, such as these:

- What I like least about youth ministry is—
- Regarding a balance of my youth ministry job and my personal life, I—
- The hardest thing about being in youth ministry is—

The range of expressed concerns was so extensive that a total of 70 items had to be included in our survey. This list enabled every respondent in our survey to find items that adequately described their concerns.

The patterns of response that youth ministers in the survey gave these items caused them to form 12 clusters—six clusters that can be identified as external concerns, or ones a congregation can alter; and six clusters that are internal concerns, which describe inner battles many youth ministers face.

The internal concerns are listed here in order of severity—concerns that seriously undermine the work and confidence of a youth minister:

Six clusters of congregationally created concerns
- Time Conflict: Job demands versus personal needs
- Time Conflict: Administrative duties versus youth contacts
- Disconnect between Youth and Church
- Disinterested and Apathetic Youth
- Inadequate Salary and Youth Budget
- Lack of Personal Support in Ministry

When concerns are not remedied

The concerns are usually personalized by youth ministers, even when there is no actual basis in fact for the youth worker's poor perception of himself or herself. This fallout is personalized by Mark DeVries, associate pastor for youth and families at First Presbyterian Church, who relates this anecdote in Family-Based Youth Ministry:

> **Several years ago I heard the surprising news that my good friend Jim, an incredibly well respected youth pastor in Texas, was leaving the youth ministry. This guy was one of the most effective youth ministers I had ever known. He had over 200 teenagers meeting weekly in small discipleship groups and creative programming that drew young people from all over the city.**
> **Certainly, there was nothing shocking about youth workers changing jobs. But I wondered why Jim was quitting—and quitting not only his present position but also youth ministry altogether. Did he get a better offer somewhere else? Was he moving on to become a "real" minister? Maybe he was going to start a profitable curriculum business? I thought of all the possibilities, but his answer hit**

me cold. "I am leaving," he said, "because I feel this overwhelming sense of failure."

Sense of failure? I was stunned. This man had been a model for me, someone whose ministry I was actively seeking to imitate. And he tells me he feels like a failure. It just didn't make sense.

But since Jim left youth ministry, his words have begun to make more and more sense to me, and I am starting to see that his experience may actually be more the norm than the exception. In fact, as I talk with more and more "successful" youth ministers, I am seeing that almost everyone suffers from a frustrating sense of failure. All have wondered more than once, Am I really making any difference?[1]

After reading the list of 70 concerns, another youth minister wrote—

Unfortunately, I can completely identify with most of the frustrations of the ministers mentioned in this study. The struggle to please parents, keep elders happy with growing numbers, and at the same time point to the truth of the cross—quite frankly stresses me out in some fashion throughout a normal day.

Although feelings of failure may not make sense and are in fact irrational, those feelings still constitute a very real roadblock for many youth ministers. So real, in fact, that when youth ministers in the study answered survey items describing concerns, they answered in ways that caused the items to form distinct clusters. Each cluster described one of those "irrational" feelings that most people in youth ministry know only too well.

Yet these feelings of inadequacy, brought on by any of the six concerns listed above, can be reduced in strength and even eliminated—but only by asking congregations to become intentional in eliminating concerns that contribute to youth ministers' feelings of inadequacy.

The thesis of this chapter is that if congregational leaders take the initiative to eliminate or mitigate these six concerns, the work and effectiveness youth ministers will be vastly enhanced. More than that—congregational initiative will cultivate volunteer leadership, develop realistic expectations of staff, bring youth and adults together in a sense of mission, give responsibility and meaningful tasks to youth, and encourage a community of believers.

Time Conflict
Job demands versus personal needs

Of the six external concerns, the most pervasive and widely felt is time conflict. It is the feeling that hours in the day are too few for all that needs to be done.

The 2,131 youth ministers who filled out sentence completion questions in 1996 were very conscious of this struggle, evidenced by their responses to this sentence-completion item: Regarding a balance of my youth ministry job and my personal life, I—

An unprecedented number, a total of 46 percent of the respondents, wrote: "It is a continuing struggle to balance the two." No single item gained such a uniform response.

It may be difficult for members of a congregation to understand the unique demands that are placed on conscientious youth ministers. Yet what is it that that effective youth ministers seek to do?

The information below comes from a Search Institute study that began by developing criteria for effective youth leaders. Once the criteria had been established and ranked, we asked the heads of national youth organizations to nominate high school youth workers who exemplify the highest-ranked criteria.

Ninety-one youth leaders were named, 75 from 11 major denominations and 16 from Young Life. These 91 workers then told us through questionnaires why they intervene in the lives of youth, how they approach them, and what accounts for their effectiveness. The eight methods they described explain why a youth ministry is time-intensive: *being available, showing interest, building relationships, communicating, leading, teaching, creating a community,* and *encouraging involvement.*

Approaches used by outstanding youth leaders

Being available
> Going to their events when adults are welcome
> Spending time with them and their friends
> Working and playing with them in various activities
> Taking kids to away games
> Inviting them home for dinner
> Initiating interviews

Showing interest
> Remembering their names
> Learning about their world
> Being able to speak their language

Listening to their music
Adopting their symbols
Finding areas where one might help
Making phone calls and writing letters regarding their
accomplishments

Building relationships
Exhibiting deep, sensitive, personal concern for them
Helping them if they ask
Coming to know them—their home life, school, friends
Participating with them as an equal
Sharing one's own feelings about life

Communicating
Talking to them every opportunity one can about a personal faith
Quietly listening and waiting for youth to share personal feelings
and faith
Listening with the third ear for emotions
One-to-one counseling

Leading
Discovering and using their talents and interests
Involving them in planning, decision-making, and executing
Facing them with the issues
Giving them provocative, challenging books to read and discuss
Offering them a host of options
Getting them interested in trips, projects, and studies that benefit
them
Creating celebration and experiences for free expression
Getting them to camps and retreats

Teaching
Training them to reach out to others on a one-to-one basis
Educating parents for helping roles with their youth
Teaching Scripture, presenting the message of Christ
Teaching a class relating the Bible to youth and culture
Personally confronting each youth with the claims of Christ

Creating a community
Helping them to get to know each other
Developing teamwork among youth in their activities
Making them aware of others in the community who may be
experiencing loneliness, deprivation, and friendlessness
Helping forgiveness and acceptance to happen

Encouraging group awareness and sensitivity in everyday life
Developing groups who share at the deepest possible level

Encouraging involvement
Involving kids in volunteer work, seminars, schools, and inner-city
   communities in order to encourage growth and faith experiences
Service projects in other localities
Getting young people involved in congregational life
Creating opportunities for kids to think about and discuss their
   concerns
Discussing current issues and trying to do something about them

Not involved in this list are the activities now being recognized as an additional responsibility of a youth minister—that of working with parents and helping them communicate faith in their home. For many this represents a paradigm change. The task of shifting responsibility for faith development from church to home means that the youth minister must become involved with parents in a new way.

This list impressively demonstrates that youth ministry can consume all of a youth worker's time and energy. The inner conflict it creates is described in the five items that make up the cluster "Time Conflict Created by Job Demands." They describe facets of what is for many, a serious issue.

CLUSTER
Time conflict created by job demands

- The job demands are more than time allows.
- I have too little time for myself.
- I do not have time to pursue hobbies or interests beyond my ministry.
- What I want to do often interferes with what needs to be done.
- I often have to leave tasks undone.

The item "Job demands are more than time allows" ranks second highest among all 70 concern items in this section of the survey. Note in figure 2.1 how many respondents say this concerns them:

A total of 46 percent are much concerned (very much and quite a bit) about this issue; another 34 percent are trying to cope with it. This concern is so pervasive that only 13 percent say it is not an issue for them.

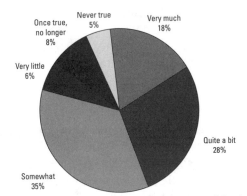

Figure 2.1—Percent concerned over time conflict created by job demands

Another of the cluster's five items—I have too little time for myself—ranks fifth highest among all 70 concern items. This particular item proved to be troubling 35 percent of the respondents either very much or quite a bit. Without question we are dealing here with a most pervasive and troubling issue.

Interestingly, none of the groups identified in our study stand out as being more troubled by this concern than others. The one exception is youth ministers who are deeply devoted to their Lord's mission of reaching the lost. This is reflected in the one item that refused to correlate with any of the 12 clusters:

When busy, I sacrifice my devotional time. This concerns me.

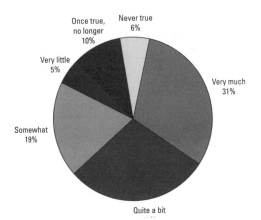

Figure 2.2—Percent concerned over sacrifices of devotional time

This item drew the highest number of responses for all 70 concern items in the survey. Note that a total of 60 percent expressed great concern over their loss of devotional time because of job demands. No other item is as great a concern to youth ministers as this one. Notice also how very few (6 percent) are not concerned over this issue.

Southwestern Theological Seminary's professor of youth education, Wesley Black, writes about the devastating effect this neglect can have on one's ministry:

> **During the busy activities of leading youth ministry, directing the youth choir, and filling in for the minister of music who had moved to another church, I forgot to attend to my own spiritual needs, I substituted planning youth Bible study sessions for my own personal devotional bible reading. I spoke with God only in public prayers, forgetting to converse with him in private. Sharing my testimony and witnessing became routine duties to perform. I faced this dilemma during a retreat for youth ministers sponsored by our state convention.[2]**

This concern over the "Time Conflict Created by Job Demands" cluster can be intensified by three other factors—separate clusters themselves—that show their association by intercorrelating significantly with the "Time Conflict Created by Job Demands" cluster of items. (The higher the number, the stronger the correlation; correlations of .50 and higher are worth considering.)

Clusters correlating with time conflict	Correlation
Administrative demands	.57
Strained family relations	.54
Feelings of inadequacy	.52

Each of these (which will be considered subsequently) bears a relationship to the troublesomeness of the "Time Conflict" issue. Without question, "Time Conflict Created by Job Demands" may be the most vexing of all concerns experienced by youth ministers.

What congregations can do

First of all, a congregation should set boundaries that apply for *all* employees, not only youth ministers. Furthermore, leaders within a congregation can adjust their expectations so that the duties of a position can be carried out within the limits of a normal week. Youth ministers can be told that no more than a certain number of hours per week are expected of them.

Consideration also needs to be given to extended duties beyond the regular week, such as weekend retreats, which vastly increase the time served away from one's home. A policy that makes provision for compensatory time would be a blessing to a stressed youth minister.

A practice that recognizes the importance of a youth minister's home life is dividing the day into thirds—morning, afternoon, and evening—with the employer limiting the youth minister's tasks to no more than two-thirds of a day. For instance, if the day's schedule included an evening activity, the youth minister was not to come into the office until noon that day. This was standard practice for years at a Youth for Christ chapter north of Chicago. Denver's Youth for Christ program went so far as to actually forbid their staff from being in the office when kids were out of school.

Not only do such expectations honor a youth minister's private time, but they communicate to youth ministers that congregations and supervisors recognize that some of the most important work with young people takes place during the time that most of the work force are unwinding for the day. Churches that insist their staff keep eight-to-five office hours simply do not appreciate the nature of youth work and will likely contribute to time-conflict frustration.

The need to release responsibility

I asked Methodist youth pastor Gordon Gathright in Hastings, Minnesota, who once had charted his time at 80 hours a week, how he was now coping. I knew that in his church the job could use up all 24 hours of his day. His immediate answer was: "I now give responsibility to my adult leaders."

His church budgets $5,000 for training volunteer leaders, he said. His 25 adults and 15 youth in leadership positions spend a weekend or two a year in leadership training, during which times Gathright gives away responsibility. Once a month Gathright meets with these volunteer leaders for two to three hours at a supper meeting, which provides an opportunity for them to report, pray together, and plan.

In *Reaching a Generation for Christ*, Richard Dunn and Mark Senter offer this axiom: "Long-term growth of a youth ministry is directly dependent on the ability of the youth worker to release ministry responsibilities to mature and qualified lay workers."[3]

It is important for these volunteer adults to realize that they are not being recruited to help a youth minister carry out tasks, but rather to share God's workload—a distinction revealed in the words God used when he asked Moses to gather seventy elders of Israel to help bear the burden of the people: "Gather for me seventy of the elders of Israel."

Releasing responsibilities to those who sense God's call means shifting the authority to minister while still sharing responsibility for the quality of that ministry. Real authority is given to volunteer workers so that they do not need to fear being second-guessed by the professional worker.

Finally, a congregation can give its youth minister a sabbatical. More and more churches are recognizing the need for those in full-time ministry to occasionally pull away from the demands of their work for an extended period in order to spend time in spiritual renewal and professional development. Usually one to three months is awarded every several years, which allows a youth minister to return with a renewed passion and sense of vision. Sabbaticals only work, of course, when volunteers have been equipped and empowered to carry out the ministry.

Concern 2
Time Conflict
Administrative demands versus youth contacts

Administrative tasks are disturbing when they prevent youth ministers from spending the time they covet with their young people. This apparently happens with sufficient frequency to form our second troublesome issue. Here are the items that clustered together because enough youth ministers felt keenly about this issue of administrative demands:

CLUSTER
Time Conflict: Administrative demands versus youth contacts

- Administrative expectations hinder my time with youth.
- I spend too much time in my office.
- I cannot spend as much time with youth as I want.

These items identify the vexing concern created by administrative expectations that robs time otherwise spent with young people. One aspect of this concern relates to the youth that have dropped out for one reason or another.

Item: *I regret not spending more time with youth who have dropped out of our youth ministry.*

This particular item, whose specific focus kept it from being correlated with the other three, is an important one. It ranks fourth highest of all 70 concerns. It identifies another possible reason why administrative demands pose a troublesome conflict.

However, this regret may be due also to the basic approach that youth ministers have established: if they are trying to do everything on their own, without involving a cadre of volunteer leaders, the result will be less contact with youth. This is to be expected.

Figure 2.3 reflects a fair estimate of just how widespread is this concern of youth ministers over a time conflict between administrative demands and youth contacts:

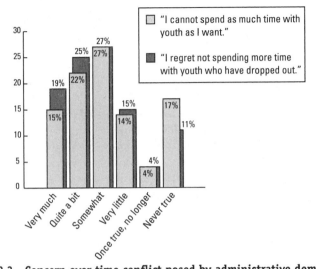

Figure 2.3—Concern over time conflict posed by administrative demands

As noted above, administrative demands pose a significant concern for at least two out of five in the study; less than one in five do not regard it as a vexing concern.

The ones troubled most by this concern are those serving in congregations of over a thousand members. Though their score is significantly greater than youth ministers serving in congregations fewer than 500 are, the difference is not large.

Aside from this one relatively small difference, "Time Conflict: Administrative demands versus youth contacts" are felt quite uniformly by all respondents whether they have advanced in education or not, are seminary trained or not, whether they work in small communities or large ones, whether they are young or old, male or female, veterans or novitiates in youth ministry.

What congregations can do

It may be true that most youth ministers are creative, right-brained, action-oriented people by nature and by training—which is all the more reason for them to work under an administrator or with an assistant who is gifted in administration.

The church can provide secretarial assistance through volunteers who give a certain number of hours each month fulfilling clerical tasks necessary to the church's youth ministry. Such a practice could save a great deal of a youth minister's time. Yet such volunteers for this kind of task are not easy to find in many churches—which means that other ways to cope with administrative demands need to be considered. Two ways are suggested here:

Use lead teams

Administrative details can easily overwhem most youth ministers, who become responsible for arranging trips, outings, and special events in addition to their standard week-to-week programs. When Richard Ross, now youth consultant with the Southern Baptist Convention's LifeWay Ministries, was a Nashville youth minister, he was troubled by how administrative details separated him from the youth he wished to serve. He found that an increasing amount of his time was being spent managing events, preparing for "the next big thing."

What troubled him was how event management left him with too little time for—

- Establishing relationships and sharing his faith with lost teenagers.
- Counseling with troubled teenagers.
- Coordinating the programming and personal ministries for parents.

In order to move away from event management and its endless details, Ross developed a "Lead Team" concept: the formation of teams of youth and lay adults whose task is to assume responsibility for activities Ross had traditionally handled. Each Lead Team assumed ultimate responsibility for an event—a mission trip, weekend retreat, family festival, or vacation Bible school. The Lead Team functioned only as long as it was needed to prepare for and carry out the designated project.

I was present in Ross's church one Sunday evening and saw these Lead Teams in action, as they planned some significant and complicated youth events. It was clear to me that they, not their youth pastor, were the ones making things happen. Ross had freed himself to do what he had been trained to do. The Lead Team approach to delegation has now been propagated to many hundreds of churches in the Southern Baptist Convention, and with positive results.

Involve youth

There is also the possibility of securing help from gifted young people for some clerical tasks and information gathering and disseminating, but particularly for developing and maintaining Web sites for their youth groups, now that increasing numbers of youth ministers and youth recognize the value of an Internet presence for a youth group. While this task can be very time-consuming, using students can allow youth ministers to nurture relationships as well as get the job done.

One youth minister tells how he delegated administrative tasks to a student, and the effects of that delegation:

> **Andy walked into our student ministry in his eighth-grade year. He didn't even know that God existed. His parents were recently divorced, and he was beginning to experiment with alcohol and drugs.**
>
> **Over the past several months Andy became attached to our ministry. Almost a year and many conversations later, I had the opportunity of leading Andy to Christ.**
>
> **Several times a week I get a phone call from him or he stops by my office and sincerely asks me how I am doing. He is willing to do whatever is needed, especially if it requires a computer. He helped us put together a worship CD.**
>
> **Besides all kinds of data entry, publications, administrative, and other "slave" work, Andy has been leading one of our accountability groups of student leaders. And about a month ago Andy told me he feels that God is calling him into pastoral ministry.**

Concern 3
Disconnect between Youth and Church

The disinterest of adults in the congregation in the church's teenagers can dishearten youth ministers. Adults too often have a stereotypical assumption that youth *do* not want meaningful relationships with a church's adults—an assumption that is dead wrong. Youth actually do want such relationships. Yet this erronous perception, held also by even many of the teenagers' parents, is characteristic of our culture today.

Evidence of this is found in a 1997 national study entitled *"Kids These Days: What Americans Think about the Next Generation."* When asked to describe teenagers, two-thirds of the thousand adults surveyed came up with negative adjectives like *rude, wild,* and *irresponsible.* Only 37 percent believed that today's teenagers might eventually make this country a better place.[4]

That this attitude, found also in the church, troubles youth ministers becomes evident in the following six items. The fact that they correlated to form a cluster means they are viewed similarly by youth ministers in the study.

CLUSTER
Disconnect between Youths and Church

- There is little interaction between adults and youth in our church.
- I have a hard time getting parental involvement in my ministry.
- Youth ministry seems disconnected from the rest of our church.
- Youth feel that adults in the church just do not understand them.
- I do not have the volunteer youth leaders I need.
- It is difficult to keep senior high youth interested.

Just *how* troubling an issue this can be is seen in the percentage responses to the item drawing the highest response of the six items:

I have a hard time getting parental involvement in my ministry.
This concerns me.

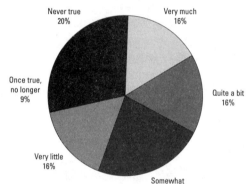

Figure 2.4—Percent concerned over lack of parental involvement

One-third of the respondents (32 percent) are much troubled by this lack of parental involvement. Another 23 percent are aware of it and are "somewhat" troubled. Here is an issue troubling more than half (55 percent) the youth ministers—which is probably on the low side. Should our hypothesis be correct that a disproportionate number of *non*respondents (48 percent) are the frazzled and overworked who are ready to resign, then the true percentage of youth ministers troubled over this issue would probably be higher.

It is significant that only about one in five has *not* been concerned about parental uninvolvement. After all, parents ought to be the most interested and supportive of all congregational adults. Should they become supportive and interested in their church's youth ministry, it would make a great difference in how youth ministers feel about their work.

Those most troubled about the youth-church disconnect

Generally, youth ministers serving youth groups numbering less than 40 tend to be far more troubled with this issue than those serving groups over 100.

(Here you meet standard scores. Remember that 50 is the average score for all 2,416 youth ministers. For those serving groups of less than 40 youth, the average score is over 53. This means they expressed considerably more concern than average over the six items in this measure. By way of contrast, the average score for those serving groups over 100 is down to 46.1, which means that they are much less troubled by this issue.)

Concern over lack of parental involvement

Size of youth group	Standard scores
Youth ministers serving groups of less than 40 youths	53.3
Youth ministers serving groups of 41 to 100 youths	49.0
Youth ministers serving groups of 101 or more	46.1

The difference between scores 53.3 and 46.1, which is highly significant, means that the "Youth-Church Disconnect" is most troubling for persons serving small youth groups.

The most important information here may be that youth ministers are generally alike in their concern over this issue. With the exception of small-group youth ministers (see sidebar this page), no differences in scores appear between groups when compared on the basis of education, region, size of community, seminary education, or approach to youth work. We are generally dealing with a concern that is real to all youth ministers.

After having read a preliminary version of this manuscript, one youth minister wrote about her frustrations over this "Youth-Church Disconnect" issue.

About small youth groups

This contrast in scores between youth ministers serving youth groups of 40 or less young people and those serving groups of more than 40 occurs a number of times in this report. In fact it occurs more times than for any other variable. (See figure 9.1 on page 228). Because we will be seeing many comparisons based on youth group size—comparisons that seem to put youth ministers of small youth groups at particular professional peril—it will be helpful to identify four factors that could be at work behind the scenes:

• **Youth groups that are failing are most likely to be included in the category of 40 or less youth.** Youth vote with their feet. If things are not going well, the group that should be numbering 50 may now be averaging an attendance of 15. It is plausible that this category, more than any of the others, includes more of the youth groups that are disintegrating.

• **Small churches whose youth program is being led by the senior pastor are not included in this study.** Some of these churches through volunteer leaders have excellent youth ministries. But they are not included because their congregation is too small to hire a youth minister. Scores might be higher for youth groups numbering less than 40 if such churches had been included.

• **Churches with small youth groups tend to be those that can afford to hire only the young, inexperienced, and often untrained youth minister.** This the study finds to be true. The significance of this is that those with less experience (see figures 9.10 and 9.11 on pages 237 and 240, respectively) are less competent in job performance, confident leadership, effective youth relationships, theological grounding, developing adult volunteers, being motivated by God's call, and their ability to respond creatively to the youth culture.

My struggle is with the disconnection of students with the congregation as a whole. It breaks my heart to hear terms like "big church." Shouldn't we be teaching students how to worship, what communion means, and the elements of worship through modeling them? How are we supposed to pass down the heritage of our faith if we separate the students from the adults? How are students supposed to feel a connection to the body of Christ as a whole and have an understanding of a commitment that supersedes their parents?

I am not against age-appropriate teaching, but my struggle lies with age-appropriate teaching at the expense of connecting students to the whole body of Christ.

Those youth ministers who are concerned about the "Youth-Church Disconnect" tend also to have youth groups with a ho-hum attitude toward their church. This characteristic correlates significantly (correlation coefficient of $r=.63$) with "Youth-Church Disconnect." (Whenever a correlation approaches .50 or larger, there is a statistical relationship worth noting.)

It is easy to see why some youth ministers become devastated when they bump against the wall of a "Youth-Church Disconnect:" it is often because the youth group includes a bunch of "Disinterested and Apathetic Youth" (see the discussion of the next cluster, beginning on page 60).

Something radical that congregations can do

A congregation needs to assume responsibility for removing these huge impediments to an effective youth ministry and not expect the youth minister to do it—a process that starts with adopting a whole new approach to how the congregation views its ministry.

In *The Godbearing Life: The Art of Soul Tending for Youth Ministry*, Kenda Dean (assistant professor of youth, church, and culture at Princeton Theological Seminary) and Ron Foster (pastor and PTS instructor) advocate a concept of youth ministry that can change how adults in a congregation view their youth: that Jesus Christ calls young people into ministry, not into a youth program.

> **Youth ministry is primarily ministry— ministry because youth are called to bear the gospel in their own right. Adolescents have their mission fields as well as we do, and they look to the church for guidance in how to be the person God calls them to be—both in and in spite of their culture.[5]**

Adults in a congregation need to begin viewing their youth as potential Marys, Timothys, Marks—Godbearing teenagers in the New Testament whom God called to be part of his saving purpose. Rather than viewing the congregation's youth ministry as an effort to keep them off the streets, protect them from the evils of society, or keep them interested in their church, a congregation needs to begin viewing their youths as important partners in bringing others into a saving relationship with Jesus Christ.

The director of youth ministry and spirituality at San Francisco Theological Seminary, Mark Yaconelli writes about congregations that show a low level of interest in their ministry to youth:

> **Why are we so eager to hand the spiritual development of our young people to the first person we can find who can locate the New Testament and needs a little part-time work? Have we forgotten that one of the most sacred of human activities is sharing the intimacies of our souls, our values, and the visions of our hearts with children? This is not a**

• **A higher percentage of the youth ministers serving youth groups of less than 40 are females (48 percent versus 35 percent males).** Fewer of the females have seminary training (39 percent versus 52 percent), fewer identify themselves with a conservative theology (40 percent versus 77 percent). The study shows that female youth ministers operate under greater handicaps than do male youth ministers.

These possible explanations can help deter one from concluding that effective youth ministries are unlikely in churches where the youth group is 40 or less. I write this having interviewed three volunteer youth leaders—three young adults who took over the youth program in an Episcopal congregation of 200 members in Buena Vista, Colorado. They did this as a calling from God. In the space of nine months, they had reached 35 youth that were now coming once a week for the equivalent of Bible study discussions (using the Alpha Program). They estimated that 80 percent of these youth are from unchurched, dysfunctional homes. The two that I saw on Sunday serving as acolytes had both been on drugs and now were free and committed to Jesus Christ.

These considerations should be kept in mind as you see repeatedly in this study that youth ministers serving the smallest groups tend to fare the poorest.

> **task for overloaded students; it is the privilege of
> every congregation.**[6]

Yaconelli notes that congregations have fallen in the trap of giving
total responsibility for the spiritual development of their young people
to a charismatic youth leader, hoping that the young, attractive,
recent-from-college-or-seminary graduate will be "able to mediate the
holy through his or her spiritual charisma."

This winsome-and-attractive-youth-leader approach tends to imitate
the parachurch ministries originally developed by organizations like
Young Life and Youth for Christ. When the approach is used in a congregational setting, this personality-driven and entertainment-emphasized
approach has often relegated adults to the roles of drivers and chaperones. It is easy to see how this shift of responsibility to a charismatic
youth leader has encouraged the attitude reflected in the items of
"Youth-Church Disconnect."

In his congregation of 80 members, Yaconelli invited six adults to
engage themselves in youth ministry as a spiritual practice. Rather than
serving as chaperones or committee members, they became an intentional spiritual community. They met for an hour before the weekly
youth meeting to share their lives, read Scripture, pray, and discern
their call. It was their understanding that this desire for God was their
greatest witness to their youth.

What has been the outcome of this approach? Yaconelli writes:

> **Gathered to nurture young people in faith, we
> soon realized that we were being transformed by
> this ministry. The most surprising development was
> that people began to make long-term commitments
> to working with youths; they attested to finding
> the ministry enriching rather than draining. At
> present we have 19 people, each devoting three
> hours a week to the ministry. Our whole church is
> experiencing renewal.**
>
> **These "fruits" capture the essence of this
> new/old approach to adolescent spiritual develop-
> ment. Rather than entertaining them, we are invit-
> ing youth to be transformed. Rather than providing
> a solitary youth leader, we offer a community of
> disciples who seek to walk with youths toward a
> deeper intimacy with God. Rather than handing
> young people statements of faith, we give them the
> space and tools to recognize and act with One who is
> beyond all theological formulations. We are claiming**

> this work as a church, inviting young people into
> the intimacies of our hearts and rediscovering the
> indescribable power of the Risen Christ who forms,
> sustains, and calls us by name.[7]

A group of Southern Baptist youth ministers in Texas initiated the discipleship event "DiscipleNow" during the 1970s that is still popular. This unique involvement of youth and adults now pervades Southern Baptist churches and has even caught on in churches outside the Convention.

DiscipleNow is a weekend discipleship retreat in the homes of congregation members. Church members host a small group for a weekend; an outside leader (who also stays in the home) leads the small group in training and recreation; church members bring meals to an assigned home during the weekend; other volunteers drive youth to service projects on Saturday.

The event culminates in a Sunday worship service, during which students make commitments based on their experiences. Host families, meal and transportation providers, and other volunteers are also recognized during the service. As a result of connections made at the DiscipleNow weekend, informal mentoring relationships between the church's adults and its youth are often initiated and strengthened.

After reading these potential remedies to the "Youth-Church Disconnect" in a preliminary draft of this book, a youth minister in graduate school had this to add:

> It is a paradigm shift for me to think that youth
> ministers are not the ones solely responsible for the
> youth ministry in a congregation—that they are
> rather an extension of the church's ministry to
> young people. It is plain that youth ministers must
> begin to see themselves as serving the congregation
> as they seek to serve young people, rather than see-
> ing themselves as simply called to serve the young
> people. To see youth ministry in this way (which is
> probably the more correct way) means drawing on
> the considerable resources of a congregation to
> accomplish more effectively a congregation's goals
> for its teenage ministry.

Mark Senter makes the interesting observation that Young Life's Mike Wilson in Eastern Europe is *not* promoting a leader approach, with its ready-made bag of Young Life tricks. He is rather serving as a consultant, theologian, counselor, and brother in ministry to the adults who work with youth. His ministry to adult leaders is as an equipper of lay ministers. "The key to ministering to the coming generations of young people," Senter adds, "is the equipping of volunteers in local settings."[8]

Disinterested and Apathetic Youths

Few things are more devastating for youth ministers than disinterest and apathy among members of their youth groups. The concern it creates is compounded (as we have already noticed) when it includes adult disinterest. The relatively high correlation ($r = .63$) between a "Youth-Church Disconnect" and "Disinterested and Apathetic Youth" indicates that when you have one, you usually have the other, too. The two factors present an imposing obstacle to the morale of any youth minister.

Disinterest takes many forms. It can be seen in a young person's body language, offhand comments, absences, or failure to follow through on what has been promised. It is a behavior that characterizes youth who lack motivation, a sense of mission, or a feeling of ownership for the youth program. They are youth who have not been gripped by the gospel and a living relationship with Jesus Christ.

One way this disinterest is shown is by a marked discrepancy between rhetoric and what is actually supported. Youth may ask for a weekend ski trip, so the youth minister schedules it—but is later forced to cancel because most students withdrew their reservations when their friends decided not to go. Such thoughtless actions tend to be viewed by the youth minister as acts of unkindness.

My *"Study of Generations"* (1980) tested the expectation that youth more than adults would be involved in acts of kindness. We assumed this to be so because of young people's strong identification with the needs of people. But the study found them far *less* likely than adults to perform specific acts of service.[9] Their rhetoric is not always matched by what they do—which makes it difficult for a youth minister who is trying to respond to their interest and suggestions.

Karen Jones, coauthor of this study and Huntington College professor of youth ministry, tells about a discouraged youth minister at a Southwestern Baptist Theological Seminary gathering:

> **One youth minister—call him Jason—expressed his deep concern over his group's small size. He said he found it hard to get them to attend anything except fun events. When they did show up, they seemed bored. Nothing he tried seemed to help. Other conferees offered their suggestions,**

telling Jason about ways they had overcome this in their own ministries. The discouraged youth minister brushed aside all of the suggestions, stating that he had tried all of the suggestions—that he had tried everything. Jason even indicated the possibility of leaving youth ministry altogether.

One attendee suggested that the problem might actually lie with Jason's planning. Was there anything taking place during his meetings that might cause youths to be interested? Did Jason give his students any motivation to attend?

Most of the conferees were quick to remove any blame on Jason's part, probably because it was their consensus that youth ministers beat themselves up too much when youths are disinterested. One wonders if it is the youth culture and not the youth minister that is at fault.

A notable manifestation of youth disinterest and apathy is found in the following five items. What they describe creates a concern in the minds of youth ministers, causing them to ask, *How do I motivate such unresponsive kids?*

CLUSTER
Disinterested and Apathetic Youth

- The youth show little interest in church or their youth ministry.
- I find it hard to motivate my youth.
- Our youth ministry is primarily adult-led.
- I'm not sure if my youth ministry is successful.
- I am not seeing results from my ministry.

What is interesting about the items that form this cluster is their content. Adult-led youth ministries are associated with disinterested youth. Also, not seeing results from one's ministry is also associated with disinterested and apathetic youth. There is no question but that this concern undercuts the confidence of a youth minister.

How widespread is this concern of youth ministers? An estimate is available in the item drawing the highest response of the five:

I find it hard to motivate my youth. This concerns me.

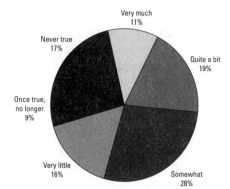

Figure 2.5—Percent concerned over disinterested and apathetic youth

Note that 30 percent of the youth ministers identified this issue of finding it hard to motivate their youth as troubling them *very much* or *quite a bit*. An additional 28 percent said it concerns them "somewhat." This represents over half the sample. Only 17 percent—a low percentage—discarded these items as something not characteristic of the youth they serve.

Who are most aware of disinterested and apathetic youth?

It is those working with fewer than 40 youth in their group. They contrast strikingly in their concern with youth ministers serving over 100 youth. The difference is 8½ standard scores. When the numbers of youth in attendance are low, it is apparently easy for a youth minister to conclude that it is due to their lack of interest. On the other hand, when over 100 youth show up for meetings, it is easy to conclude that the youth are interested—even though the numbers may represent a lower percentage of that church's youth.

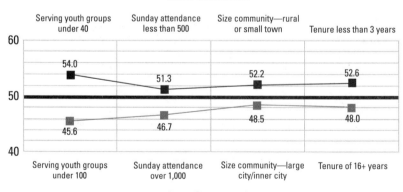

Figure 2.6—Groups compared on concern over disinterested and apathetic youth

In figure 2.6, all differences between the top and bottom scores in each size or tenure grouping would have happened by chance only once in a hundred times.

Two groups of youth ministers showing highest concern are a puzzle:

- Those serving congregations that draw fewer than 500 people at a Sunday morning service.
- Those serving congregations located in rural or small towns.

For some reason, church attendance and size of community are strongly related to youth ministers' concern over "Disinterested and Apathetic Youth" (see figure 9.15 on page 245). Do small churches and churches in small towns have less success in challenging their youths to be followers of Christ?

Added confirmation for this puzzling phenomenon is seen in the fact that *least* concern is expressed by youth ministers serving congregations whose Sunday morning attendance is over a thousand, and in large cities.

Three factors can be singled out as contributors to why youth ministers serving the largest churches are the least concerned about disinterest and apathy among their youth. These youth ministers, as will be seen later in this book, tend to gain the most favorable scores in all evaluations of their youth ministry. Why is that? Why do youth ministries seem to improve as church size increases?

If we cannot definitively answer these questions, we can at least advance some reasonable assumptions:

We can assume that large churches can afford to hire those who have already distinguished themselves as youth ministers.
These stars among youth ministers have the ability to establish attractive and meaningful ministries because they are among the most experienced and professionally mature, and the best-trained. The evidence shows that they relate well to both youths and adults, they know what to do, and they can be innovative while remaining theologically grounded (see figure 9.16 on page 246).

Our measures of these people show them to score significantly higher in—

- Being motivated by a sense of calling.
- Displaying competent job performance.
- Confident leadership.
- Ability to develop volunteer leadership.
- Effective relationships with youth.
- Ability to relate to parents and adults.

(See chapter 9 and figure 9.15 on page 245 for more information on those serving in larger churches.)

We can assume that congregations able to draw an average of a thousand people or more each Sunday have a preaching ministry that inspires and energizes people.

These are probably missional churches where preaching is done with a passion that people come to know Jesus Christ. One can assume also that the music in these congregations establishes an atmosphere of reverence and excitement about the faith.

This kind of energizing Sunday service has a positive effect on youth as it does on adults. It was my observation while serving as youth director for our church body that youth who were responding best to their congregation's youth program were members of a church where there was great preaching and inspiring worship services.

We can assume that large churches generally have more resources, facilities, and adult volunteers available for their youth ministries

Because large congregations are usually located in a large urban center, their membership tends to include a large number of adults whose training and background equip them in a special way to serve as volunteer leaders with youth.

It is not difficult to understand why inexperienced youth ministers express high concern over "Disinterested and Apathetic Youth." Those with a tenure of less than three years are simply less able to energize youth than those with 16 years or more of experience. Experience enables youth ministers to work with adults and parents in a congregation in ways that help awaken youths' interest.

Not only size of youth group, but also a youth minister's denomination indicates how troubled he or she will be by apathetic youth group members. As seen in figure 2.7, those in Lutheran churches express the highest level of concern; those from parachurch and Episcopal churches express the least.

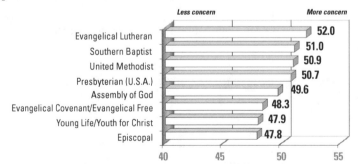

Figure 2.7—Youth ministers' concern over disinterested and apathetic youth

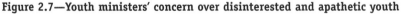

Clearly, the perceptions of youth ministers vary by denomination; by size of youth group, congregation, and community; and by tenure. Finding an explanation for these variations could provide direction for those who serve as youth ministers and those who serve as their support group.

We tried to probe more deeply into factors associated with greater or lesser concern over "Disinterested and Apathetic Youth," using an analysis known as Automatic Interaction Detection—a complex computer analysis that shows which factors most strongly predict a concern over "Disinterested and Apathetic Youth." Figure 2.8 displays a simplified form of the results of this analysis.

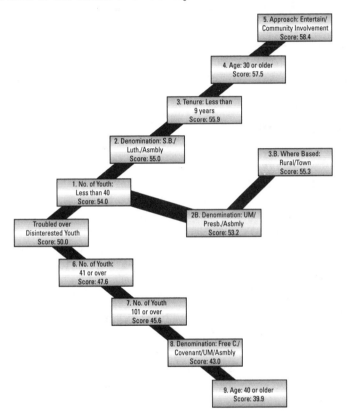

Figure 2.8—Analysis how factors contribute to youth ministers' concern over disinterested and apathetic youth

What the analysis tells us (scores below 50 indicate decreasing concern about apathetic students; scores above 50, increasing concern):

- Size of youth group contributes first and foremost to this concern. The smaller the youth group that is being served, the more troubled the youth minister (score: 54).

- Ranking next in significance is denominational affiliation. Scores for youth ministers serving small groups rise on the average to 55 if they are Southern Baptist, Lutheran, or Assembly of God youth ministers.
- Within these denominational groups, those in youth ministry for less than nine years average a concern score of 55.9. And those with this tenure who are younger than 30 register a score of 57.5.
- The most troubled, however, are the youth ministers (within the groups described above) who use entertainment as their youth work approach, or who encourage community involvement. This small group registers a high concern score of 58.4.

Such information should alert congregational and denominational youth leaders to the persons especially needing special support and assistance—for these are the youth ministers most likely to consider leaving the profession.

What congregations can do

Make the purpose pointedly spiritual.
The first need is to make sure one's teenagers are being introduced to a very particular relationship—namely a relationship with Jesus Christ. With this appeal should come a sustained effort to enlist them in the missionary movement of Jesus Christ. They need to hear "God's invitation to participate in the divine transformation of the world."[10] God can work through them just as he enabled the Virgin Mary, Timothy, and Mark to live Godbearing lives.

Find creative ways to bulk up the size of the youth group.
A second need is to look at the issue of numbers. Because small numbers strongly predict youth disinterest, ways need to be found which bring more youth together. Small churches can combine with others for monthly meetings. Seven Lutheran churches and one Presbyterian church near Binford, North Dakota, joined hands to form Tri-County Parish—an arrangement that enabled them to have three pastors and an intern. The youth pastor who serves the entire parish now sees a number of interested youth attend the events, when before very little was happening.

A youth minister in Huntington, Indiana, writes of something similar:

> **Five small churches in a rural area became concerned over the lack of youth ministry being done in their congregations. One of the churches was considering shutting its doors because of a lack of**

enthusiasm and growth. So leaders from these churches met together to chart a better future for themselves.

They decided to shut down one church, absorbing its members into the other four congregations. The vacant church building was then made available as a youth center for the combined youth ministry of the four remaining churches. Together they had enough resources to hire an experienced youth minister, who now meets weekly with the pastors of the four churches for accountability and encouragement.

All four churches supply adult volunteers for activities at the youth center. Presently around 200 high school youths can be found at this youth center on a weekly basis.

Find alternatives to entertainment-based ministry—like small groups for discipleship and Bible study.

In addition to combining resources, congregations can consider an approach that is being used with success in both small and large churches. It is the small group approach where six young people and two adults form a group for Bible study and discussion. The focus of these group meetings is on learning how to become disciples of Jesus Christ.

The focus of traditional youth ministry programming, on the other hand, is entertainment, usually in the form of one speaker and a large audience—a model that attracts youth with a heavy fare of fun activities. It is an approach adopted by youth ministers when they noted the success of Young Life and similar parachurch youth organizations in attracting large numbers of young people. Yet now the weaknesses of this approach are being recognized by many of today's current youth ministry writers and practitioners.

Coauthor Dave Rahn reports that when he first began to direct Campus Life clubs for Youth for Christ, he was given two resources to help him do his job: a manual of potential meetings and a "hot seat"—a stool with screen mesh for a seat, which was wired to a battery and coil off a Model T. Club directors (i.e., Campus Life youth workers) would hold a button switch which when depressed would send a harmless but jarring electrical shock through the person on the stool.

As fun and popular as this gimmick was to use, Dave was given some advice about the limitations of the hot seat. "The hot seat may attract kids to Campus Life," he was told, "but it takes spiritual substance to keep them involved. Don't let the entertainment become the dominant reason why youth attend."

When Young Life founder Jim Rayburn said, "It is a sin to bore a kid," he was reacting to some of the staid approaches being used in churches he had observed. But as Mark DeVries rightly says,

Keeping teenagers from ever being bored in their faith can actually deprive them of opportunities to develop the discipline and perseverance needed to live the Christian life. It might be more of a sin to suggest to young people that the Christian life is always fun and never boring.[11]

One is reminded of the words of Christ: "If anyone would come after me, he must deny himself and take up his cross and follow me. For whoever wants to save his life will lose it, but whoever loses his life for me and for the gospel will save it" (Mark 8: 34-35).

Gordon Gathright, pastor of youth and family for Hastings United Methodist Church, discovered this. He was one of those who used fun and entertainment to attract young people to his youth group. But when it came time to squeeze a religious message into the life of the evening, he found it hard to challenge the kids.

Though 40 to 50 teenagers came to these group meetings, the faces were always changing—he was not seeing the same ones each time. More disconcerting was the lack of desired outcomes—instead of commitment, he saw biblical illiteracy. Few actually encountered Jesus Christ.

Finding some students who really wanted to connect in a significant way with their peers and with a faith-oriented adult, he shifted to a small-group approach in which six young people met with two adults. After two years of struggling against naysayers, he now has a youth program where 125 sixth-through-twelfth graders meet weekly in a small group.

Twelve of these young people joined Gathright in praying that a Bible study fellowship could be established that would be an outreach to the community. After struggling through a small beginning, their Wednesday evening fellowship now draws 50 to 70 youth, half of them unchurched. After some icebreaker games and 40 minutes of praise singing, one of the youth gives a 20-minute message. Then everyone assembles in small groups to discuss the message.

I asked Gordon about the results of his small-group approach. He listed them:

- More kids at worship.
- More kids willing to share their faith.
- Stronger youth leadership.
- More who are willing to identify themselves as disciples of Christ.

- More that are Biblically informed.
- More who are interested.

And none of these occurred with any regularity during his entertainment-driven programming.

His youth activities reflect the mission statement he developed with his youth, one that is intentional about making disciples of Jesus Christ: "We call and equip youths and their families to be faithful, hope-filled followers of Jesus Christ, and empowering them to be leaders in their world."

In keeping with this mission statement, some youth activities of the past were discontinued because they did not contribute to the declared mission. Others were added. For instance, now each small group is asked to be involved in a regular mission project. For some, *regular* means often as once a month.

I find it significant that the national survey of randomly chosen youths in the mid-1950s (described in chapter one) did not show boredom as a prominent characteristic of church youth. What characterized youth work then? Not entertainment or fun activities organized by a youth minister, but personal involvement and responsibility. Youth of the church were members of a league or fellowship that they ran themselves. They elected their officers and project secretaries and sent them to workshops for training. These youth were totally responsible for carrying out the mission of their youth organization. Could this be a major reason why the vast majority viewed their church as a vital factor in their life?

Assessing the effectiveness of the entertainment approach

There is more than anecdotal evidence for the ineffectiveness of the entertainment approach, and good reason why this approach contributes to an apathetic youth group. To determine the relative effectiveness of the entertainment approach, we formulated an item that described four contrasting approaches to youth ministry (based on four of Richard Niebuhr's five descriptions of how Christians relate to their culture[12]). Each description required a couple of sentences. We asked respondents to choose the description that best described how they wanted their youth to relate to today's culture. Here are summary descriptions of these four approaches to youth ministry:

Four Approaches to Youth Ministry
- Arranging events to protect youth from temptation
- Trying to win youths' interest through entertainment and fun
- Involving youth in both community and church responsibilities
- Challenging youth to transform society by living out Christ's gospel

Our description of the entertainment approach, which 265 youth ministers identified as characterizing their approach to youths, was this:

My emphasis is to establish a relationship with youth and gain their interest in church. Therefore, I avoid turning them off through a heavy religious diet, but instead stress gaining their interest and participation through entertainment and recreational events.

The ineffectiveness of this approach is apparent in our data. In fact, it ranks as the poorest approach in almost every category of the study and poorest in achieving the desired outcomes of a youth ministry.

To illustrate, note in figure 2.9 how the youth ministers evaluated the degree to which their youth take part in public prayer, witness, educational and ministry opportunities. The higher the score, the higher the evaluation.

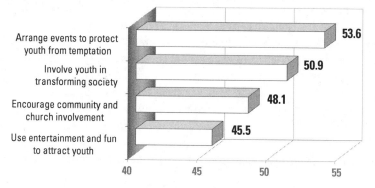

Figure 2.9—Youth approach and youths' activity in public witness

Youth who regularly are faced with exciting events, novel and entertaining, soon come to expect that everything should be fun. Their expectations no longer include the need to accept responsibility, or to work through difficult ministry situations. Because they view their congregation as their parents' church and not something for which they are responsible, they do not become involved in congregational activities. Nor do they seek out Bible studies, service, or learning situations.

A purpose-driven approach as remedy for apathetic students

One approach to disinterested and bored youth is to put them to work, to give them responsibilities, to challenge them with the exciting possibility of helping to transform society and make life better for someone else.

Doug Fields, youth pastor at Saddleback Church in Southern California, insists that a healthy youth ministry is a purpose-driven youth ministry—which means pursuing and reflecting the purposes commanded by Jesus and manifested in the early church.

In his book, *Purpose-Driven Youth Ministry,* Fields identifies five purposes for his youth ministry: evangelism, worship, fellowship, discipleship, and ministry. He views a healthy youth ministry as one that constantly encourages students to discover their gifts and put them into practice through ministry and mission opportunities.[13]

Once his youth have arrived at a statement of purpose, he creates a game to help everyone memorize the statement so that it becomes the guiding purpose in all the youth events. Central to the approach of his youth organization is evangelism. To accomplish this he involves the youth in programs designed to reach the uncommitted. For these he employs four principles:

- A positive environment
- An element of fun
- Student involvement
- An understandable message[14]

Mike Rinehart, pastor at Grace Lutheran Church in Conway, Texas, writes about his experience with youth programs in Paul Hill's book *Up the Creek with a Paddle.*

A few years ago I was running two programs for junior high youths at my church. One was high content for the highly committed. It provided depth for those who were searching for it. The other was a low-content, sloppy, gross, filled-with-lots-of-surprises program designed to attract new youths and be an entryway to the congregation.

While our numbers were higher for the sloppy-gross program, what surprised me were the weekly visitors that were showing up for the high-content program. The moral? How about this: today's youths are attracted to high-energy fun and games, but deep inside they crave more than just fun and games. They're searching for community—genuine Christian community, complete with trust, love, and conversation on the stuff of their everyday lives.

Here's the problem: youths usually cannot articulate what it is they want or need, because—like adults—they don't know.[15]

Rinehart at Grace Lutheran further adds:

There are four basic keys to a balanced youth ministry that need attention if a church wishes to keep its program healthy. Think of them like that old four basic food groups: worship, outreach, learning, and fellowship—WOLF (or FLOW spelled backwards)

- *Worship.* The best youth ministries have focused on getting youths to worship through choirs, drama groups, services, and so forth. They offer opportunities for youths to worship with youths while off at retreats or by having a strong devotional time at the beginning or end of youth meetings or events.
- *Outreach.* In washing the disciples' feet Jesus showed them that the greatest must be the least, and that being one of his followers meant being a servant. After a steady diet of servant projects, youths soon discover that it means a lot more to them than going to the amusement park, and they can have just as much fun.
- *Learning.* No youth program is complete unless it challenges youths to grow in their understanding of the Bible, the Christian faith, the world they live in, and how these three interrelate. Youths don't want extra school (which is how they often view the church), but they do want to learn; some just know it.
- *Fellowship.* Churches that ignore this do so at their own peril. Adolescence is about relationships. Friends are central to youth. If enduring friendships are not built, youths will gravitate to other places where they can be established.[16]

Concern 4
Inadequate Finances

Somehow, youth work in the church has been viewed as the popcorn stand that one passes on the way to the main arena of church endeavor. The lower estimate of its importance is reflected in the number of dollars appropriated for salaries and youth programs.

The tragedy is that some gifted and committed youth ministers are forced out of the profession due to a lack of financial support. These men and women must take other jobs to support their families because the compensation given them is not adequate. Others who stay on and struggle with inadequate finances battle the feeling of being a second-class citizen in work of the Kingdom.

Coauthor Karen E. Jones tells of her experience at Huntington College.

During my years as professor of youth ministry, I have met with hundreds of prospective students and their parents. During our conversations the issue of finances has surfaced repeatedly. Overwhelmingly, the top questions raised by parents about their sons' and daughters' prospective careers in youth ministry are these: Will they be able to find a job? Will they be able to support themselves and a family on a youth minister's salary?

The issue is an important one, because we are facing the largest teen population ever to be on our horizon. Salaries should be adequate so that those who respond to God's call to enter this field are able to stay.

Group magazine editor Rick Lawrence, when reporting on a 1999 survey by his magazine of youth minister salaries, included this significant question: *Do you have an additional job outside the church?* One third (32 percent) answered yes. This means that a third of those in the study were moonlighting to make ends meet. (Contributing to this high percentage, however, is the fact that 16 percent of *Group's* sample were part-time youth ministers.)

The good news in the survey is that 1997 salaries, compared to those given in 1990, were up 22 percent for males and 32 percent for females. Though this increase is impressive, the bad news is that the average new salary of $26,625 is still not enough to support a family.[17]

The significance of this issue is found in how youth ministers responded to the items given below—items that trouble many youth ministers, items that identify not only the dilemmas created by an inadequate salary and fringe benefits, but also the dismay felt when the youth budget is too small to accomplish what needs doing.

<u>Concern</u>
Inadequate Finances

- I am not paid what I deserve.
- Our youth programs do not receive enough funding.
- My health and pension benefits are not adequate.
- Money is too often a deciding factor in our youth ministry.
- I have a hard time paying all my personal bills.

An estimate of how many youth ministers writhe under the feeling of being underpaid and undersubsidized is seen in their responses to the following item. It is the one drawing the highest response of the five items:

I am not paid what I deserve. This concerns me.

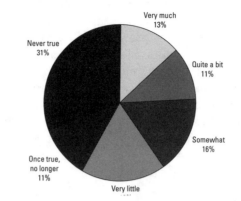

Figure 2.10—Percent concerned over inadequate salary

As can be seen in figure 2.10, salary is a pressing concern for one out of four (24 percent) and an issue for at least an additional 16 percent. Only one in three (31 percent) say this has never been a concern of theirs. Here we have another congregationally oriented concern—that is, a concern that a congregation can alter.

We get a better idea of the financial pressures youth ministers experience when we look at their fringe benefits. According to *Group's* 1999 survey of youth ministers, approximately half receive no fringe benefits—not even for car or travel expenses. Lacking fringe benefits, then their base salary is, of course, less livable.

Fringe benefits given youth ministers in 1999

- Nearly half (47 percent) receive no car or travel allowance
- Nearly half (47 percent) are given no continuing education
- Half (51 percent) are given no pension or retirement contribution
- Half (52 percent) are given no professional supplies or book allowances
- More than half (57 percent) receive a housing allowance
- Most (64 percent) receive no contribution to social security
- More than a third (38 percent) receive no health insurance

As mentioned earlier, this *Group* survey included part-time paid youth pastors, who represented 16 percent of the sample. Obviously, some of these would not be eligible for fringe benefits. But even subtracting them from consideration, we become aware of the fact that a significant number of youth ministers receive no fringe benefits.[18]

Those most concerned over inadequate finances

There is something dismal about this cluster "Inadequate Finances,"
because they correlate with "Burnout" (see chapter three, page 109). The
"Burnout" items describe a loss of enthusiasm for one's work, weariness in
spending time with youth, and a reoccurring thought of leaving the profession. This correlation suggests that there is a connection between
receiving a low salary and struggling to keep one's personal vision alive.

Congregations fail to realize the devastating impact that inadequate
finances can have on youth ministers. They begin questioning their
worth. They gradually develop a low opinion of their abilities, and their
vision of trying to reach young people for Christ and service in his
church is dulled.

I know this feeling well. As a college pastor I was at the bottom of
an already low salary scale. With a wife and two children, I found that I
did not have enough money to purchase groceries at the end of the
month. I had no recourse but to go to the bank and make short-term
loans. I remember well my feelings: *Am I not doing an adequate job to
be given a living wage? Why is my income so low—is it because I am not
worth more?* I hated the low self-esteem it gave me.

What congregations can do

Fortunately, this concern of youth ministers can be eliminated by alert
and thoughtful congregations. Salaries can be raised and fringe benefits
given. Even a few members of a congregation can do a lot, unofficially,
to prick the balloon of financial concern. This is what happened for a
couple youth workers, reported in *Group* magazine:

> **My wife and I have been renting a two-bedroom
> duplex from an elderly couple in our community for
> four years. The rent wasn't much to begin with, but
> neither is my salary. About eight months ago, one of
> her sons—a wealthy businessman—offered to pay our
> rent indefinitely. It's all the more unexpected because,
> though he was raised in a Christian home, he isn't a
> follower of Christ. (Brian Wilcox, Minnesota)**

> **My wife and I were married right out of college, and
> we immediately went into the ministry. Back then
> every piece of furniture we owned was a hand-me-
> down. Our bed was so old it would bend in the mid-
> dle. When a family in our church practically adopted**

us as their own children, their gift to us for our
first wedding anniversary was a brand new bed.
(Dennis Poulette, Florida)

One youth minister receives a vacation each year after their big
winter youth discipleship weekend—a gift from a prominent member
of the community who is also a member of the congregation. Though
no longer a parent of a teen, this person recognizes the long hours
the youth minister has worked on the event, particularly the hours
spent away from his spouse. He recognizes that the church cannot
afford to reward him financially and that the discipleship event with
its long hours is considered part of his job responsibilities. This busi-
nessman is also aware that in the business world, such work constitutes overtime and is therefore recognized with comp time or bonus-
es, or both. His gift, therefore, not only recognizes outstanding work,
but also the stress and time way from his home. It is an attempt to
help the youth minister and spouse nurture a relationship that had to
be neglected.

Congregational leaders need to review what they are providing their
youth minister and take the necessary steps for making sure that the
salary and fringe benefits provide an adequate income. Laborers are worthy of their hire.

Concern 6
Lack of Personal Support in Ministry

A sixth concern of youth ministers is the low respect they sense being
given their area of work. It is an attitude youth ministers have con-
fronted for some time.

Southwestern Theological Seminary professor of youth education
Wesley Black tells of his rude awakening to the low importance being
accorded his youth ministry.

In the first church I served as a youth minister, I
worked almost totally with the youths. There were
few adults who volunteered to help—but I did most
of the planning and promotion. I also did most of
the work.

When I talked with the pastor, I discovered that
the church always looked upon youth ministry as
one of the extracurricular activities that went along
with the study, ministry, and worship of the rest of
the church. Youth ministry was simply planning the
fun element while others ministered in serious

ways. It was seen as a program separate from the
life and work of the church.[19]

This perception of youth ministry is reflected in casual and well-mean-
ing comments, writes Jay Kesler, former president of Youth for Christ:

> When people would ask me what I did, and I would
> tell them I was a youth worker, they would often say,
> "What do you plan to do when you grow older?" or
> "Have you ever thought of going into the ministry?"
> Over the years I began to counter with, "I am in
> youth work just like the president of the state uni-
> versity is in youth work, or the principal of the high
> school, or the math teacher."[20]

Kesler found it necessary to address the low respect reflected in
people's remarks by referring to the importance of his work.

A youth minister wrote the following entry in his personal journal
following a staff meeting:

> Today in staff meeting we were discussing the new
> youth intern that will be coming on staff in a week.
> One of the pastors indicated that the intern had a
> degree in recreation management but no formal
> training in ministry. Then one of the staff persons
> said what drew a round of laughter: "That sounds
> like a youth pastor." I am personally sick of the lack
> of respect I get at this church.

Former Group Publishing staff worker Jolene Roehlkepartain found a
contrasting evaluation of youth ministers when she conducted a survey
of 535 families in 20 rapidly growing churches in 20 cities across North
America. The study—whose purpose was to find out what attracts people to a church—discovered that for four out of every five respondents,
the church's youth ministry is a very important factor. Only preaching
outranked the youth program in contributing to people's decision to
join their current church.[21]

Notwithstanding the acknowledged impact of a vital youth ministry
on church growth, the common congregational attitude, subtle but real, is
this: youth ministry is less important than what is being carried out by
other pastoral staff members. In general, it occupies the lowest position
on people's totem pole of respect and importance. Unfortunately, youth
ministers are fully aware of this attitude, and it troubles them. That is
why the following five items correlated to form the cluster given below.

CLUSTER
Lack of Personal Support in Ministry

- I feel less appreciated than other staff members.
- The church views youth ministers with less respect than other staff members.
- I lack the affirmation that I would like.
- Sometimes it is hard to know who my real bosses are.
- It seems like my job description is always changing.

Fortunately this concern is not as widespread as the ones we have already considered. This is seen in the percentage responses to the item drawing the highest response of the five:

The church views youth ministers with less respect than other staff members. This concerns me.

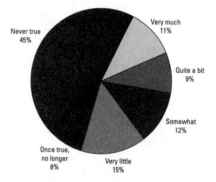

Figure 2.11—Percent concerned over low respect

As seen in figure 2.11, the most significant percentages are the 45 percent and 8 percent. They indicate that more than half the youth ministers sense respect and affirmation from their congregation But the issue is troubling for 20 percent—one in five—and a concern felt to some degree by another 12 percent. These two groups represent a third (32 percent) of the sample.

Those especially conscious of low respect

Youth ministers especially conscious of low respect are those whose youth group is smaller than 40, and whose church has less than 500 in Sunday attendance, and is located in a rural area or small town. In a way this seems strange. One would think that youth ministers working in a small, more personal situation would be better known and appreciated. But it is not so. The ones most conscious of being respected and appreciated are youth ministers working in congregations over a thousand. Apparently they are the ones most likely to be thanked and honored for their work.

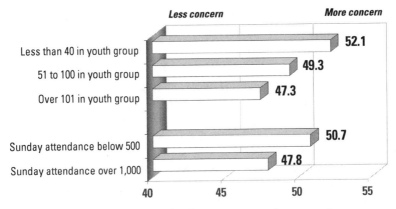

Figure 2.12—Variation in concern over low respect

Though the differences between top and bottom groups are not large, it is unlikely that they would have occurred by chance. Clearly, respect for the importance of a youth minister diminishes for those serving smaller youth groups, in smaller churches.

This concern over "Lack of Personal Support in Ministry," though not widely felt, does have a network of contributing concerns, indicated by how they correlate with "Low Respect." Each of these contributing concerns might, at times, contribute to the feelings underlying this concern—as these, which demonstrate a relationship:

Clusters correlating with lack of personal support	Correlation
Disinterested Youth	.47
Inadequate Finances	.54

What congregations can do

Willow Creek Community Church's director of Student Impact, Bo Boshers, writes in *Student Ministry for the 21st Century* about how to find support in a church—support that he gets, first of all, from a prayer team support.

> I'll never forget a gift I received from a student leader in Southern California. This mature, godly young woman gave me a gift of prayer: the commitment to pray for me, my family, and the ministry every day for an entire year. She followed up regularly, adding new prayer requests to her list. Her gift marked my life and my ministry.

I decided from then on that I would search for a few men and women each ministry season who would commit to pray for me and the ministry. Building a prayer team has become a meaningful, vital part of my ministry.[22]

In a large congregation in California, I learned from the youth minister that he had three prayer groups that met with him each week at different times. The fact that he took the time to tell me about them showed how much he appreciated the support they gave him.

Beyond a prayer team, a second source of support and respect for a youth minister is the church council, board of deacons or elders, or other ruling body. This group of elected leaders is a congregation's opinion makers. Their offhand comments and commendations can help create a climate of respect for a youth minister. This group needs to spend some time thinking into ways by which they can increase congregational respect and appreciation for the difficult and trying work of a youth minister.

A most important person—the key person, in fact—in creating a climate of respect and appreciation for a youth minister is the senior pastor. When he or she makes public statements of appreciation for what is being done, those words of praise and commendation set a tone and climate that, over time, come to characterize the congregation.

Another valuable source of support is a network of parents that a congregation helps establish. These people can become knowledgeable regarding the problems, issues, and difficulties a youth minister faces. Gaining their advice and counsel becomes another way by which their support is solidified.

Summary

This chapter has focused on a foundational aspect of a transformational youth ministry—that of congregation taking the initiative to erase six concerns that are troubling to youth ministers:
- Time conflict: job demands versus personal needs
- Time conflict: administrative duties versus youth contacts
- Disconnect between youth and church
- Disinterested and apathetic youth
- Inadequate salary and youth budget
- Lack of personal support in ministry

Congregational leaders can take steps to mitigate the time conflict and lessen the disconnect between adults and youth. They can personally challenge the youth to become missional agents, and become involved in outreach activities.

A congregation can decide to provide adequate finances for the youth minister, as well as create a climate of appreciation and personal support. And, mercifully, leaders can establish boundaries of time within which the youth minister is to serve. This will include providing volunteers to assist in program and administrative tasks—ones usually left with the youth minister. For these volunteers to be effective, however, there needs to be a continuing education program that equips a growing number of such people.

Efforts to mitigate these six troubling concerns will increase the effectiveness of youth ministers and encourage them to stay on their jobs longer. This initiative is foundational because it enables a youth ministry to get off the ground and move.

THINK IT OVER, TALK IT THROUGH

1. What illustrations can you come up with for each of the six congregationally created concerns?

2. What advice would you offer to youth ministers who are concerned about how their own devotional time seems to get squeezed out by the job?

3. What should a congregation do if they discovered that their youth minister was among the 31 percent who are *very much* concerned that their devotional time is sacrificed in the busyness of the job?

4. What do you think is a reasonable percentage of each week's time that youth ministers should spend in administration and planning?

5. What are the best indicators to monitor the strength or weakness of the youth ministry's connection to the rest of the church?

6. What can youth ministers do when their congregations are unaware of their concerns?

7. How do you think your own congregation or organization measures up against the concerns discussed in this chapter?

Notes 2

1. Mark DeVries, *Family-Based Youth Ministry* (Downers Grove, Illinois: InterVarsity Press, 1994), 15-16.

2. Wesley Black, *An Introduction to Youth Ministry* (Nashville: Broadman Press, 1991), 170.

3. Richard Dunn and Mark Senter, *Reaching a Generation for Christ* (Chicago: Moody Press, 1997), 150.

4. Steve Farcas, with Jean Johnson, *Kids These Days: What Americans Really Think about the Next Generation* (New York: Public Agenda, 1997), 8-9.

5. Kenda Dean and Ron Foster, *The Godbearing Life: The Art of Soul Tending for Youth Ministry* (Nashville: Upper Room Books, 1998), 17.

6. Mark Yaconelli, "Youth Ministry: A Contemplative Approach," *Christian Century* (April 21-28 1999): 450.

7. Yaconelli, 452, 454.

8. Mark Senter III, *The Coming Revolution in Youth Work: And Its Radical Impact on the Church* (Wheaton, Illinois: Victor Books, 1992), 185.

9. Merton Strommen, *A Study of Generations* (Minneapolis: Augsburg Publishing House, 1980), 247.

10. Dean and Foster, 64.

11. DeVries, 27.

12. *In Passing on the Faith: A Radical New Model for Youth and Family Ministry* (Winona, Minnesota: St. Mary's Press, 2000), Dick Hardel and I devote an entire chapter to Niebuhr's five descriptions (pages 262-277), which we apply to five different ways youth ministries are being conducted.

13. Doug Fields, *Purpose-Driven Youth Ministry* (Grand Rapids, Michigan: Zondervan Publishing House, 1998), 47-50.

14. Fields, 117.

15. Mike Rinehart, "W.O.L.F.: The Balanced Ministry Proverb," in Paul Hill (ed.), *Up the Creek with a Paddle: Building Effective Youth and Family Ministry* (Minneapolis: Augsburg Fortress, 1998), 55-56.

16. Rinehart, 55-56.

17. Rick Lawrence, "The Money Game," *Group: Empowering Youth Leaders for Real-Life Ministry* 26, 1 (November/December 1999): 73-74.

18. Lawrence, 73.

19. Black, 37.

20. Gary Dausey (ed.), *The Youth Minister's Source Book* (Grand Rapids, Michigan: Zondervan, 1983), 9.

21. Jolene L. Roehlkepartain, *Youth Ministry: Its Impact on Church Growth* (Loveland, Colorado: Group Publishers, 1989), 7.

22. Bo Boshers, *Student Ministry for the 21st Century* (Grand Rapids, Michigan: Zondervan Publishing House, 1991), 51.

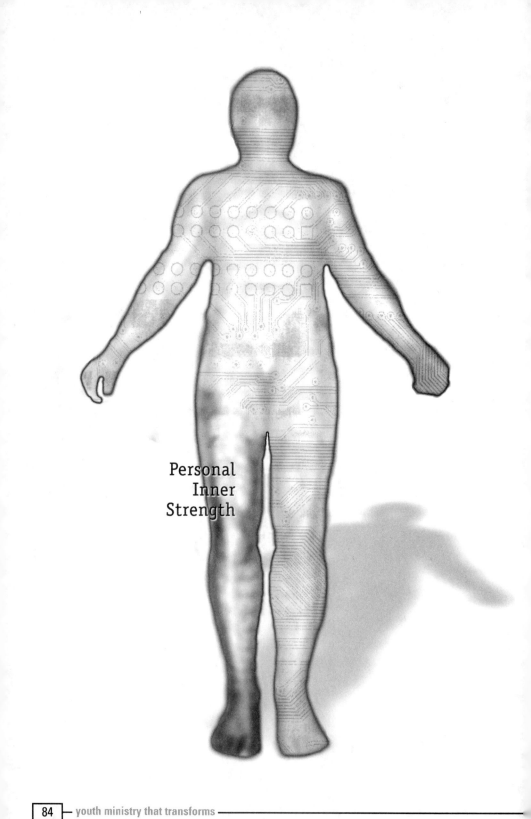

Personal
Inner
Strength

Chapter 3

Personal Inner Strength: To Offset Six Concerns Debilitating Youth Ministers

Merton Strommen

This chapter, about youth ministers and the personal inner strength they bring to their job, calls attention to another foundational aspect of a transformational youth ministry—one that undergirds all that a youth minister does. If we think of those who "wait on the Lord as mounting up with wings like an eagle," we can also think of them as able to "walk and not faint"(Isaiah 40:31).

"Congregational Initiative" (what a youth minister's church or organization can do for him or her—the subject of the previous chapter) and "Personal Inner Strength" (what youth ministers can do for themselves—the subject of this one) are the two legs that enable a youth minister to walk and not faint. Personal Inner Strength especially can counter the spiritual fatigue that can overwhelm youth ministers, making them vulnerable to the six debilitating concerns discussed in this chapter. Youth ministers must assume responsibility for undergirding all they do with the resources of God and his power.

Youth ministers and spiritual fatigue

There is a spiritual fatigue that can overwhelm youth ministers, which makes them prey to debilitating concerns. Kenda Dean writes about this in *The Godbearing Life: The Art of Soul Tending for Youth Ministry*.

> After a few years of ministry—three, to be exact—
> the program I worked with began to seem weary. If
> God made me gung-ho, God also made me tired—
> and not because I needed more sleep. My soul was
> empty. I was running on fumes, and the ministry
> entrusted to my care was too. The depressing truth
> was that youths were not the only ones who needed
> more substantial faith; so did I. Here I was, sup-
> posed to be teaching them to pray, immersing them
> in Scripture, involving them with the poor—and
> when was the last time I did any of that for the
> sake of my soul and not for the sake of my job? God

**knew I was faking it and I knew I was faking it, but
I didn't know how to stop faking it without drop-
ping up altogether.**[1]

A spiritual fatigue such as this can affect the spirit of a youth minister,
resulting in feelings and self-evaluations that undermine a person's
effectiveness. They include these six concerns:

- Feelings of Personal Inadequacy
- Experiencing Strained Family Relations
- A Growing Loss of Confidence
- Feeling Unqualified for the Job
- Feeling Personally Disorganized
- Experiencing Burnout

These six concerns, voiced by the 2,416 youth ministers in the survey,
have a ring of reality. So it seemed to a youth minister who, after
reading an early version of this manuscript, wrote—

**My first reaction to this book was to wonder if
someone had been listening in on my conversations
and rantings for the past 12 years. The material
accurately describes what I and many youth ministers I know experience regularly. I am happy to
encounter this material at a time when our church
is getting ready to hire an associate youth minister,
over whom I will have oversight. Now I have a more
complete understanding of what this person is
going to need to succeed in this ministry.**

Concern 1
Feelings of Personal Inadequacy

"I see my associates achieve some degree of success or receive some
recognition, and I smile and congratulate them enthusiastically," a
youth minister writes. "But inside, I'm eating my heart out. Why do I
feel this way?"

Feelings of inadequacy touch the lives of a significant percentage of
youth ministers. They create a desperate need for outward evidences of
success, coupled with an unconscious drive for perfection. The three
items that formed this first cluster all speak of this emotional hazard to
the effectiveness of a youth minister.

CLUSTER
Feelings of personal inadequacy
- I have a fear of failure.
- I am too critical of myself.
- I feel the emotional strain of my work.

Such feelings can come from sensing the overly high expectations of parents and pastor, from feeling a lack of respect from adults in the congregation, from believing that humility is the same as self-condemnation, and from believing that self-love is sinful.

An estimate of how many are conscious of these feelings is found in the number responding to the third item:

I feel the emotional strain of my work. This concerns me.

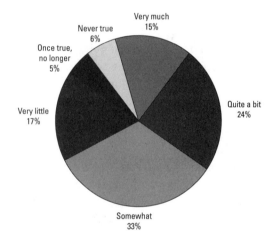

Figure 3.1—Percent concerned over emotional strain

As figure 3.1 illustrates, 39 percent of the respondents indicated high concern about these feelings. That is almost two out of five—a fact that needs to be taken into consideration when seeking to assist those in the profession. Significant, too, is the fact that only 6 percent said this was never true for them.

Who especially is troubled by feelings of inadequacy?

Those new to their job, in general—which fact suggests that the job should include a three-month orientation period during which the person works under the guidance of a mentor. It is significant that the longer people serve as youth ministers, the less likely they will be troubled by this concern. The contrast in scores is striking.

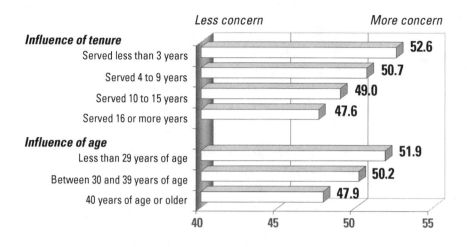

Figure 3.2—Concern over feelings of inadequacy, by tenure and age

As seen in figure 3.2, youth ministers serving less than three years have a standard score of 52.6, whereas those serving 16 years or more register the lowest score of 47.6. This difference of five standard scores is significant. And as might be expected, a similar contrast in score appears between those younger than 29 and those older than 40.

Here again we see the powerful influence of tenure and age (but especially tenure), both of which make an enormous difference in how youth ministers feel about themselves. The longer one serves as youth minister, the higher one scores on measures of competent job performance, confident leadership, effective relationships with youth, theological grounding, achievement in developing adult volunteers, being motivated by God's calling, ability to relate to parents, and making a creative response to the youth culture. (For documentation see figures 9.6 and 9.10, on pages 233 and 237, respectively.) Tenure is an important contributor to how a youth minister evaluates self. (For documentation see figures 9.7—9.10).

One gains further insight into feelings of inadequacy by examining what may intensify them. (I write *may* because correlation does not mean causation. Correlation means only that there is a relationship.) Note what correlates most closely with "Feelings of Inadequacy."

Clusters correlating with feelings of inadequacy

Conflict of time	.52
Lack of personal support in ministry	.49
Disinterested and apathetic youth	.49
Growing loss of confidence	.54
Burnout	.51

The first three of these factors (which we examined in the previous chapter) show how interlocked a youth minister's feelings tend to be with what a congregation does or fails to do. When the job demands too much time, when people give the impression the position is not important, when the youth reflect an attitude of disinterest—when these occur, there is a strong likelihood that the youth minister will experience feelings of inadequacy.

As these feelings mount, one can expect to see an increased "Lack of Confidence" in the youth minister, as well as symptoms of "Burnout." At this point youth ministers begin wondering if they should move on to another congregation or leave the profession.

We should note that there is an advantage to accumulating years of experience as a youth minister. One can surmise that a youth minister learns something (maybe very much) at each place of service. We can also assume that the less able drop out of the profession, with the result that the fittest are the ones who survive.

One youth minister writes that, although the years bring a type of maturity that blunts sharp feelings of inadequacy, they still pose a real life issue.

> **Each of my past four years have given me greater feelings of confidence in my abilities as a youth pastor. However, feelings of inadequacy still sneak up on me from time to time. But they are not as frequent as they once were. Yet I am still concerned about these feelings and my desire for the approval of others. At times it can be what drives me to succeed, and at other times what drives me crazy. I can tell myself that it doesn't matter. Nevertheless, I want to be recognized for my hard work and gifts. Combating these feelings is an ongoing challenge.**

What youth ministers can do

Stephen Covey of *7 Habits of Highly Effective People* fame quotes a maxim central to the changes he proposes: "Sow a thought, reap an action; sow an action, reap a habit; sow a habit, reap a character; sow a character, reap a destiny."[2]

The thoughts he wants to become habits focus on seven natural laws of growth—laws that help one move from total dependence, to independence, and finally to interdependence. These habits for effective leadership are in essence an antidote for feeling inadequate. (The first three habits he calls "private victories," because they move one from dependence to independence.)

- Be proactive. That is, assume responsibility for your own life. Subordinate your feelings of inadequacy by taking initiative and responsibility for making things happen.

- Begin with the end in mind. Start with a clear understanding of your destination. Recognize that you must first arrive at a mental creation. Then comes the second or physical creation, where you start doing what will achieve your destination. To help in this process, write a personal mission statement.

- Put first things first. Learn to say yes to important priorities and no to other things, even if they're urgent ones. This requires time management: identifying activities that are both important and urgent as well as important activities that are not urgent. It also involves identifying activities that are not important but have a note of urgency, as well as those that are neither important nor urgent. Consider these when doing monthly and daily planning.

- Think win/win. Create solutions that are mutually satisfying and beneficial for all concerned. This means considering different points of view with the idea of arriving at a new and better ways of doing ministry.

- Seek first to understand, then to be understood. Genuinely try to understand the other person—a process that involves empathetic listening until you begin to see the world they see, and understand how they feel. Seeking to be understood means making effective presentations that inspire trust, show an awareness of feelings, and are logical in what you communicate.

- Synergize. Create a synergistic culture by involving people in the analysis and solution of problems. The effort will release creativity and a commitment to what is created. It involves teamwork, team building, the cultivation of gifts, and the development of creativity in the youth and adults with whom one works.

- Sharpen the saw. Preserve and enhance the four dimensions of your nature—physical, spiritual, mental, and social-emotional. The physical requires attention to exercise, nutrition, and stress management; the spiritual involves prayer, worship, study of God's Word; the mental includes reading, writing, and visualizing; and the social-emotional demands time for service, friends, fun activities, and music.

A thorough reading of Covey's popular book will show you how these seven habits can become part of your destiny and can replace feelings of inadequacy.

Finally, a youth minister can look to a support group of fellow youth ministers for bolstering. In the words of one who gained encouragement through colleagues:

> **When I began my youth ministry career 10 years ago, a friend of mine told me to keep every note of encouragement that I received and place it in an "encouragement file." Then, whenever I faced a discouraging time, I should take out the notes and read them. So I began collecting notes. Some years brought many more notes than others.**
>
> **It's been a little over ten years now, and I never read one of them. Frankly, when I was discouraged, the notes seemed too shallow. Instead, when I was discouraged, I turned to people around me who had been in ministry longer than me. There was great comfort found in the experience of those who had gone before me. They knew best what I was feeling and what I needed.**

This youth minister's response to discouragement is a key concept in learning how to counter feelings of inadequacy: to take advantage of the support that is available from more experienced youth ministers.

Concern 2
Experiencing Strained Family Relations

In our sample of 2,416 youth ministers, 81 percent are married—four out of five. Unfortunately for some, their job as minister and its excessive time involvement creates conflict between spouses.

Marital conflict for this reason is the subject of Richard Laliberte's article "Men and Women Managing Conflict." Thanks to videotapes of couples he has made for research purposes, Laliberte narrates a typical conflict:

> **It often starts with the woman bringing up an issue: "We have a problem with money" or "You don't talk to me" or "We need to spend more time together" Often the man perceives what she's saying more negatively than she's intending. Next, the guy— even if he is staying in the discussion—often sig-**

nals in the same way that he's not interested in talking. He withdraws, perhaps by turning away from her, rolling his eyes and saying to himself, "Here we go again." The woman then pursues the discussion, often in an increasingly negative way, and the man withdraws more.

In many cases, the man may try to cut off discussion by agreeing with her prematurely—"Yeah, you're right so tell me what to do and I'll do it." This buries the issue and it will likely come back to haunt the couple later on. Or sometimes he may come back with something negative, like "You're always attacking me. You're just like your mother," and all of a sudden they're off into an increasingly negative cycle of attacks and counterattacks.[3]

Chuck Neder echoes this problem in his soliloquy "Too Busy: Reflections of a Person Going Mad with the Busy Addiction":

Too busy to stop. To smell the roses. To enjoy a sky full of stars. To notice little eyes that look to me longing for time with daddy. To notice hands across the bed that reach out to be held.

Too busy to spend time with the Lord. To pray with my wife. To tuck in my children. To call my friend. To thank the many who help me. I am a busy person with so many important things to do. Do I know or do I care that my busy life destroys relationships, kills the dreams of my spouse, discourages and alienates my children?

I protest to anyone who says, "Slow down! You're sucking the life out of all who love you!" They are to blame. Don't my kids know my busy schedule doesn't have time for them? Doesn't my wife understand that my wedding vows are less important than my busy schedule? Haven't they got it? I never see them because I'm working for Him and for them.[4]

This busyness, caused by the never-ending demands of a youth ministry, has caused many youth ministers to identify with the cluster of items given below.

CLUSTER
Strained Family Relations

- I often experience conflict at home over my job.
- My spouse has difficulty understanding my ministry.
- Conflicts often arise over how much time I spend at home and at work.
- My family gets only leftovers of my time.

An estimate of how many youth ministers struggle with job time versus family time is seen in the item that drew the highest number of responses:

My family gets only leftovers of my time. This concerns me.

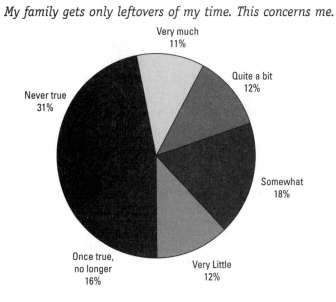

Figure 3.3—Percent concerned over family getting only leftovers of time

From figure 3.3 we can assume that most of the 30 percent who say this issue *never* concerns them are unmarried.

However, for a small number—one-fourth of the sample (23 percent)—a spouse who feels cheated out of family and marriage time is a real and troubling situation. There is no question that the time demands of a youth ministry indeed strain the marriage relationship for many youth ministers. Theoretically, all youth ministers need to do to save themselves from dilemma is to establish some boundaries on the days and hours that their students can expect their youth leaders to be "on call." But this is difficult to do in reality. Youth work is a never-ending job.

What is interesting about this concern is that no group of youth ministers is more concerned over this issue than others—that is, it affects everyone equally. No marked differences in scores appear when we compare youth ministers on the basis of age, education, size congregation, denomination, gender, or seminary education. This issue can creep up on any youth minister.

One naturally wonders if youth ministry causes divorces, directly or indirectly. The only indication in the survey of this is the number in the study who have been divorced. Fortunately, this number is a relatively low 4 percent—an extremely low percentage when one considers that 70 percent of the youth ministers are between 30 and 60 years of age and living in a country where the divorce rate is nearing 50 percent.

The seriousness of this concern over "Strained Family Relations" is twofold:
• First, an embattled family life has a dampening effect on the spirit of a youth minister. He or she cannot readily enter into the life of the youth group with freedom and enthusiasm if there is a nagging sense that a spouse back home is unhappy.
• Second, because youth ministers work with parents of their students, they need to face realistically the personal problems that fester in their own homes. How else can they encourage parents to address similar issues which threaten their family unity?

What youth ministers can do

First and foremost, youth ministers must view their families as part of their ministry. From the beginnings of the Christian church, the family was considered a holy and sacred place for prayer, worship, and ritual. In the late fourth century, St. John Chrysostom referred to the family as *ekklesia*, the Greek word for *church* in the New Testament.

Youth leaders have a ministry to carry out in their own home—the domestic church—that resembles the ministry they ask parents to carry out with their children and youth. The two ministries are inseparable. What one learns in relating to spouse and children equips one for a larger ministry with families in church.

A family is not merely a collection of separate individuals who simply happen to share the same last name and street address. A family is an organism in which the attitudes, values, and actions of each member interact with those of all the other members.

Case in point: although parents may try to hide their conflicts from the children, it is doubtful that they really succeed. In *Family Crucible*, family therapist Augustus Napier says he frequently finds that the problems of a troublemaking child or adolescent can be traced to some strain in the husband-wife relationship that is upsetting the balance of family life.[5]

Using a Search Institute survey of high school youth, we tried to identify the factor that most powerfully predicts family disunity. Through a complex analysis of data, we found our answer: *My father and mother do not get along with each other. This bothers me.* This factor outranked 39 others in predicting family conflict.[6]

This simple statement turned out to be our most powerful predictor of family disharmony or conflict. Which is to say, whenever husband and wife are at odds with each other, the whole family suffers. The children are prone to become psychological orphans within their own home.

A youth minister plagued with this problem needs to assume responsibility for changing, for the good of both the youth ministry and the family. A good place to begin in assuming responsibility is meeting with one's senior pastor. He or she is only too familiar with this difficulty in dividing responsibility between home and calling, and will likely give a sympathetic ear and assist in achieving a better balance between work and home.

Secondly, this job family tug of war can be eased by talking and consulting with one's associates in youth ministry.

> **I have sought out some very healthy accountability relationships in my current ministry. I meet with one other fellow youth worker regularly for the purpose of asking the tough questions. He knows me well, and has permission to go at me when things aren't right. Whether on the phone, on the golf course, or over a cup of coffee, I have come to look forward to our times of talking. God has used this relationship to keep me healthy.**

Not to be overlooked is the help that can come through seeing a professional counselor or therapist. The issue of "Strained Family Relations" is too important not to.

Concern 3

A Growing Loss of Confidence

I asked a very successful youth minister with 30 years of experience about his first three years in a youth ministry.

"That was when I lost my self-confidence," he replied. "I was actually intimidated by the high school students. I began asking myself, *Is this what I really want?*"

Closely allied with feelings of inadequacy is a growing lack of confidence in one's ability to perform effectively. At such times a youth minister tends to regard evaluations and comments of others as all-important.

Note how the clustered items describe persons whose lack of confidence has made them subject to the evaluations of youth and parents.

CLUSTER
A Growing Loss of Confidence
- I often judge my youth ministry success by numbers.
- I am intimidated by parents.
- I look to my youth to give me a personal sense of approval.

Those most troubled with this feeling evaluate themselves and their ministry by headcounts and youth approval, shrinking from constructive criticism and parental feedback.

Interestingly, less than half of those in the study say that "Youths affirm me often." Most lack this form of support—a support they would appreciate.

Doug Fields is forthright in describing the battles he fought within himself over feelings of inadequacy and lack of self-confidence:

> **Even though I worked exhausting hours, the job wasn't getting done the way everyone seemed to want. Previously unspoken expectations surfaced, and they fueled my workaholic personality to fix everything, even though I couldn't specifically identify the problems. My desire for doing ministry had long moved from pleasing God to appeasing people. I wanted to be liked by everyone, and that desire moved me to feel that I could never do enough to please everyone.[7]**

The apostle Paul was conscious of this tension when he wrote: "Am I now trying to win the approval of men, or of God? Or am I trying to please men? If I were still trying to please men, I would not be a servant of Christ" (Galatians 1:10).

This tension is very real for people in the serving professions. Robert McGee, a professional counselor, writes about how he has battled this tendency.

> **My desire for the approval of others has often been so great that I sometimes joke about having been born an approval addict. Growing up I felt inadequate and tried to win the approval of others, desperately hoping that this would compensate for the negative feelings I had about myself.**

But the conditional approval of others has never been enough to satisfy me. Instead, being praised only reminded me of the disapproval I might encounter if I failed to maintain what I had achieved. I was thus compelled to work harder at being successful. I occasionally find myself falling into this pattern of behavior even now, despite my knowledge, experience, and relationship with God.[8]

How extensive are these feelings among youth ministers? An estimate is available in the item that drew the highest response of the three.

I often judge my youth ministry success by numbers. This concerns me.

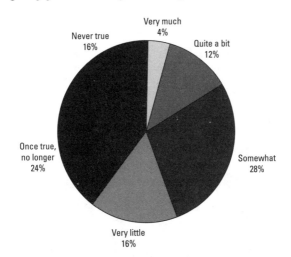

Figure 3.4—Percent concerned over judging success by numbers

The percentages in figure 3.4 indicate that this concern—battled by only 16 percent of the youth ministers—is not as widespread as "Feelings of Personal Inadequacy". What is interesting is the higher percentage (24 percent) who say that using numbers to evaluate their ministry was once true for them—which means we are dealing with an occupational hazard that many youth ministers must face and overcome.

Who are most vulnerable to these feelings? As is true for those troubled with "Feelings of Personal Inadequacy," it is the youngest and those newest to the profession who are concerned by their tendency to count success by numbers.

Little experience and young age also point to lack of confidence, as seen in figure 3.5. The higher scores of the inexperienced and the young contrast strikingly with veterans of 16 years' experience or more, and with persons over 40 years of age.

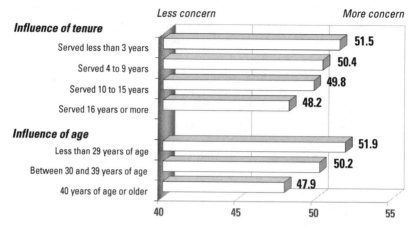

Figure 3.5—Concern over lack of confidence

The diminishing scores evidence the increase in confidence that comes as youth ministers gain experience and years of maturity. It underscores the importance of providing mentors for youth ministers during their vulnerable first three years. They especially need the support and encouragement that a veteran in the field can give them.

What youth ministers can do

I find it significant that the apostle Paul, when writing to his protégé Timothy, reminds him of the potential that is his: "For God did not give us a spirit of timidity," Timothy's mentor writes him, "but a spirit of power, of love and of self-discipline" (2 Timothy 1:7).

We see how God transforms the lives of those choosing to follow him. Peter, the fisherman, whose desire for approval led him to deny Christ, later became a pillar in the early church. In his second New Testament letter he gives the reason for the transformation that took place in his life:

> **His divine power has given us everything we need for life and godliness through our knowledge of him who called us by his own glory and goodness. Through these he has given us his very great and precious promises, so that through them you may participate in the divine nature and escape the corruption in the world caused by evil desires. (2 Peter 1:3-4)**

The apostle Paul was also conscious of these "precious and very great promises" when he wrote to the Corinthian church:

> **For in him (Christ) every one of God's promises is a "Yes." For this very reason it is through him that we say the "Amen," to the glory of God. But it is God who establishes us with you in Christ and has anointed us, by putting the seal on us and giving us his Spirit in our hearts as a first installment. (II Corinthians 1:21-22, RSV)**

Many have found an effective antidote to lack of confidence in memorized promises of God that one can rehearse when threatened by a vexing situation. Consider what it can do for your spirits, for example, when the following words occupy your mind.

"So do not fear, for I am with you; do not be dismayed, for I am your God. I will strengthen you and help you; I will uphold you with my righteous right hand" (Isaiah 41:10).

Not only the sustaining power of God's promises, but also the supporting help of a mentor or fellowship group can help youth ministers take responsibility for combating the debilitating effect of declining confidence.

A youth minister attests to this fact, after reading about troubling personal issues in many youth ministers' lives:

> **From my own perspective, it seems that these issues are largely a reflection of our relationship with Christ. If it is God who has called us to full-time ministry, then it is God who will sustain us and give us the strength to carry out his mission. But spiritual warfare is alive and very much a reality, and Satan knows our weaknesses. If he cannot convince us that we are not good enough for the job in order to disable us, then he will try using every method imaginable. This is where mentorship and friendships of utmost spiritual integrity are crucial—especially friendships, where discernment and love are present.**

Additional sources of strength are found in prayer groups youth ministers can join, in a regular time for private meditation and prayer, and in opportunities for fellowship and talking shop with other leaders.

Mentors (whether formal or informal) of youth ministers should know what contributes to this lack of confidence among novitiate youth ministers. Such factors include the following three, two of which are familiar. The one new to our discussion is unusually intimidating—"Feeling Unqualified for the Job". The fact that these three bear a relationship with a "Growing Loss of Confidence" suggests that when you have one of these feelings, you may have all three.

Clusters correlating with a growing loss of confidence

Feelings of personal inadequacy	.54
Disinterested youth	.54
Feeling unqualified for the job	.47

One might think that the two feelings *inadequacy* and *unqualified* would be one and the same. But, interestingly, they emerge as distinct feelings—which may mean that when answering the survey, respondents were conscious of these two as separate realities and reflected this fact in the way they answered the items.

Concern 4
Feeling Unqualified for the Job

Many youth ministers feel ill equipped for their job, theologically or professionally. They feel unqualified to be serving as a youth minister. Even though the number who feel this way is not great, it represents for some a formidable roadblock to a successful youth ministry.

A contributing reason for feeling unqualified is the enormity of the task. Richard Dunn, former Christian education professor at Trinity Evangelical Theological Seminary, tells about one of his graduates who summed up his experiences after six months on the job: "You told us that ministry was hard, but I never really believed you," the graduate said. "Now I know what you mean. In fact, it is *harder* than you said it would be."

One of the difficulties is trying to understand a changing population. Even the most seasoned youth leaders are at a loss to explain the why of student behavior—both positive and negative. The rapidity of social change, the diversity of contemporary culture, and the complexity of students' lives suggest that what worked before may not be the most effective approach now.[9]

How do we best communicate the gospel to the present generation? How does one understand today's youth in order to minister to them? What are the words and concepts that we should use? These are the kinds of questions that push youth ministers to the wall.

The items that capture this feeling of not being up for the task are found in the cluster given below. They correlate tightly with each other to indicate a consistent awareness in the minds of respondents who feel unqualified. Each item, brought together by the computer, describes a feeling that is very real to some youth ministers.

CLUSTER
Feeling Unqualified for the Job
- I feel like an amateur doing my job.
- I do not feel professionally equipped.
- I feel uncertain about my abilities in ministry.
- I feel inadequate discussing theological issues.
- I feel incompetent when teaching the Bible.

This impressive and sobering list of items describes some of the ways youth ministers feel unqualified for their job.

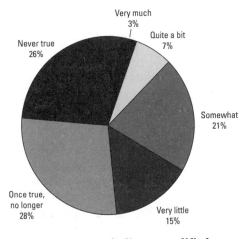

Figure 3.6—Percent feeling unqualified

Note in figure 3.6 the number responding to the highest-ranking item—those who *once* battled feeling unqualified for their job. Though only one in ten (10 percent) are sharply troubled by these feelings, a total of 28 percent have had to cope with this feeling in a way they remember. This means that persons new to the profession are the most susceptible to such feelings. And, as we will learn later, they are the ones most interested in opportunities for professional growth.

Practical skills are the aspect of leadership where youth ministers feel particularly unqualified. They want further training that enables them to counsel both youth and parents, as well as skills that enable them to spiritually nurture youth. They wish for greater understanding in how to train adults for mentoring. These are all areas where youth ministers feel particularly unqualified.

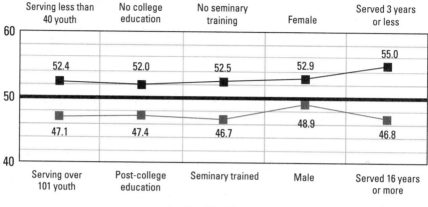

Troubled Most

Serving less than 40 youth	No college education	No seminary training	Female	Served 3 years or less
52.4	52.0	52.5	52.9	55.0
47.1	47.4	46.7	48.9	46.8
Serving over 101 youth	Post-college education	Seminary trained	Male	Served 16 years or more

Troubled Least

Figure 3.7—Those feeling unqualified

Who are the ones most likely to be troubled with feeling unqualified? Note the striking list of contrasting scores in figure 3.7. For some reason those who serve large youth groups feel much more qualified than those serving small groups. It may be that those hired by larger congregations are those who already have a track record of several years during which they have demonstrated special ability. As indicated before, these are no doubt the stars among youth ministers.

More understandable is the heightened sense among college or seminary graduates of feeling qualified. The differences in scores are considerable between those with this training and those without it.

Especially interesting is women's *lesser* sense of being qualified than men are. One can only wonder why. They tend to serve youth groups with more females than males in them—a situation that, seemingly, would give them an advantage.

One reason females feel less qualified may be due in part to serving in a male-dominated profession. In four of the denominations in our sample (Southern Baptist, Assembly of God, Evangelical Free, Evangelical Covenant) only 5 percent of youth ministers are females. The situation is reversed for three mainline denominations (Episcopal, Lutheran, Presbyterian), where 59 percent are female.

What does it feel like to be serving in a denomination where few females are youth ministers? One woman wrote—

> **As one of the only females attending conferences in my state, there have been many times when the men would plan recreational events for themselves**

without inviting me. Often they were things I wouldn't have participated in, even if asked, like a game of basketball. During their times together, though, they would plan and strategize—so that during later meetings, I would be left in the dark about what they were talking about. I had to ask clarifying questions, which made me feel as if I was the only one who didn't understand the issue being discussed—which, of course, was because I was the only one who didn't understand.

It wasn't that they were better or more intelligent, but only that they had dealt with the issue informally ahead of time. I knew this rationally, but I still felt very inadequate during these situations. It was as though I was the dumb female.

The greatest contrast in scores in figure 3.7 is between those new and old on the job. Clearly, those just starting are the most susceptible to feeling unqualified; they are also the most vulnerable to feelings that could propel them *out* of the profession. Their training (which may have been inadequate) has not helped them feel that they are adequately equipped for the challenging task of working with adolescents.

Which factors contribute most to feeling unqualified?

This is an important question. Even though the number of youth ministers troubled over this issue is a low 10 percent, it is a feeling that *once* plagued 28 percent. Obviously, feelings of being unqualified for the job hardly contribute to effective leadership. It is therefore important to probe more deeply to identify the factors that predict this feeling.

In figure 3.8 a computer analysis of this concern (using automatic interaction detection) identifies the factors in their order of importance as they contribute to Feeling Unqualified. Those listed first account for the most variation in scores. We see immediately the powerful influence of a seminary education, which creates the first division in scores and accounts for the greatest amount of variance (see boxes 1 and 11). Next in predictive power is gender—female youth ministers scored higher than males (see boxes 2 and 6). As noted earlier in the above anecdote, female youth ministers often feel intimidated by serving in a man's world. They miss the support that comes with serving as mentee with an older female minister.

The next ranking factor is the youth minister's denomination or youth organization. The fact that certain denominations appear more than once (see boxes 4, 8, and 10) with high scores (61.6) and low scores (45.5) means youth ministers both troubled and untroubled by feeling unqualified can be found in each organization.

It is worth noting that youth ministers who feel least qualified are in rural areas or small towns. Their score of 64.2 is 20.9 standard scores above those serving in large congregations (that is, with Sunday attendance is over 500). Note also that youth ministers whose approach to youth is either to protect them or transform society score 43.3; such a low score means that these youth ministers feel *most* qualified to do their job.

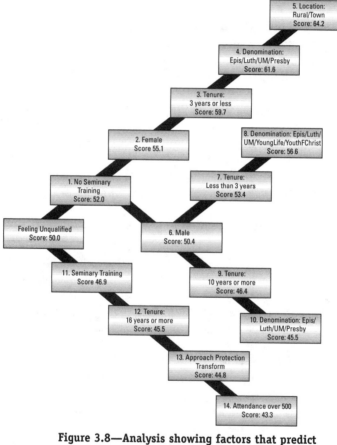

Figure 3.8—Analysis showing factors that predict
feeling unqualified

What youth ministers can do

Feeling unqualified should motivate a youth minister to take advantage of learning opportunities. This should mean going beyond merely looking for new ideas or trying to become skilled in the how-to's of youth ministry.

Assuming responsibility for professional growth means trying to increase one's understanding and knowledge of the field—all of which requires a program of reading and study. Over time a person's attention to the thoughtful side of youth ministry is bound to provide the insight a youth minister needs for becoming creative in ministering to current needs.

Helpful, too, for professional growth is mentoring by veteran peers. Their sharing of what they have learned from experience becomes a training in itself.

Books, videos, mentoring, and such can provide the conceptual tools needed to counter the feelings that often convince one of being unqualified.

Concern 5

Feeling Personally Unorganized

Here is a concern that some youth ministers aggravate by inattention—inattention, first of all, to college and seminary courses that teach organizational skills

Coauthor Karen E. Jones has observed that some students preparing for youth ministry will sometimes complain about the administrative or skills components of their courses, failing to realize the importance of organization and structure. All they think is important is the relational aspect of ministry.

> **One student recently spent time with me outside of class, airing his frustrations over the heavy emphasis on practicality and methodology. He argued that knowing the Bible and developing one's own spiritual walk should be the focus of a youth ministry preparation. His argument was that the Holy Spirit would make sure that our message reached youths and transformed their lives.**
>
> **This same rationale has motivated some seminary students to pursue divinity degrees instead of educational ministries. This low regard for administrative skills causes some students to overlook these components in their preparation or to take them less seriously. Then later, when faced with the reality of administrative demands of the profession, they lack the expertise to meet these demands. This results in frustration and overwhelming feelings of inadequacy.**

Imagine the youth minister who feels unorganized, goalless, and unprepared—a state of mind that can contribute to feeling unqualified for *any* job. As shown in the cluster below, this is the reality for many youth ministers—so real, in fact, that it caused the following three items to correlate.

CLUSTER
Feeling Disorganized

- Administration is one of my greatest weaknesses.
- I feel like I go from one idea to another idea without reason.
- People question my preparedness for youth ministry.

These items describe a person who is floundering, who is uncertain of what to do, and who is unable to structure tasks and time. The flightiness of this person is noticed by parishioners, who take a dismal view of the person's ability to make things happen.

Are many youth ministers conscious of this weakness and concerned about it? We gain a partial answer to this question by noting percentages for the item gaining the highest response:

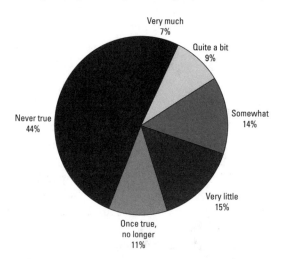

Figure 3.9—Percent troubled by administration

At most we are talking about 15 percent of the youth ministers, though another 14 percent do admit they are somewhat concerned over this tendency. Almost half (44 percent) resolutely say this is never true for them, and another 11 percent say it was once true for them but is no longer—all of means that this is *not* a concern for over half our respondents.

Still, this concern cannot be dismissed lightly. We see in another part of the survey that only 62 percent are willing to agree that they are *good organizers*. Only 42 percent are willing to agree that they are *good delegators*. We must recognize that here is an area of leadership where much learning needs to take place, especially for those new to the profession. Those who feel disorganized have yet to learn how to carefully select, train, and involve volunteer leaders in the youth ministry.

What youth ministers are most likely to feel unorganized?

Again, it is those new to their job and those serving youth groups numbering less than 40. Note the contrasts in scores for the groups listed below, all of which are statistically significant. It is unlikely that they could have occurred by chance.

Most troubled	Least troubled
Have served less than 3 years: 51.8	*Have served 16 years or more:* 48.1
Have fewer than 40 youth: 51.2	*Have 101 youth or more:* 47.9

It is likely that a youth minister's first job is in a church with an undeveloped youth program, or in a rural area or small town—for these are the kinds of churches who hire the youngest and least trained youth workers because they are the most affordable.

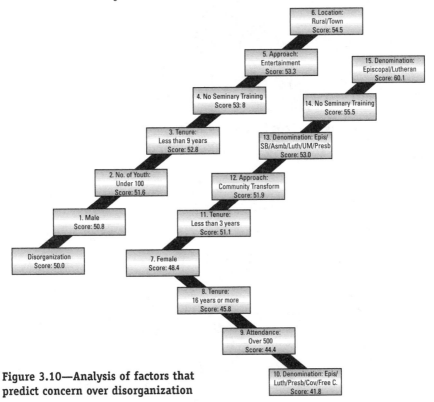

Figure 3.10—Analysis of factors that predict concern over disorganization

Figure 3.10 yields more insight: first of all, that males are more troubled over this issue than female youth ministers. This concern increases for males who serve fewer than 100 youth and whose years of service as a youth minister is less than 9 years (score of 52.8).

Within this group of males, the concern heightens for those *without* a seminary education, those whose approach to youth work is to use entertainment as a come-on, and those located in a rural area. Males with these characteristics score a 54.5—a significant concern over this issue.

Little concern among females, unless…
Female youth ministers are generally less concerned about "Feelings of Personal Disorganization," with an overall average score of 48.4. But females' scores start mounting when we single out those females who have served for less than three years, who lack a seminary education, and who are members of the Episcopal or Lutheran denominations. Those possessing *all three* of these characteristics achieve a concern score of 60.1, a seriously high number.

Female youth ministers show the *least* concern over feelings of disorganization who have served for 16 or more years, who are serving congregations where the Sunday attendance is 500 or more, and who belong to one of the same denominations that drew the highest score. The distance between the highest and lowest scores is 18 standard scores or the equivalent of 47 percentiles.

What youth ministers can do

If we assume that youth ministers have been trained to be creative and, consequently, tend to be more right-brained in their thinking, then a mentor is needed to help these youth ministers develop some left-brain skills. Because the value of mentoring has been established as a valuable assist in virtually every profession, youth ministers who feel personally disorganized should find a mentor who either has years of experience or is more organized.

The lack of such mentoring is keenly felt by a female youth minister:

> **It is highly frustrating being female in this profession—most of all because there's virtually no mentoring available for me from older females in ministry (especially youth ministry). Our staff, for example, is led by a team of male elders. I also struggle with intimidation, especially when it comes to sharing my ideas. Part of this is simply my own timidity and lack of confidence, but part of it is**

that I am not given the same respect that male ministers receive. And I need to be more creative in communicating my ideas; a few months ago I was told that my ideas are great, but that I need a "mouthpiece."

Which leads us to the final concern—one that heralds those youth ministers ready to exit the profession.

Concern 6
Experiencing Burnout

This often misused word describes youth ministers who are no longer energized and enthusiastic about their ministry, describing the feelings and attitude of persons inclined to exit the profession.

Les Parrott III, professor of clinical psychology at Seattle Pacific University, notes that burnout is especially prevalent among those who are in the serving professions. In *Helping the Struggling Adolescent,* he describes the onset of burnout in a counselor.

> Once sensitive, caring, and vibrant with enthusiasm, Jim seems to have lost the joy he once had in counseling teenagers. He doesn't admit it to others, but now he doesn't even care about the adolescents who come to see him. At times he even catches himself about to express his anger and frustration at them. The people in Jim's life have noticed the difference too. He seems far away, not so much fun anymore. Jim has the classic symptoms of burnout: feelings of futility, powerlessness, fatigue, cynicism, apathy, irritability, and frustration.[10]

Burnout is a response to repeated emotional strain. One researcher described the process of burnout as involving four stages: enthusiasm, stagnation, frustration, and apathy.[11]

Note how the items that clustered together describe the very characteristics that Parrott identified:

CLUSTER
Burnout

- I lack the enthusiasm I had when starting youth ministry.
- I grow increasingly weary of spending time with youth.
- I consider leaving the profession of youth ministry.
- I fear I am not remaining faithful to God's calling.

- I feel like a babysitter.
- I struggle to keep my personal vision alive.

These items describe the end of the road for youth ministers who are buffeted by the concerns described in this chapter. This cluster reflects discouragement, disillusionment, and disappointment—highly intercorrelated items that paint a strong, sobering picture of how some youth ministers feel.

Rick's case

A youth minister in a small city, Rick had never managed to recruit enough volunteers to assist him, so he ended up being responsible for *all* the programming and administrative details. His commitment to youth and his ministry kept him busy most hours of the day. As the work progressed, so did the amount of time and energy that was needed to keep it going. His wife and children consequently saw him rarely, except during an occasional meal together, or when they were all in church together.

From all appearances the youth ministry was a success, and Rick was a model youth minister. His frequent absences from home, however, and the constant stress from keeping all the plates spinning, left him emotionally drained. He began confiding his feelings of emptiness and exhaustion to his secretary, whom he saw more often and more regularly than his wife. The secretary's emotional support for him became addictive; he felt he needed her ear to keep from going off the deep end or walking way from the ministry.

Ironically, though predictably, it was their relationship that eventually caused him to walk. Their emotional affair turned sexual; when it was discovered, he walked away from everything—family, church, even his city. He began driving a truck to earn a living.

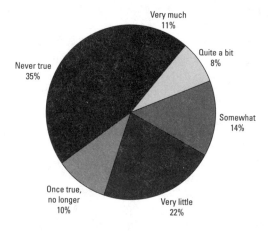

Figure 3.11—Percent considering exit from ministry

Fortunately, the number of respondents admitting to elements of burnout is not great. But their number is significant when one recognizes that they are considering an exit from the profession. Note in figure 3.11 that 19 percent—almost one-fifth of the youth ministers in the study—are considering leaving the profession. (The only survey item garnering a higher percentage is the item "I struggle to keep my personal vision alive"; see pages 109-110.) An additional 10 percent considered such an exit at one time, yet apparently changed their minds.

This information is sobering especially in light of the fact that if the entire sample had participated, the percentage could be greater. It alerts everyone to the urgency of addressing the concerns described in this chapter. Congregations wishing to keep their youth minister and enhance the effectiveness of his/her ministry need to consider how the concerns over which they have some control can be diminished.

What youth ministers in particular are inclined to burn out?
Our data show that no one group of youth ministers is particularly vulnerable to "Burnout", with one slight exception: those working with youth groups of fewer than 40 youths. As we have seen, they are among the most troubled respondents on several fronts.

One gains a better idea of the factors contributing to or associated with Burnout by noting the following:

Clusters correlating with a growing loss of confidence

Feeling Unqualified	.51
Loss of Confidence	.53
Feeling Inadequate	.51
Disinterested Youth	.61

These four related factors are the ones most highly associated with Burnout. They may contribute to a youth minister's decision to leave the profession. Which is to say, when youth ministers feel unqualified and inadequate...when they have lost all confidence in being able to resurrect a disinterested group of youths...when they can no longer cope with the pressure of not being able to do what the job demands—then "Burnout" is a likely outcome.

What youth ministers can do

Kenda Dean and Ron Foster identify a basic safeguard against burnout:

What is at stake in imagining ourselves as Godbearers with youths, is redefining ministry—youth min-

istry in particular—as a holy pursuit and not a service profession. Theologically we must work out what it means to place sanctifying grace at the center of youth ministry. Sanctifying grace is the gift of the Holy Spirit who enters us, dwells among us and makes it possible for Christ to enter the world through us. Sanctifying grace allows us to burn without becoming consumed by ministry.[12]

We must become thoughtful about how to deal with these psychological hazards. One cannot expect that they will be resolved with mere public affirmation, for it is rare for adolescents to appreciate or even recognize a youth minister's conscientious work. So one cannot bank on compliments from teenagers or rave reviews from parents and leaders in the congregation. To survive, a youth minister needs a strategic plan, a survival kit, to guard against the ravages of emotional burnout.

Parrott identifies a number of things in this survival kit. One item is to stop blaming external factors on others or shifting responsibility to others. Instead, channel your energy toward changes within your control.

Seek out a support group—compassionate people with whom you can share your concerns. Networking is an important way to stay alive. And stop measuring your work against those who seem to be able to do more with less effort.

Most importantly, take seriously the power found in God's healing presence. Believe that his strength is made perfect in your weakness (2 Corinthians 12:9). Allow him to shepherd you and your work in a way that restores your soul (Psalm 23). An authentic spirituality prevents burnout.

Les Parrott identifies the following keys for preventing burnout.

- Find an activity that diverts your attention away from your work.
- Put some variety into your daily routine.
- Balance your life with the basic ingredients of a healthy lifestyle: adequate sleep, exercise, and proper diet.
- Set limits to demanding job requirements and stick to them.
- Rely on prayer to guard you from negative self-talk. God will keep you in perfect peace when your mind is stayed on him (Isaiah 26:3).
- Have something at your office that is just for fun.
- Take time off to escape and seek new experiences—like travel, for
- Practice a relaxation technique regularly.
- Cultivate your sense of humor.[13]

It should be recognized that undergirding the lives of many youth ministers is a strong sense of call—as one youth minister puts into words:

> I am excited to say that I have been involved in youth ministry for the past 18 years. There are only a couple reasons why I continue to this day and will prayerfully continue for many years to come.
>
> The first is that God called my into a ministry with youths 22 years ago when I was participating in a summer ministry. Whenever I ask questions and struggle with the why of what I am doing, I simply turn back to God's call to serve in this way. That's enough.
>
> My second reason is that God gave me gifts and passion to work with teenagers. There is no higher calling. I have no desire to be a senior pastor or to work with children. It's teenagers, those who are between the ages of 12 and 18. I wake up enthusiastic about the possibilities for ministry on most days and thank God for that.

A closer look at the most vulnerable

We have already identified those who are most vulnerable to issues troubling youth ministers. They are the youngest (29 or less) and those with the fewest years (3 years or less) in the profession. What can congregational leaders learn about these least-experienced youth ministers that might result in giving them better support?

- They are more troubled than most youth ministers about how well they are doing.
  Compared to the overall sample, they are more critical of themselves (49 percent versus 33 percent), far more concerned over their inability to manage their time (49 percent versus 26 percent), more troubled about the emotional strain from their work (51 percent versus 39 percent), and more concerned over a lack of needed volunteers (51 percent versus 38 percent).

- About a third are troubled over how well things are going in their congregation.
  One out of five (22 percent) are not happy with the way things are going in their congregation or organization. A third of these youth ministers (34 percent) report there is considerable tension in their ministry, and 42 percent say that too much time and

effort is required to get something approved. These percentages, which indicate how many are unhappy over their work situation, are nevertheless quite similar to those reported by the other youth ministers.

- Most are serving in congregations where they feel valued and trusted. Three out of four (72 percent) serve in congregations where the Sunday morning attendance is under 500 people. And half (50 percent) work with a youth group that numbers less than 40. In these settings where they have served only a few years, they already feel trusted by their senior pastor or supervisor. Only 4 percent of these first-timers don't. And they feel valued by the parents of the youth they serve (only 10 percent do not). It is significant that a total of 85 percent say they enjoy their work.

- But many lack the ability to delegate responsibility, to equip parents for ministry, and to recruit volunteers.
Nearly a third of these first-timers (30 percent) feel they are not good at delegating responsibility. An even larger number (43 percent) feel they are not equipped to prepare parents for a youth ministry leadership. And the largest group (56 percent) admit it is difficult for them to recruit volunteers. But they hang in there. A large majority (88 percent) insists that God's call is their primary motivation for doing youth ministry.

Summary

Writes a youth minister who read an early draft of this chapter,

> I guess I shouldn't be surprised about the level of satisfaction that youth workers express concerning our profession. In talking with those who are younger, the satisfaction issue does come up on a frequent basis: "If God really called me to this ministry, why isn't it more satisfying, gratifying, and fulfilling?"
>
> It's a fair question, and one that I have to grapple with at least a couple of times a year. There do come those occasions when I wish I had an eight-hour job where I could see some production accomplished at the end of the day. If I could see a wall built, or lots of lumber cut up to be used in a fireplace—that would be of help to me from time to time.

This youth minister poignantly expresses the importance of this book's second key to a transformational youth ministry: the youth minister's personal inner strength. Unless youth ministers, who serve in a very demanding profession, draw on the rich resources found through prayer, reading of the Word, and personal counseling, they become vulnerable to spiritual fatigue.

This chapter has underlined six debilitating concerns that can overwhelm a youth minister:

- Feelings of personal inadequacy
- Experiencing strained family relations
- A growing loss of confidence
- Feeling unqualified for the job
- Feeling personally disorganized
- Experiencing burnout

These represent the Achilles heel of youth ministers.

Suggestions were given in the chapter regarding what youth ministers can do to ward off these feelings and maintain the inner strength that is essential for effective leadership. The responsibility for combating spiritual fatigue rests with the youth minister.

1. What's your theory behind the concerns represented in this chapter: Do you think persons bring them into youth ministry? Or do you think that youth ministry *causes* the concerns?

2. How could seminaries and colleges prepare future youth ministers to deal positively with the concerns in this chapter?

3. How can the information in this chapter help you predict or explain the type of youth minister who is most likely to feel personally disorganized?

4. Which of the concerns represented in this chapter do you personally feel most susceptible to?

Notes 3

1. Kenda Dean and Ron Foster, *The Godbearing Life: The Art of Soul Tending for Youth Ministry* (Nashville: Upper Room Books, 1998), 42.

2. Stephen Covey, *The 7 Habits of Highly Effective People* (New York: Simon & Schuster, 1989), 46.

3. Richard Laliberte in "Men and Women Managing Conflict," in Les Parrott III (ed.), *Relationships: An Open Guide to Healthy Connections* (New York: McGraw-Hill, 1993), 102.

4. Chuck Neder, "Too Busy: Reflections of a Person Going Mad with the Busy Addiction," in "What Is the Status of Youth Ministry?" in Richard R. Dunn and Mark H. Senter III (eds.), *Reaching a Generation for Christ* (Chicago: Moody Press, 1997), 258.

5. Augustus Napier and Carl Whitaker, *The Family Crucible* (New York: Bantam Books, 1978), 47.

6. Merton Strommen, *Five Cries of Youth*, San Francisco: HarperCollins, 1988), 53.

7. Doug Fields, *Purpose-Driven Youth Ministry* (Grand Rapids, Michigan: Zondervan Publishing House, 1998), 31.

8. Robert McGee in "Our Search for Significance," in Les Parrott III, *Relationships: An Open and Honest Guide to Healthy Connections* (New York: McGraw-Hill, 1993), 8.

9. Dunn and Senter, 33, 41.

10. Les Parrott III, *Helping the Struggling Adolescent: A Counseling Guide* (Grand Rapids, Michigan: Zondervan Publishing House, 1993), 28.

11. J. Edelwich, *Burnout: Stages of Disillusionment in the Caring Professions* (New York: Human Sciences Press, 1980).

12. Dean and Foster, 50.

13. Parrott, 32.

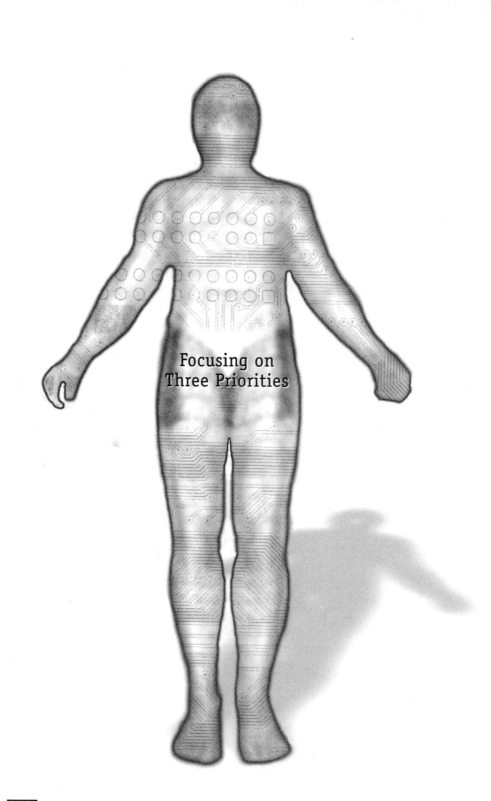

Focusing on
Three Priorities

Chapter 4

Focusing on Three Top Ministry Priorities
Merton Strommen

This chapter identifies three commanding priorities—ones that the youth ministers in the study consider to be the most important aspects of their ministry:
• Clearly stated mission statement.
• Focus on the spiritual development of youth.
• The training of volunteer leaders.
These three form the basic agenda for a youth minister.

Because these three priorities are so basic to a youth ministry, one is reminded of the words of Paul in the book of Ephesians: "Stand firm then, with the belt of truth buckled around your waist, with the breastplate of righteousness in place, and with your feet fitted with the readiness that comes from the gospel of peace" (Ephesians 6:15).

We have considered the feet or legs that enable a ministry to move—the foundational aspects of a youth ministry. Now we focus on the business of transforming the youth whom a ministry touches. This represents one of the purposes of a transformational youth ministry.

Determining Priorities

How were the top priorities determined? How did the 2,416 youth ministers indicate what they considered most important in their ministry?

The answer is found in how they responded to a list of 21 items chosen to reflect the range of objectives that can characterize a full-blown youth ministry. When answering these items, youth ministering respondents favored eight of them in ways that caused them to correlate and form three clusters—clusters that make eminent sense and identify what might be regarded as commanding priorities in youth ministry, ones that no doubt reflect the maturity of youth ministers in our sample. The three are these.

Three clusters of youth ministers' priorities
• Clear Sense of Direction
• Spiritual Development of Youth
• Recruitment and Training of Adult Volunteers

These objectives are apparently uppermost in the minds of these youth ministers, and therefore the most important. The implications of this list are powerful: note how the respondents focus on being partners with God in the mission of transforming the lives of youth.

Priority 1

A Clear Sense of Direction

Two elements are involved in gaining a clear sense of direction: a philosophy of youth ministry that is unambiguous, and a one-sentence mission statement that identifies the need, the activity, and the desired outcome. These two essentials point the way for a significant ministry.

Let two youth ministers tell how moving from a vague to a clear philosophy of youth ministry revolutionized their approach to youth.

Change through contemplation

Mark Yaconelli tells of a growing realization that nothing in his youth ministry was working. Having had the best training, he built his ministry on the latest models. His ministry was filled with enthusiastic personalities, expensive excursions, and hot lesson plans. After three years of full-time youth work, he had attracted lots of kids—but made few disciples. He was successful in creating lots of fun but little interest in matters of faith. Lots of students liked him, but few loved Jesus Christ.

"I was a wreck and my marriage was suffering," Yaconelli says. "I was working 70 to 80 hours a week, seeking to save every teen I encountered—and yet I seemed to be losing everyone, including myself. The job had become heavy, consuming, and filled with frustration."

Then during on a retreat at a nearby convent, Yaconelli became focused on being with God rather than on performing duties. He discovered what it means to rely on God alone. His experience with contemplative prayer exercises showed him a different approach to discipleship.

The change he made involved integrating contemplative exercises into his youth ministry—and this setting has given students a firsthand experience of God as a living reality. The exercises include biblical meditation, icon prayers, chanting, music meditation, guided imagery, centering prayers, and prayers of discernment.

Realizing that youth want to hear from God directly, Yaconelli considers spiritual exercises evangelistic. He finds them especially effective with unchurched youth. When they are listening to Scripture in a quiet setting, they experience the God they long for. Their experience of his presence is followed by an eagerness to learn the stories and concepts of the Christian faith

Yaconelli's new philosophy of youth ministry is to provide opportunities for youth and leaders to be listening to God. He creates settings where God is given a chance to enter into the conscious life of participants. And when God does this?

"When spiritual exercises are regularly used, leaders and students experience transformation," Yaconelli claims. "Slowly the ministry begins to revolve around the movement of the Spirit rather than the chaotic wanderings of our own egos and anxieties. Suddenly we become what we've always hoped to be—disciples."[1]

Change of philosophy

Doug Fields lacked a philosophy of youth ministry when he began his career. Eager to succeed, he was driven to always do more, looking for the bigger and better in everything he did. He characterizes his approach as basically hype. His was a continual search for new ideas. He looked for the program that would please parents, bring students out in droves, and help them grow spiritually. "I wanted an instant program to bring quick success," he says.

There came a time when, alone and depressed in his car, he felt the supernatural presence of God. "I sensed God saying, 'Doug, you'll never be able to do enough to please everyone. Focus on me. Rest in me. Abide in me. When your heart is turned toward me, we can work together and do some good things.' That was it. That was the moment that revolutionized my ministry."

His philosophy of youth work changed to embody the following principles:

> • **Recognize God's power through personal humility. When good things happen, I need to recognize that they happen because of God's power, not my own.**
> • **Submit your abilities to God and allow his power to work through who you are. Rest in the truth discovered by the apostle Paul: "My grace is sufficient for you, for my power is made perfect in weakness" (2 Corinthians 12:9).**
> • **Focus on being a person of God before doing the work of God. God is more concerned about your spiritual health than about your youth ministry hype. When you seek God, you will see supernatural elements within your ministry that no flashy idea could ever produce.**[2]

These two men have established a philosophy of youth ministry that centers in a partnership with God—where it is God who empowers, guides, and acts. It is a philosophy that takes seriously the promise, "Seek first his kingdom and his righteousness and all these things will be given to you as well" (Matthew 6:33).

The phrase *"all these things"* can well include interested youths, youth ownership, their public sharing of faith, their orientation to service, a commitment to discipleship, and more.

An unambiguous statement of philosophy

Paul Hill, director of Wartburg Lutheran Seminary's Center for Youth Ministries and 30-year youth ministry veteran, does not mince words when stating his philosophy of youth ministry.

> **The primary purpose of youth and family ministry is to be tools of the Holy Spirit in faith formation. We want to help our youths grow up believing in the person (God as a human being, manifested in Jesus); power (God defeats sin and death and restores life through Jesus' death and resurrection); and purpose (Jesus' believers are called to discern and do his will) of Jesus Christ. The essence of youth ministry is evangelism. Those who work with youths are evangelists and missionaries.**
>
> **I can hear your thought process: "Evangelism? Missionaries? Those are old, out-of-date words. This sounds like you are trying to shove something down the kids' throats." This is an understandable reaction. Many Christians are squeamish when it comes to proselytizing. Many of us just can't help it—we are missionary shy.**
>
> **Good excuses and explanations to be sure, but the fact remains that youth and family ministry is primarily a work of evangelism. Our children don't spring from the womb reciting the Small Catechism; it must be taught. Our children are not born with a Christian chromosome that predetermines they will believe in God; God is experienced through the Holy Spirit. Our children do not automatically gravitate to a life in Christian community; they must be invited. Our children do not voluntarily sacrifice all to be disciples; they must see the work of God's kingdom in the effort of the adults around them.[3]**

In *Effective Youth Ministry* Roland Martinson, professor of pastoral care and youth ministry at Luther Theological Seminary, tells why such philosophies of youth ministry equip one to minister to youths.

Adolescents seek symbols that represent the hopes and dreams of their expanding world. They search for movements which concretely focus their beliefs and needs. Some chase experiences that stretch the boundaries of their imagination and consciousness. They look outside themselves for heroes and art forms which represent truth, power, and love. Broadened sensitivities, deepened comprehension, and new enthusiasm provide them with great capacities for commitment and adoration. Shifting worlds, expanding possibilities, and unfolding needs push them to reach out for security and direction.[4]

Establishing a mission statement

Following a change in philosophy of youth ministry comes the need for a clear statement of mission. Such a statement should be a single, clear sentence. Whoever hears it should know *why* your youth ministry exists and *why* it is important to you.

Ideally, the statement identifies the need, the desired result, and the approach used to achieve that result. Bo Boshers of Willow Creek Community Church's Student Impact offers his mission statement:

To turn irreligious high school students into fully devoted followers of Christ.

This streamlined mission statement has two of the three elements: the need (*irreligious high school students*) and the desired result (*fully devoted followers of Christ*).

Boshers also has what he calls a "vision statement," which is also a kind of mission statement:

A unique community of students and leaders committed to letting God change their lives, change their friends' lives, build the church, and impact the world.[5]

Here are all three elements: the need (transformation of students, leaders, church, world), the desired result (changed lives, a stronger church, a saved world), and the means to that result ("a unique community").

Another illustration of a one-sentence statement of purpose was developed by a youth task force at Oak Grove Lutheran Church in Minneapolis:

The purpose of our youth program is to foster a Christian community of youth who are committed to Jesus Christ, involved in the study of God's word, participants in the life of their congregation, and living beyond themselves through a life of service.

Mission statements such as these communicate quickly why a youth ministry exists, what it wishes to accomplish, and the means by which it will achieve its goal. Each statement becomes the basis for evaluating the ministry's effectiveness and provides the rationale for determining what to include or omit from a youth program.

The importance of arriving at a mission statement—and then communicating it to congregational leaders—is illustrated by a youth minister who was trying to operate without one.

> **Two years into my first youth ministry experience, the local high school asked me to coach the boys' volleyball team. To me, it was an official invitation to be in contact with students on campus every day. It was the perfect combination for me—I could hold my church youth ministry position, and I could be with students, on their turf. I though it would be professional to let my church know about the offer, so I told the head of personnel.**
>
> **I didn't expect the reaction I got. A meeting of the entire deacon board was called the following week—and my presence was required. They wanted to know why I wanted the coaching position. Did I not have enough to do? Was I unhappy with the youth ministry? With the church? With them?**
>
> **Needless to say, I feared for my job. So before the meeting I wrote down my rationale for being involved on the high school campus as a youth minister. Over the course of that week, my rationale developed into a full-blown mission statement with theological underpinnings. When it came time for the meeting, I clearly communicated my vision for youth ministry. It saved not only my job, but my career too. Now, ten years later, I still make sure that I take as many opportunities as possible to refine and communicate my youth ministry vision.**

Importance given to a clear ministry direction
In the computer analysis of survey data, two items formed a separate cluster to state unambiguously how necessary a priority it is to have a clear philosophy and mission statement. These two items, which the 2,416 youth ministers ranked high in importance, identify something

that has been wanting in many youth ministries.

CLUSTER
Importance: A clear sense of direction
- Agreeing on a philosophy of youth ministry.
- Developing a clearly defined mission statement.

Both items drew high and similar responses from the youth ministers when they were asked,

How important is the following statement to your youth ministry?

Agreeing on a philosophy of youth ministry		Developing a clearly defined mission statement
	Extremely important	
43 percent		43 percent
	Very Important	
35 percent		31 percent
	Quite Important	
13 percent		16 percent
	Somewhat Important	
7 percent		9 percent
	Not Important	
1 percent		2 percent

Almost 80 percent of the youth ministers placed high importance on arriving at a philosophy of youth ministry and almost 75 percent on developing a mission statement. They recognize that a rationale must undergird what they do and that a clearly defined mission must serve as their focus. It is evident that a program of hot ideas and entertaining activities falls short of good youth ministry.

Wartburg Seminary professor and Center for Youth Ministries director Paul Hill underscores how an effective youth ministry must have a guiding vision.

To have a vision is to have power. To have a vision is to be powerful. To have a vision that is of God is to lead with power. Martin Luther, Mother Teresa, and Martin Luther King, Jr., each had a vision. For Luther it was of a church that does not sell Jesus but shares Jesus. For Mother Teresa it was a vision of God who calls God's people to care for the outcasts. For Dr. Martin Luther King, Jr., it was a dream

of a common humanity rooted in mutual respect. Their visions have moved nations, institutions, and millions of people. Importantly, none of these people held political office, commanded armies, or possessed great wealth. Yet their accomplishments have reshaped the world. Vision is that powerful and that important.[6]

What youth ministers give greatest importance to this priority?

Specifically (as you can see in figure 4.1), the parachurch ministries Young Life and Youth for Christ. Incidentally, their scores on *achievement* of this priority are an exact parallel. Conversely, just as Presbyterian youth ministers give the lowest rating on importance to a "Clear Sense of Direction," they also occupy the bottom in their estimate of how well this is being achieved in their ministry. Apparently this aspect of youth work has not been emphasized in the training of Presbyterian youth ministers.

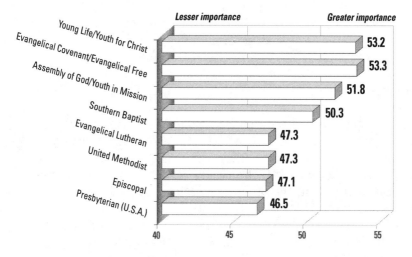

Figure 4.1—Importance accorded a clear sense of direction

In fact, it can be said that how a denomination's youth workers perceive the importance of a "Clear Sense of Direction" and how they perceive their *achievement of it* exactly parallel each other. That is, those giving higher importance to this aspect of youth ministry show higher ratings of achievement; by the same token, those giving lower ratings of importance evaluate their youth program lower in achieving this outcome.

A youth minister serving with Youth for Christ tells about the important place a mission statement has occupied in his thinking and ministry.

**Youth for Christ handed me my mission statement
when I got involved with the organization years ago.
It continues to this day to be a compass for me as I
minister to teens. My goal is to share the life-changing message of Jesus with students. If they come to
a point of salvation, I work hard on helping those
students take steps towards the church—for I have
built good relationships with churches in my area.
Our ministry is about reaching every student in our
area. Sounds pretty impossible, but with God and an
army of his soldiers, the task is a challenge instead
of an impossibility. And it all starts with our mission statement.**

Denomination or organization is only one predictor of how important a "Clear Sense of Direction" is to a youth minister. There are four
others, as figure 4.2 depicts: theological orientation, size of congregation, number in one's youth group, and size of community.

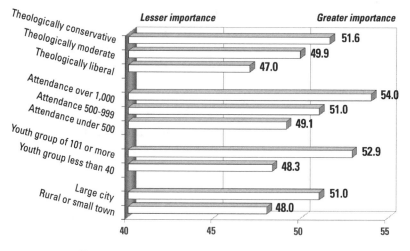

Figure 4.2—Comparisons on clear sense of direction

We note again that the more conservative the youth minister's
denomination or organization, the greater the importance to that youth
minister of a clear philosophy and mission. More significant is the factor
of size of congregation: youth ministers serving in the few churches
whose attendance is over a thousand on Sundays (11 percent of the
total) are the ones most likely to make this a priority. Furthermore,
these churches are usually found in large cities.

The Spiritual Development of Youth

The most compelling of the three priorities is the spiritual development of youth. This is true not only for the youth ministers, but also for youth ministry professors in U.S. colleges and seminaries.

Daniel Lambert found this out by using the Delphi Method for his doctoral dissertation.[7] He involved all those who were teaching in the 70 schools that offer youth ministry as a major area of study on the graduate or undergraduate level. Full-time and adjunct youth ministry faculty were included, along with 1998 members of Youth Ministry Educators. A total of 192 were identified.

These potential participants were asked by letter to write responses to the question, *What aspects of youth ministry would benefit most from systematic research?*

A total of 46 percent responded by sending in research ideas. These were processed and then sent back, requesting respondents to evaluate each of the 160 research ideas using a seven-point Likert scale to indicate the importance of each item.

To this second mailing there was a 72 percent response (of those participating the first time). The 162 items that they evaluated were then listed in their order of declared importance and sent a third time to the respondents, who were asked a final time to review the list and change the rank order of items or leave them as presented.

What is impressive is the fact that in this list of topics developed by the Delphi Method, the three candidates for systematic research drawing highest ratings (ranks one, two, and three) all refer to faith development.

Round-three results: Top-ranked items
- Longitudinal studies on teen faith after a youth group—what factors affect teen faith and how we better prepare them for life after youth group?
- Parents' role in faith development.
- What is the profile of a ministry whose students are most likely to remain active in the cause of Christ beyond high school?[7]

This is impressive evidence of how united youth ministry professors are in their conviction that special efforts are needed to learn more about faith development among our youth.

We find the same conviction among the youth ministers in the study. The following three items that were included in the survey ranked highest in importance.

CLUSTER
Nurturing the spiritual development of youths

- Helping youths make a commitment to Jesus Christ.
- Providing help for teaching biblical concepts of right and wrong.
- Seeing that God is at work changing lives.

This three-item measure ranks first in importance to the respondents. An indication of how intensely this aspect of youth ministry is viewed by youth ministers can be seen in their response to "Helping youths make a commitment to Jesus Christ," as depicted in figure 4.3. This exceptionally high response indicates the importance this aspect of ministry holds in the minds of youth ministers. But what does commitment to Christ include?

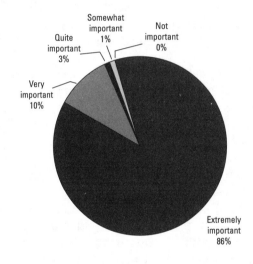

Figure 4.3—Percent according importance to helping youth make a commitment to Christ

What is included in a commitment to Christ?

We believe that commitment involves much more than a decision to follow Christ. Youth who are committed to Christ can evidence the ten characteristics listed below, which are characteristics identified for adolescents as determined by research at Search Institute, reported in *Five Cries of Youth* and *Five Cries of Parents* and explored more fully in *Passing on the Faith: A Radical New Model for Youth and Family Ministry.*[8] These ten serve as a description of what can be sought by the time youth graduate from high school.

Ten Characteristics of Youth Committed to Jesus Christ
1. Trust a personal Christ
2. Understand grace and live in grace
3. Commune with God regularly
4. Show moral responsibility
5. Accept responsibility in a congregation
6. Demonstrate unprejudiced and loving lives
7. Accept authority and responsibility
8. Develop hopeful and positive attitudes
9. Embrace the rituals of a Christian community
10. Engage in mission and service

These characteristics resemble the ones the apostle Paul enjoined Timothy to embody: "Don't let anyone look down on you because you are young, but set an example for the believers in speech, in life, in love, in faith and in purity....pursue righteousness, godliness, faith, love, endurance and gentleness. Fight the good fight of the faith" (1 Timothy 4:12, 6:11-12).

Characteristics like these ten can serve as prayer goals, so that they can become evident in a youth minister's students by the time they graduate from high school.

These are not unreasonable expectations, but ones that ought to be sought when fostering the spiritual development of youth. They include much more than the three items above that describe our second priority (helping youth make a commitment to Jesus Christ, providing help for teaching biblical concepts of right and wrong, seeing that God is at work changing lives). If a richer assortment of items on spiritual development had been included in the survey questionnaire, more items would have been drawn into this cluster. These three here simply indicate that this aspect of ministry, though thinly defined, is of extreme importance for most youth ministers.

Needless to say, the spiritual development of youth is not the sole responsibility of a youth minister, but is only one aspect of a congregation's effort to foster such characteristics. The youth's parents are important partners in the spiritual development of youth. The spiritual nurture given in their home makes a most telling impact on young people. In fact, parents who talk about the faith in their home and involved their children in service projects double and sometimes triple the probability that their children will evidence the characteristics of commitment. (Evidence demonstrating this is found in *Passing on the Faith: A Radical New Model for Youth and Family Ministry,* by this writer and Richard Hardel.)

Not to be overlooked is the congregation's program of Christian education, its worship, and its functioning as a faith community. Research has shown that each aspect of congregational life makes a discernible impact on the faith life of young people.

This means that youth ministers are only part of a team of individuals who are praying that these ten characteristics become a reality for all youth. This team notwithstanding, the spiritual development of students still needs to be at the front of a youth worker's ministry.

Variation in perceived importance

Variation appears in the importance given this priority when youth ministers are classified by denomination or youth organization. It shows in how they responded to the item "Helping youths make a commitment to Jesus Christ." A ranking of 5 indicates that this is *extremely important* to a youth minister; a 4 means *very important*.

How important is commitment to Jesus Christ in your youth ministry?

Average rating	#	Youth ministers organizational group
4.98	265	Assembly of God
4.97	427	Young Life and Youth for Christ
4.91	527	Southern Baptist Convention
4.90	134	Evangelical Covenant and Evangelical Free Churches
4.74	326	United Methodist Church
4.51	230	Presbyterian (U.S.A.)
4.44	230	Evangelical Lutheran Church in America
4.37	73	Episcopal Church.

The differences between the three groups (indicated by the separators) could not have happened by chance. The scores identify which group of youth ministers place the greatest importance on helping youth make a commitment to Jesus Christ. First to be noted, the averages for all groups are above 4; all groups consider commitment to be *very important*.

An average, however, conceals the fact that many score higher than the average and many score lower—which means that in the distribution of scores that resulted in the average of 4.37, some gave ratings of *extremely important* and others gave ratings of *quite important*.

Two groups worthy of special note for their evangelistic emphasis are Young Life and Youth for Christ. Both rank near the top in terms of the importance they accord the objective of bringing youth to a personal commitment: both are topped (though only slightly) by Assembly of God youth ministers in achieving this outcome.

Jim Rayburn began Young Life, a leader-centered and evangelism-focused organization, in 1941. His passion for youth is reflected in a prayer that author Emile Cailliet heard him pray.

> Good Lord, give us the teenagers, that we may lead them to thee. Our hearts ache for the nine million young people who remain untouched by thy gospel, and for the tragically large proportion of those who, having once been led to attend Sunday school, have dropped by the wayside and now find themselves without spiritual guidance...Oh thou Holy Spirit, give us the teenagers, for we love them and know them to be awfully lonely. Good Lord, give us the teenagers.[9]

His prayer reflects what Christian Schwarz calls a "passionate spirituality"—being "on fire" and practicing the faith with joy and enthusiasm.[10] Youth ministers who are motivated by this "passionate spirituality" are the ones most likely to see young people joining them in the faith.

It was not until 1962 that the Youth for Christ philosophy was modified to reach beyond committed students to the unchurched, non-Christian students. Their Campus Life strategy came to be that of equipping the Christian student to establish a one-on-one relationship with an unbeliever.[11]

As is obvious from the responses of those in the Lutheran, Presbyterian, and Episcopal church bodies, an evangelism that stresses commitment to Christ is not a first priority for some. Hence it is no surprise that fewer in these church bodies give the highest rank to achieving the outcome of "Spiritual Development."

This difference in both perceived outcome and declared importance no doubt reflects differences in theology by denomination. Some Lutheran youth ministers may insist that their youths are children of God through baptism. Appeals for youths to make a commitment to Christ is therefore a denial of their covenant relationship. Still, youth ministers with such theology are nonetheless encouraged by their theology to emphasize daily renewal—that is, one should repent each day and be renewed in a personal relationship with Christ. In a real sense this theological orientation calls for a *daily* commitment to Christ.

Differences in perceived importance by theological orientation and approach

How important their students' "Spiritual Development" is varies not only by the youth ministers' denominations, but also by where on the liberal-to-conservative theological spectrum they are, and also by their approach to youth work. Of all the factors considered, these two—theological orientation and approach—are the only factors showing significant differences in the importance youth ministers give to "Spiritual Development."

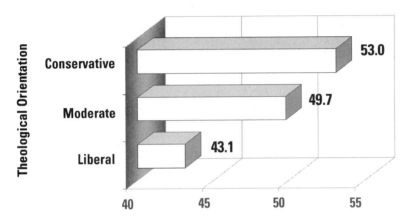

Figure 4.4—Importance accorded spiritual development

As seen in figure 4.4, respondents classified themselves as theological conservatives, moderates, or liberals. The differences that appear in their standard scores, based on this theological self-classification, are considerable: ten standard scores.

The scores indicate that youth ministers with a theologically liberal orientation place less importance than those with a conservative theology on the "Spiritual Development" of their youths. From these scores one gains a fair idea of who are most likely to passionately foster the ten characteristics of "Spiritual Development".

Differences also appear when youth ministers are classified on the basis of how they approach youth work. As is obvious here, those who try to interest their youths with a diet of entertainment and fun activities place less importance on the "Spiritual Development" of their youth.

Classification of youth ministers, by approach	Standard scores
• Arrange events to protect	53.9
• Seek to transform society	50.6
• Community involvement	48.7
• Gain interest through entertainment	47.1

Youth ministers who are trying to protect their youth from the evils of society are apparently motivated by an earnest and deep concern over their spiritual welfare; they consequently rank high in the "Spiritual Development" priority.

This earnestness also characterizes youth leaders of the Seventh-day Adventist church, who in the past at least has consciously tried to protect their youths with prohibitory standards. An evaluation based on a national study of Seventh-day Adventist youth showed a number of positive features—such as faith scores higher than other church bodies and fewer youth involved in at-risk behaviors.

Unfortunately, the negative side of this was demonstrated in an overwhelming number of this denomination's youth having adopted the idea that acceptance by God is based on their behavior. The church's emphasis on prohibitive standards was essentially creating a law-oriented Christianity among their youth.

The benefits of a protective youth ministry
Lest we dismiss too quickly the protective approach to youth ministry, it may be well to consider the argument advanced by Miroslav Volf, Henry B. Wright Professor of Theology at Yale University Divinity School, in the *Christian Century* article "Floating Along?" Volf admits that he has thought naïve those who try to define their Christian subculture by replicating the world of their pious grandparents.

However, he realizes that the most vigorous and coherent counterculture today is the one constructed by conservative Christians, who buck the popular notions of what constitutes a fulfilled life.

We are drowning in floods of consumer goods and are drenched in showers of media images. We live in a smorgasbord culture in which everything is interesting and nothing really matters. We have lost a vision of the good life, and our hopes for the future are emptied of moral content.[12]

He then speaks appreciatively about the Scheibners, a family who has chosen to be "selective separatists"—choosing "not to participate in those parts of the culture that do not bring glory to God." Volf suggests that "instead of complaining about the particulars of a robust funda-

mentalist counterculture, we should ask ourselves: Why are we seemingly incapable of creating a viable and vibrant alternative?"[13]

Whatever one thinks of the protectionist approach, youth ministers
who use it nevertheless register the highest concern about their students' spiritual development—especially compared to youth ministers
who say they use an entertainment approach. The efforts of these youth
ministers who try to slip in a little religion at opportune times are
apparently not motivated by a deeply felt passion for youths' spiritual
development.

Priority 3
The Recruitment and Training of Adult Leaders

The significance of our third priority is identified by Mark Senter: "The
key to ministering to the coming generations of young people is the
equipping of volunteers in local settings."[14]

Barry St. Clair underscores this point: "A broad ministry can only
stand on a broad foundation of volunteers."[15] So does Doug Fields: "A
youth ministry without adequate leadership can never be healthy but
one with an abundance of quality leaders will always have the potential
for health."[16]

The point is that a youth minister cannot do it alone. It is important to have assistance, just as Moses realized after listening to the
counsel of his father-in-law Jethro (Exodus 18).

Recruiting the right volunteers

Hear Kenda Dean and Ron Foster in *The Godbearing Life:*

> **What youths need more than gung-ho adults are
> Godbearing adults, people whose own yes to God has
> transformed them into messengers of the gospel. We
> gather people for God so that God can give them
> what.we cannot: a share of God's spirit, the spirit
> that empowers ministry.[17]**

This is the kind of recruiting that is needed, as Paul Hill agrees:

> **If we want spiritual kids we need spiritual adults. If
> we want Christian seeds to grow, then we need
> Christian farmers to nurture that seed. It has been
> observed that faith is caught more than it is taught.
> And it is caught by youths observing, living, grow-
> ing, exploring, questioning, and engaging faith in**

the adults around them. In other words, youth ministry is best spelled A.D.U.L.T. R.E.N.E.W.A.L.[18]

Though everyone in the congregation is a potential volunteer leader, one still must be selective. The critical process of selection may involve a series of steps such as those proposed by Barry St. Clair, who warns of the need to protect both the young persons as well as the at-risk volunteer. Therefore he proposes the following steps to screen out potential problems:

• *Require written applications.* This application form should include a question about possible abusive activity. Thus the application can serve as a filter that allows vulnerable volunteers to quietly withdraw.

• *Interview every volunteer.* The volunteer should be pointedly asked, "Have you ever abused or molested a child or young person?" Watch for evidence of deception.

• *Avoid using people new to the church.* Certain abusers move from place to place, hoping their reputation will not catch up with them.

• *Network with other youth ministers.* They may be helpful in understanding local laws and resources.[19]

The screening process must do more than eliminate those who can harm young people. It needs also to be a way of finding those who genuinely love the Lord, enjoy young people, and sense God's call. It needs to identify adults with a mature faith who also have the ability to share that faith with others, especially teenagers.

Training volunteer leaders

This is a weak link in many youth ministries. Karen Jones has noted this from reports by students who observe veterans.

> **My youth ministry students are required to interview a full-time youth minister and observe three or more events or meetings during the course of a semester.**
>
> **One thing they observe time and again is the ineffective use of volunteer leadership. Though volunteer leaders usually attend the youth function, rarely do they lead in a significant way. Very few of the youth ministers interviewed say they have training or regular planning times with their volunteer leadership.**

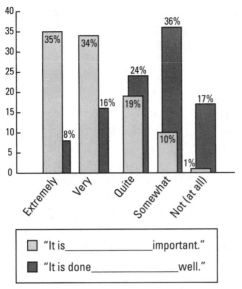

Figure 4.5—Importance versus achievement

In the general developing of adult volunteers, how important is the specific act of *training* them systematically? As figure 4.5 above depicts, 70 percent of the 2,416 youth ministers involved in the study said it is of *high importance*—a priority activity that needs special consideration. Although this item ("developing a systematic plan") drew a slightly higher response than the other two cluster items ("recruiting adults for one-on-one mentoring" and "equipping small-group leaders;" see below), it shows a marked disparity between declared importance and degree achieved. Conclusion? The training of volunteer adult leaders is not being done very well, although it is recognized as highly important.

CLUSTER
Developing Adult Volunteers
- Recruiting adults for one-on-one mentoring with youth.
- Equipping adult volunteers who lead small groups
- Developing a systematic plan for training volunteer youth workers.

Recruiting adults for one-on-one mentoring of youth

The power in a mentoring relationship was made explicit through a major national study in 1992-1993 involving six agencies of Big Brothers/Big Sisters. Through a comprehensive and scientifically valid research effort, an evaluation was made of the outcomes of mentoring approximately one thousand 10-to-16-year-olds (70 percent of whom were African American and almost all living with a single parent).[20]

The randomly selected experimental and control groups were compared after a period of 18 months to see if mentoring resulted in—
- Less use of drugs and alcohol
- Less hitting of someone else
- Improved school attendance
- Improved attitudes towards completing school work
- Improved peer and family relationships

The results were highly positive. For instance, among minority Little Brothers and Little Sisters, 70 percent were less likely to initiate drug use than were those in the control group. They skipped half as many days of school as did the control youth, they felt more competent about doing schoolwork, and their GPAs showed modest gains. The study concluded that a mentoring relationship is most successful when an adult spends time with the young person at least *three times a month, four hours each meeting, for at least a year.*

"The Big Brothers/Big Sisters findings provide evidence that here is something that works," said Gary Walker, president of Public/Private Ventures. "It works by engineering the hardest of all things to engineer—namely, a human relationship. The study shows that positive youth development means having an adult friend."[21]

Mentoring for faith development
The power with which a mentoring relationship can change behaviors of inner-city youth applies equally well in fostering the ten characteristics of "Spiritual Development". Faith-oriented adults can have a life-shaping influence on young people when close relationships are established through mentoring.

The General Conference Mennonite Church has pioneered the use of a mentoring program. Two denomination-published books incorporate what Mennonite congregations have learned over the years about mentoring: *Side by Side: A Mentoring Guide for Congregational Youth Ministry and One on One: Making the Most of Your Mentoring Relationship.*[22] With a tradition of mentoring programs behind them—and with the resources of the Canadian Mentor Strategy National Training Leaders—Mennonite congregations are uniquely equipped to assist their communities in establishing their own mentoring programs. The influence can be huge: the CMSNTL newsletter of June 1995 reports that a core of 30 National Mentor Leaders trained more than 2,200 new mentors, which were later paired with 130,000 students.

Equipping adults to lead small groups

Dave Rahn has shown how adult leaders of small groups of student leaders can vastly enhance their evangelism capabilities. A study carried out with Terry Linhart sought to determine what would make student leaders more effective in peer evangelism. Their research revealed that when students had "regular accountability meetings with adults, the adults not only helped student leaders grow in their faith but also contributed to their success in being able to influence their friends for Christ."[23]

The findings of this study are significant. The majority of students who were effective in evangelism were the ones who met regularly with adults. Those who reported having no impact on their friends coming to Christ were the ones who did not meet with an adult.

In *Student Ministry for the 21st Century*, Bo Boshers makes a strong case for developing a small-group ministry. At his large Willow Creek Community Church, he has stressed the building of balanced small groups while de-emphasizing large group activities.

> **I believe God designed small groups so that every student could have a shepherd here on earth. Small groups provide an opportunity for students to become more like Christ and to experience care, acceptance, and true community. One of the principle functions of a small group is discipleship.[24]**

Boshers believes that small groups maximize life change, stop program-driven ministry, keep the ministry small even in a big context, disciple leaders and students, and build community. His idea of a small group is five students (all from the same high school) and an adult leader.

Boshers provides ongoing training for his adult leaders through a monthly all-leadership meeting. His agenda: 30 minutes on how to effectively minister to students, followed by 30 minutes where leaders huddle around tables to share concerns, ideas, and prayer. The session ends with 20 minutes of worship.[25]

Who especially stresses developing adult volunteers?

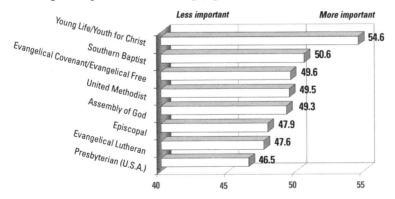

Figure 4.6—Importance of developing adult volunteers

When the youth ministers are classified according to denomination/ youth organization, considerable difference appears in the importance accorded the development of adult volunteers, as can be see in figure 4.6. Clearly, Young Life and Youth for Christ are the most serious about this priority. They not only rank well above the denominational groups in this regard but also excel in achieving the objective of "Developing Adult Volunteers."

However, both denominational and parachurch youth ministers have a long way to go before they can say they are doing well in developing volunteers. This becomes very evident in the low response of their combined groups to the following two items.

Developing Volunteers: degree achieved

Equips adult volunteers who lead small groups	Recruits adults for one-on-one mentoring
Done extremely well	
7 percent	4 percent
Done very well	
17 percent	9 percent
Done quite well	
28 percent	16 percent
Done somewhat well	
34 percent	37 percent
Not done at all	
15 percent	35 percent

What we have here is an unfinished agenda for youth ministers. Only a small percentage have developed their recruitment and training programs to where they are willing to say they are doing very well in both areas.

Summary

This chapter has focused on the life-transforming aspect of a youth ministry—the three priorities deemed most important by the 2,416 youth ministers in the study:
- Clear sense of direction
- Spiritual development of youth
- Training of adult volunteer leaders

It is well to note that these three priorities draw the same evaluation of importance from youth ministers irrespective of their years in service, whether seminary trained or not, whether well educated or not, whether male or female, or serving in any region of the country. Somehow these factors have not influenced the degree of importance youth ministers give these three priorities.

What then is most likely to make these priorities more compelling for some youth ministers than for others? The answer is denomination/youth organization and size of congregation. These two details about a youth minister can help one predict the degree to which these three priorities represent a compelling agenda for a youth minister.

THINK IT OVER, TALK IT THROUGH

1. Generally speaking, how do personal priorities develop?

2. What has led so many youth ministers to identify the three priorities in this chapter as most important to them?

3. What are the benefits and limitations of having one's personal mission statement coordinate with the youth ministry's mission statement?

4. What explanation would you suggest for why a youth minister's theological orientation affects the importance to him or her of developing youth spiritually?

5. What can you do to avoid becoming someone who values highly the recruitment and training of adult volunteers, but doesn't seem to do it very well?

6. How does your denomination or parachurch organization seem to measure up to the three priorities described in this chapter?

7. If you could pick any three priorities you might wish were widely embraced by the youth ministers of your denomination/organization, what would they be?

Notes

1. Mark Yaconelli, "Youth Ministry: A Contemplative Approach," *The Christian Century* (April 21-28 1999): 450-454.

2. Doug Fields, *Purpose-Driven Youth Ministry* (Grand Rapids, Michigan: Zondervan Publishing House, 1998), 10-11.

3. Paul Hill,ed., *Up the Creek with a Paddle: Building Effective Youth and Family Ministry* (Minneapolis, MN: Augsburg Fortress, 1999), 1-2.

4. Roland Martinson, *Effective Youth Ministry* (Minneapolis: Augsburg Publishing House, 1988), 52.

5. Bo Boshers, *Student Ministry for the 21st Century* (Grand Rapids, Michigan: Zondervan Publishing House, 1997), 114, 118.

6. Hill, 18.

7. Daniel Lambert, "Determining the Research Needs in North American Christian Youth Ministry: A Delphi Study," dissertation (University of Cincinnati: 1999), 49.

8. Merton Strommen, *Five Cries of Youth* (San Francisco: HarperCollins, 1988), 123; Merton P. Strommen and A. Irene Strommen, *Five Cries of Parents* (Minneapolis: Youth and Family Institute of Augsburg College, 1993), 138; Merton P. Strommen and Richard A. Hardel, *Passing on the Faith: A Radical New Model for Youth and Family Ministry* (Winona, Minnesota: St. Mary's Press, 2000), 19.

9. Emile Caillet, *Young Life* (New York: Harper & Row, 1963), 4.

10. Christian Schwarz, *Natural Church Development: A Guide to Eight Essential Qualities of Healthy Churches* (Emmelsbull, Germany: C & P Publishing, 1998; Published in USA by Carol Stream, Illinois: ChurchSmart Resources, USA edition, 1996), 26.

11. Mark H. Senter III, *The Coming Revolution in Youth Ministry: And Its Radical Impact on the Church* (Wheaton, Illinois: Victor Books, 1992), 130.

12. Miroslav Volf, "Floating Along?" *The Christian Century* 117, 11 (April 5, 2000), 398.

13. Volf, 398.

14. Senter, 185.

15. Barry St. Clair in "How Can We Find and Support Volunteers?", Richard R. Dunn and Mark H. Senter III (eds.), *Reaching a Generation for Christ* (Chicago: Moody Press, 1997), 263.

16. Fields, 271.

17. Kenda Dean and Ron Foster, *The Godbearing Life: The Art of Soul Tending for Youth Ministry* (Nashville: Upper Room Books, 1998), 52, 91.

18. Paul Hill, "Youth Ministry Is Spelled A.D.U.L.T. R.E.N.E.W.A.L.," paper (2000).

19. St. Clair, 268.

20. Hayes Tierney, *Making a Difference: An Impact Study of Big Brothers/Big Sisters* (Philadelphia: Public/Private Ventures, 1995), 2.

21. Gary Walker, *Meeting of the Funders of the Big Brothers/Big Sisters Study* (Nov. 15, 1995), 1.

22. For more information about these books or their mentoring program, contact the General Conference Mennonite Church: www2.southwind.net/~gcmc/.

23. Dave Rahn and Terry Linhart, *Contagious Faith: Empowering Student Leadership in Youth Evangelism* (Loveland, Colorado: Group Publishing, 2000), 46.

24. Boshers, 173.

25. Boshers, 174-182.

Evaluating
Priority Outcomes

Chapter 5

Evaluating Priority Outcomes: An Example
Merton Strommen

This chapter introduces the concept of evaluating how well youth ministry priorities are being achieved—that is, the extent to which youth are actually being transformed. Our example is of a careful 1980 effort to evaluate the youth ministries in that year. We believe that an example that does *not* use material from our current study is useful in providing a backdrop for evaluating the outcomes of today's youth ministry, as described in chapters 6 and 7.

The question behind the two-decades-old study was this: *What is the impact being made on youth by Protestant youth ministries?*

To find an answer to this implied question, a concerted effort was launched involving a two-year project. Sponsored by Princeton Theological Seminary and funded by the Lilly Endowment, its project directors surveyed what was known about youth, the condition of youth work in churches, and the location of promising youth programs.

Using the findings of this 1980 study as a base, D. Campbell Wycoff and Don Richter, authors of the resulting report "Religious Education With Youth," arrive at this sobering conclusion:

> **Youth Ministry in 1980. For all the efforts that the churches have made to work with youths, what is being done currently remains rather ineffective in reaching youths at their points of need, in engaging them responsibly in the life and work of the church, and in getting at the vital contribution that they must make to its present and future.**
>
> **Denominational youth organizations have largely been dismantled in recent years. Responsibility now rests largely with local congregations not only for the quality of youth work, but indeed for its very existence...The churches are, for the most part, ineffective in reaching a significant number of youths. Youth leaders flounder.**[1]

Why this discouraging evaluation? Two reasons can be given, both of which contributed to the sad state of youth work at this time.

The dismantling of denominational youth organizations

The first reason has to do with the dismantling of denominational youth organizations. Mainline denominations—such as the Methodist, Presbyterian, and Lutheran churches—actually discarded their historic youth organization in the late sixties and early seventies, despite the fact that these organizations had served them well over the past 50 years. One reason for this is the debates in the National Council of Churches about future directions in youth work. The head of the World Council of Church's department of youth work, Albert van den Heuvel, said in the course of these debates that in the mid-fifties that youth work had become paternalistic and should therefore come to an end.[2]

The thinking of many youth leaders in mainline Protestant denominations found expression in the resulting committee report "We Have This Ministry: A View toward Youth in the Church's Ministry":

> •**The church furnishes the orientation and forms the context of ministry.**
> • **Youth are full members of the church, not members in training.**
> • **The mission of the church—the place where the church fulfills its objective—is in the world.**
> • **The cult of "bigness" and "success" subverts the church's understanding of its life and work.**[3]

It was this thinking that launched the era of "Youth Ministry" as opposed to youth work. Adopted by most denominations, the "Youth Ministry" approach was to integrate youth into the life of the church and involve them in carrying out its mission of addressing world ills. Each congregation, rather than the denomination, was to address the needs of its own youth and develop a program unique to its situation.

Professional youth leaders, convinced that their youth fellowships or leagues were only preserving "the institution and the old morality of their fathers, rather than involving youths in the mission of God to the rest of the world of need," decided to dismantle their national headquarters. This meant ceasing the publication of manuals and handbooks, program resources, membership cards—in essence, the structure and the tools that made the youth fellowships possible.

Local congregations were told that they were free to develop their own dynamic ministry and that they should plan to do so without denominational support. What the denominations did offer were leadership events that would foster creativity and skills in human relations. Personal growth and skill training were viewed now as the primary preparation needed by youth leaders in a congregation.

The dismantling did not go altogether smoothly. When professional youth leaders in Lutheran Church–Missouri Synod proposed the demise of their Walther League, the young people objected; leaders pushed the decision through anyway.

Contributing to the denominations' conviction that a new era in youth work was needed was Margaret Mead's 1970 book, *Culture and Commitment*. It was the anthropologist's contention that a radical break had occurred during the 1960s between youth and adults, and that young people would no longer follow adult leadership. The professional leaders took Mead's theory as gospel and assumed that communication was no longer possible between adults and youth.

The Southern Baptist exception
An exception to this radical shift in youth ministry is found with the Southern Baptist Convention, whose youth leaders continued to supply local congregations with books, resources, and training through their Baptist Sunday School Board.

I incorporated items from Margaret Mead's book in my 1980 national "Study of Generations" (whose results were published in the book so titled) to test whether or not Mead's theory was valid. The resulting data showed that her much publicized "generation gap" was true for 20 percent of the youth population at most. It was a fallacy youth leaders swallowed hook, line, and sinker.

It is a fact of history that the radical shift into the "Youth Ministry" approach did not foster the broad-based, popular support previously enjoyed by the denominational youth organizations. The approach of asking youth to address social issues that adults had failed to solve did not rally the support of either youth or adults. Severe losses appeared in the youth enrollments of church bodies adopting this approach—mostly mainline denominations—even though the overall U.S. youth population was increasing.

Charles Courtoy, former director of youth ministries for the United Methodist Church, and whose doctoral dissertation focuses on this period in history, arrives at a telling conclusion. He concludes that the new "Youth Ministry" emphasis was abortive because it minimized if not disregarded personal salvation, while focusing on social injustices. Its failure came from having disregarded what traditionally had been the essence of youth work.

1980: What parents and youth ministers wanted from youth ministry

If the scuttling of denominational youth departments is the first reason for the dismal evaluation of youth work before 1980, a second reason is a shift in the expectations of parents, Christian educators, and youth ministers. What had been youth ministry's traditional goals and objectives for more than half a century had by 1980 lost their luster and were no longer on center stage.

We can conclude this from a 1980 study by Dean Hoge, research sociologist at Catholic University in Washington, D.C. Participants in his study were representative samples supplied by six groups: the Roman Catholic Church and five denominations—Southern Baptist, United Methodist, Episcopal, Presbyterian, and Church of God (Anderson, Indiana). Each of these ecclesiastical groups supplied 150-175 representative educators and 150-175 parents of adolescents. The educators were parish-based youth ministers or religious educators.

(It should be recognized that this was not a national study involving random samples, so generalizations for the entire country cannot be made from its findings. But the study is large enough to provide a straw in the wind that that approximately indicated what results people coveted most from youth ministry.)

Hoge first collected outcome statements from various sources—statements that described the characteristics adults wished to see in their youth after participating in a parish education and youth ministry program Then he carefully pretested the resulting 62 items. Respondents in this study rated the 62 statements of desired outcomes by indicating which they deemed most important. When the resulting data were factor-analyzed, Hoge found that the items had formed ten distinct clusters—clear indicators to him of what these adults hoped would be outcomes of their congregation's parish education and youth ministry. They describe what adults before 1980 cherished as outcomes within their congregations:

- Conversion
- Personal religious life
- Moral maturity
- Importance of sacraments
- Loyalty to denomination and parish
- Christian fellowship
- Universalizing faith (i.e., is open to other religions in the world)
- Reflective understanding of Christian truth
- Social justice
- Charismatic experience

As one would anticipate, the priorities for adults varied by denomination. Those from a conservative theological orientation—in particular, Southern Baptists and Church of God—gave a high priority to "Conversion and Personal Religious Life," and a low priority to "Universalizing Faith. Those from the other denominations gave less importance to Conversion and Personal Religious Life," and more importance to "Universalizing Faith."

The results demonstrated that a change had taken place during the century between the birth of denominational youth organizations and 1980. This change is especially seen in the way they ranked items describing a Personal Religious Life:

CLUSTER
Items in the Personal Religious Life (1980)
- Sees prayer and reflection as worthwhile.
- Sees God's role of the world as demanding a personal surrender to his will.
- Lives each day with a sense of divine forgiveness.
- Has a daily private prayer life.
- Values the Bible as inspiration for personal spiritual growth.
- Has a personal relationship with Jesus Christ.

Adults in, say, 1920 would have given these items high ratings of importance. But not in 1980, when the parents, youth ministers, and educators in 1980 in four of the ecclesiastical groups rated them well below items describing "Moral Maturity"—which means they viewed moral living to be more important than living a life of personal faith. Here are the combined ratings for each ecclesiastical group (1 is "highly desirable"; 2, "quite desirable"; and 3, "somewhat desirable").

Combined rankings (1980)

Personal Religious	Moral Maturity	Denominational identification
1.25	1.3	Southern Baptist
1.5	1.5	Church of God
1.8	1.4	Presbyterian
2	1.6	Methodist
2.1	1.6	Roman Catholic
2.2	1.5	Episcopal

Here are the "Moral Maturity" items that gained the highest ranking of importance by parents, youth ministers and educators in the 1980 study.

Moral Maturity (1980)
- Has a healthy self-concept about his or her value and worthiness as a person.
- Takes a responsible view toward moral questions such as drug use and sex behavior.
- Understands sexual feelings and has responsible ways of handling them.
- Is acquiring knowledge about human sexuality and has formed a

responsible Christian approach in sexual matters.
- Distinguishes between the values of the popular culture and the values of the gospel.

It is significant that the item given the highest priority—the first item above—has little to do with the young person's relationship to Jesus Christ.[4] Winning young people for Christ and his Church, a primary emphasis at the turn of the century, was not longer a primary focus for these respondents.

A reason for this shift in desired outcomes may well be attributed to an earlier shift in the purposes being advocated by denominational youth departments. As early as 1950 the Methodist Church had begun scaling down the evangelistic nature of Methodist Youth Fellowship, as one can see from their purposes in that year:
- To build Christian character.
- To provide young people a chance for self-expression.
- To train leaders.
- To develop friendships.
- To promote the welfare of the church.[5]

A similar set of purposes was established for the Pilgrim Fellowship, the official youth organization of the Congregational Christian churches.[6] Other Protestant denominations followed suit.

One recognizes in such statements of purpose a movement away from a focus that characterized all denominations beginning in 1880. In short, by 1950 there was an official shift among some denominations from evangelism to developing upright, moral youth. No doubt this shift in official emphasis influenced congregations during the 1960s and 1970s to yield the results that appeared in the two studies of 1980.

It is understandable why Wyckoff and Richter gave their discouraging evaluation of the youth work in 1980. Congregations formerly served by denominational youth professionals now had to fend for themselves. The youth ministers they hired tended to view their work as a stepping-stone profession. There was no dominant educational or theological approach to guide them when developing a ministry unique to the needs of their congregation's youth. The only theological context for many was a liberal theology that focused on moral, responsible living.

Whether the situation has improved will be examined in the next chapter.

Summary

This chapter, which evaluates how well youth ministries in 1980 succeeded in transforming the lives of youth, identifies a low point in the life of Protestant churches. Denominational youth organizations that had been relatively effective were largely dismantled. Congregations that now carried full responsibility for their youth ministries were notably ineffective in reaching their youth and involving them in the life and work of the congregation.

Significantly, the vision and clear sense of mission that characterized churches in the 1920s was being muted by denominational leaders. Moral maturity emerged as a priority, setting aside the urgency of bringing young people into a conscious and living fellowship with Jesus Christ.

THINK IT OVER, TALK IT THROUGH

1. What lessons can denominations learn from the example discussed in this chapter?

2. Do you observe any major pendulum swings in our approach to youth ministry today that we may need to be more cautious before embracing?

3. What was happening in youth ministry in your own particular religious heritage during the time period described in this chapter?

Notes 5

1. Campbell Wyckoff and Don Richter, *Religious Education Ministry with Youth* (Birmingham, Alabama: Religious Education Press, 1982), vii.

2. Charles Courtoy, "An Historical Analysis of the Three Eras of Mainline Protestant Youth Work in America," dissertation (Divinity School of Vanderbilt University: 1976), 76.

3. Courtoy, 81.

4. Wyckoff and Richter, 136.

5. Clarence Peters, "Developments of the Youth Programs of the Lutheran Churches in America," dissertation (Concordia Seminary: 1951), 58.

6. Peters, 57.

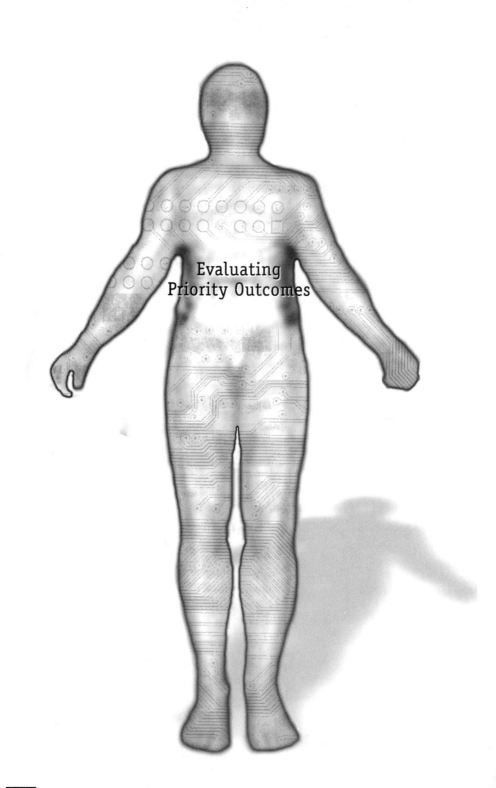

Evaluating
Priority Outcomes

Chapter 6

Evaluating Priority Outcomes: What Is Youth Ministry Achieving Today?

Merton Strommen

This chapter continues the focus on evaluating priority outcomes by answering the question: What is youth ministry achieving today? It does so by examining the evaluations of achievement given by youth ministers to outcomes they deem important.

One naturally wonders if youth ministry is more effective today than it was in 1980. We wonder if the outcomes being sought by youth ministers today have changed substantially since 1980.

As will be seen in this chapter, the answer to both questions is yes. Good things are happening in many congregations and there is a notable shift back to what has been a historic emphasis in youth work. The desired outcomes of youth ministers who participated in the study shows a marked contrast to what was reported in 1980.

Evidence for this conclusion comes from the evaluations of the 2,416 youth ministers. Their evaluations of what has been achieved in their own youth group tell us a lot. Two things need mentioning: their *pattern of response,* and their *ratings of items.*

The pattern of their response (their unconscious favoring of certain responses) caused the items to cluster in meaningful ways. Each cluster (based on the content of its items) describes an outcome they cherish, one that is prominently in their minds.

The second source of information comes from the ratings given items in each cluster. These ratings tell us, in the youth minister's opinion, how well each outcome is being achieved. Granted, we only have their perception. But who is in a better position to give us an opinion?

In this chapter we will consider how they evaluate three aspects of their youth ministry. The focus will be on what they see being achieved in outcomes important to them. The next chapter will focus on changes (transformations) they hope to see in their youth.

Outcomes being achieved through today's youth ministries
- The Spiritual Development of Youth
- Youth Owning Their Ministry
- Strengthened Family Relationships

Of the outcomes listed above, "Spiritual Development of Youth" emerges in the minds of today's youth ministers as the easily most important.

Achievement
The Spiritual Development of Youth

The survey included 21 items that describe important aspects of a well rounded ministry. Respondents were asked to respond to each statement twice: first to indicate how important that activity is for an effective youth ministry; and secondly, to evaluate how well that aspect of youth ministry is being achieved in their congregation or club.

The three items describing spiritual development, as noted in chapter four, drew the highest ratings, both in terms of their perceived importance and in terms of how well they are being achieved.

CLUSTER
Nurturing spiritual development

- Providing help for teaching biblical concepts of right and wrong.
- Helping youth make a commitment to Jesus Christ.
- Seeing that God is at work changing lives.

As is evident by the way these items correlated to form this cluster, youth ministers associate the teaching of biblical concepts of right and wrong with helping youth make a commitment to Jesus Christ. The two are strongly correlated.

A similar association was made by the youths that reported in the study "Five Cries of Youth." Their response to the survey items showed that they, too, associate a sense of moral responsibility with a consciousness of God's presence.[1] One can expect young people that have a personal relationship with Jesus Christ to be conscious of their moral responsibility to live as his disciples.

The third item in the cluster focuses on an ultimate outcome for a youth ministry—seeing God change the lives of young people. It represents youth ministers' greatest thrill. This became evident at the Leadership Conference in Atlanta in 1996 when 2,131 youth ministers responded to the item stem *The biggest thrill in youth ministry is—*.

Almost half (45 percent) identified as their greatest thrill seeing God's activity in the lives of their youth. They completed the item stem by writing: such things as *seeing lives changed, seeing a young person receive Christ, seeing God move in teens lives,* and *growth.*

As is obvious from their ratings, this aspect of ministry is viewed as a crucial part of a youth minister's work. It is the most important of all ministry outcomes. It relates to the Great Commission of making disciples of all nations. It is what Doug Fields in *Purpose-Driven Youth Ministry* identifies as a non-negotiable task. "When youths see evangelism modeled by their leaders and diligently taught from Scripture," he writes, "they gradually understand its purpose and make it a priority".[2]

How well is this outcome being achieved?

How well do the youth ministers believe this objective is being accomplished? Their answer, based on averaging their responses to the above three items, ends up halfway between *very well* and *quite well*. Though one could wish for a higher evaluation, this rating should be recognized as the highest given for all seven outcomes. It sounds like a return to youth work in the early 1900s.

One can arrive at a more precise idea of how well the 2,192 youth ministers evaluate this important outcome of ministry by noting percentages for the item drawing the highest response (of the three): *Helping youth make a commitment to Jesus Christ.* (This statement also drew the highest evaluation of all 21 items.)

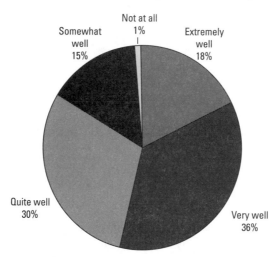

Figure 6.1—Degree spiritual development of one's youth is achieved

Here we see how well these youth ministers believe they are achieving their overriding purpose. But a caveat is warranted at this time: note should be taken of the fact there is considerable variation in how much this goal is both desired and achieved. An indication of this variation becomes available when we separate youth ministers on the basis of their denomination. This should not occasion surprise after seeing how denominations differed in 1980 with respect to their desired outcomes.

Denominational differences

Striking differences do occur between the responses of youth ministers serving in the ten denominations and two parachurch youth organizations. Though their sample sizes are small, they were randomly selected from lists supplied by each participating denomination. It is reasonable to generalize about denominations on the basis of this data.

(Though precision is sacrificed when the sample for a given denomination is small, one still has a fair estimate of what is true. A random sample as small as 230 [as is the case for Lutheran youth ministers] or 528 [as is the case for Southern Baptist youth ministers] still gives a fair estimate of what is true in each church body. We know this to be true having compared findings from a large sample with findings from a small sample drawn from the large one. The results were very similar.)

One of the largest contrasts in scores shows Lutherans scoring lowest on this measure of achievement and Assembly of God scoring highest.

The difference in standard scores between the highest and lowest scoring denominations is a full 10 standard scores.

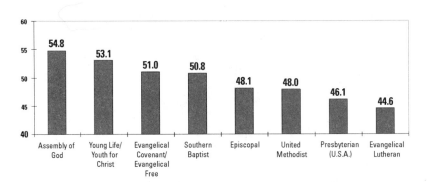

Figure 6.2—How well spiritual development in youth is being achieved, by denomination

The clear indication is that denominational youth ministers differ in how well they believe they are achieving the outcome of spiritual development among their youth (as defined by these three items).

The strange effect of youth group size

For reasons previously noted, the number of youth involved in a youth ministry makes a significant difference in achieving this outcome. The evaluations of youth ministers on "Spiritual Development" vary markedly according to the size of their youth group. The larger the youth group, the higher youth ministers evaluate their youth's spiritual development. Here we see a difference in scores of over seven standard scores, a highly significant difference.

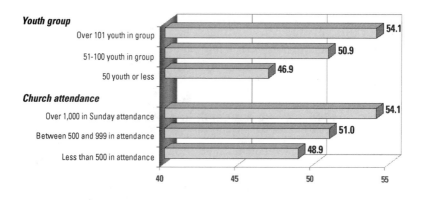

Figure 6.3—How well spiritual development in youth is being achieved, by size of youth group and congregation

What is especially strange is the finding that size of congregation is also associated with variation in these evaluations. Those whose average Sunday morning attendance exceeds 1,000 draw the highest evaluations on "Spiritual Development." Here the difference in standard scores is over 5, something not likely to have happened by chance. This suggests that the morning service can play an important role in the spiritual development of youth. Services that draw over 1,000 people on a Sunday can make a similar impact on the youth.

The lower evaluations by youth ministers serving groups of 40 or less might be expected. In some cases they may be low simply because the congregation's youth are seen as being disinterested. In other cases they may be low because the youth ministers feel limited in their effectiveness.

According to Rick Chromey in *Youth Ministry in Small Churches*, small youth groups commonly do have the disadvantage of lacking money, volunteers, numbers, enthusiasm, as well as lacking a sense of contentment when looking at the youth program of large churches. However, they have the advantage of more opportunities for involvement, personal contact with adults, the experience of family, intergenerational activities, and a place where people are considered more important than performance.[3]

Christian Schwarz addresses this issue in his book *Natural Church Development*. Basing his conclusions on his studies of 1,000 congregations in 32 different countries, he favors small groups and small churches. His research in growing and declining churches shows that continu-

ous multiplication of small groups is a universal church growth principle. His comparison of small and large churches shows that the growth
rate of churches decreases with increasing size. From studies of his
1,000 churches he concludes that the evangelistic effectiveness of mini-
churches is statistically 1,600 percent greater than that of the
megachurch.[4]

But in this our study the findings are reversed. It is in the large
youth groups and churches with a large Sunday attendance that the
spiritual development of youth is perceived as being best achieved. Why
this is true is grist for discussion.

The impact of theology and approach to youth work

We do know that the theological orientation of a youth minister does
make a difference in the outcomes described by these three items. Those
with a conservative theology are more attuned to the issue of spiritual
development. Those with a liberal orientation give a lower evaluation to
how well these items are achieved. (Maybe they are more accurate in
their evaluation.) Here the difference based on theological orientation is
approximately five standard scores.

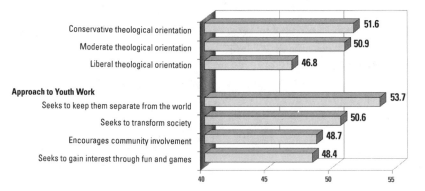

**Figure 6.4—How well spiritual development in youth is being achieved,
by theological orientation**

A meaningful difference also appears when we separate youth ministers on the basis of how they approach youth work. Youth workers
who try to arrange youth events so that their youth are kept as far as
possible from the temptations of the world evaluate their spiritual outcomes considerably higher than do those whose admitted emphasis is to
gain their interest through entertainment and recreational events. These
latter youth ministers acknowledge that they deliberately avoid a heavy
religious diet.

Here the difference in standard scores is well over five—a difference
that is highly significant.

Which factors contribute most to variation in perceived achievement?

One wonders which are most significant factors in how well "Spiritual Development" is achieved. Which combination of factors is most likely to predict high or low scores on this dimension?

An answer is possible through a data analysis known as Automatic Interaction Detection. This method of analysis, rarely used in research because of its complexity, is useful in identifying the underlying structure of a research problem.

The analysis (given here in simplified form) shows that male youth ministers differ from female youth ministers in their achievement of spiritual development in their young people. Each gender apparently responds to a different sequence of factors.

Let us focus first on how well males think they are achieving spiritual development in their youths. As shown below in figure 6.5, male youth ministers are influenced first by the size of their youth group; then secondly, by the stance of their denomination; and thirdly, by the physical location of their church.

It is apparent that some denominations or youth organizations contribute to higher scores for their youth ministers. In figure 6.5 we see the highest score going to those from the Assembly of God. Ranking second in the analysis (but not shown here) are the two parachurch groups—Young Life and Youth for Christ.

The factor of denomination, which increases the scores for one group, can also contribute to a decrease for another. This is true for Lutheran youth ministers. Even though they are serving groups with over 40 participants, their score drops to 46.6. It drops even further, namely to 44, when the averaging is limited to those serving without seminary training. (See boxes 6 and 7.)

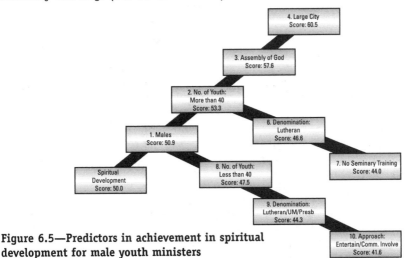

Figure 6.5—Predictors in achievement in spiritual development for male youth ministers

The three denominations associated with the lowest achievement scores on "Spiritual Development" are Lutherans, United Methodists, and Presbyterians. Youth ministers within these three denominations, who use entertainment or community involvement as their approach to youth work, show the lowest evaluations of how well "Spiritual Development" is being achieved in their youth groups.

Now let us focus on how female youth ministers evaluate their achievement in the spiritual development of their youth. Though the perceived achievement of female youth ministers is lower (47.7) than for males to begin with, the achievement scores rise quickly when three factors (boxes 2-4) are present.

The first influential factor for females has to do with denomination. Those who are members of the Assembly of God, Evangelical Covenant, Evangelical Free Church, Young Life, or Youth for Christ, show an average achievement score of 54.4 on "Spiritual Development." Those serving in these denominations are apparently more effective in fostering the spiritual development of those they serve.

A different series of factors appear for female youth ministers:

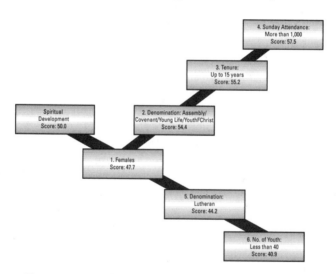

Figure 6.6—Predictors in achievement in spiritual development for female youth ministers

The second influential factor has to do with tenure. If females (in the denominations listed above) have been serving for up to 15 years, their score advances to 55.2.

The next ranking influence is size of church. Those in the denominations listed above, and serving up to 15 years, who are in churches that average over 1,000 people in Sunday services, have achievement scores that rank the highest. Females who combine all three factors give

youth ministry that transforms

high evaluations of their youth's "Spiritual Development." That is reflected in their score of 57.5.

There is a down side to this analysis as well. The female youth ministers who are members of the Lutheran church drop in their score to an average of 44.2. If at the same time they are serving in a congregation where the youth group averages less than 40, their achievement score on "Spiritual Development" drops to 40.9. That score is 17 standard scores below the highest group identified above—an enormous and certainly impressive difference.

From this analysis we see that for female youth ministers, the factor contributing most to the spiritual nurture of their youth is their denominational affiliation. For men, it is first of all the number of participants in their youth group and second, the denomination in which they serve.

Characteristics of Godbearers

What characterizes youth ministers who place a high premium on the spiritual development of their youth? We have some indication that goes beyond what has been identified already. These indicators are found in clusters that correlate significantly with "Spiritual Development of Youth." Each indicator, by virtue of its relationship with "Spiritual Development", helps describe the persons who do best in advancing the spiritual welfare of their youths.

Clusters correlating with Spiritual Development of Youths	Correlation
Has a clear youth ministry philosophy and mission	.45
Enables youth to own their youth ministry program	.45
Relates well to youth	.45

These correlating clusters of items, though not strong, and strictly relational, still suggest what characterizes Godbearers. Youth ministers who are focused in purpose, strongly oriented to helping youth own their program, and relate well to youth, are the ones most likely to see gains in the spiritual development of their youth.

Achievement
Youth Owning Their Ministry

Ranking second highest in evaluation of outcomes is this matter of the youth taking ownership and responsibility for the future of their youth organization. Too often a youth program is adult-led and adult-planned with the result that adults find themselves cajoling young people to participate.

Youth ownership was a characteristic of youth work from its beginnings when young people elected officers for their youth organization, sent them off for training, supported them in carrying out the purposes of their fellowship group, and worked to gain the participation of other youths in the congregation.

These leagues, also known as societies, trained young people in churchmanship—they prepared them for service in their congregation. It was common to see youths that had served as leaders of their youth organization later assuming leadership roles in their congregation.

This important objective has become an increasingly vital one. The current approach of many youth leaders fails in developing loyalty and a sense of ownership in a congregation. This is one of the struggles that Young Life and Youth for Christ staff experience. Their programs, though successful in attracting young people to identify with Jesus Christ, have difficulty in helping young people enter into the life and mission of a local congregation.

Bo Boshers, in his book *Student Ministry for the 21st Century*, is very strong on the importance of youth's identification with the church. He observes:

> **You and your pastor need to devise a plan to connect students with the larger church body so that when they graduate from high school they do not leave the church. We want these young adults to know they are part of the body of Christ and to understand the role they can play in the church through the use of their spiritual gifts on their journey of becoming fully devoted followers of Christ.**[5]

Given below are two items that speak to the business of helping youth to go beyond an individualistic "me and God" form of piety to one that involves a ministry. The high intercorrelation between these two items indicates that respondents gave consistent responses to both items. Though only two, they measure ownership with a high degree of reliability ($r = .84$).

CLUSTER
Youth's ownership of their youth program
- Giving ownership of our ministry to the youth
- Enabling youth to be involved in ministry

An estimate of how well this objective is being achieved can be found in the percentage response of the 2,192 youth ministers to the item drawing the highest response.

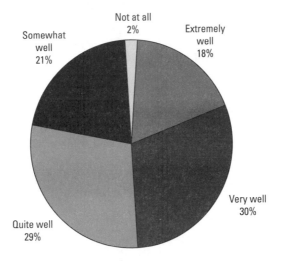

Helping youth to be involved in ministry.
How well is it being achieved in your youth ministry?

Figure 6.7—Degree youth ownership is achieved

As is evident from the responses given above, there is much to be desired in achieving "Youth Ownership."

Clearly, "Youth Ownership" is a most desirable outcome. If not given a high priority, the youth program can become adult-organized and programmed. Soon the ministry becomes a consumers' market. Like a store to which people go to buy what interests them, youths pick and choose from current offerings. When this becomes the mental attitude of a youth group, one finds little ownership, little feeling of responsibility. There is little interest in setting aside personal interests for the mission of the group.

Bo Boshers, conscious of how difficult it is for students to be fully committed to anything, wants his young people to know that he expects as much from them as they give to their other commitments. I like the way in which he explained to them that he was called to build a student ministry, not a nursery, that the purpose of his ministry is to develop fully devoted followers of Christ. He writes:

> **One time, I made this point by setting some baby rattles on a table and telling students, "See these rattles? These rattles are good for babies; they help keep babies entertained. I'm not here to entertain you."**
>
> **On another occasion, I walked students into our church's nursery and said. "This room is appropriate for babies. It's a good place for one- and two-year-**

olds to be. They enjoy it here. I'm not interested in baby-sitting; my purpose is different. I am interested in helping young men and women become difference-makers for Christ."[6]

Where youth ownership tends to be found

One would expect to find a greater sense of ownership in smaller youth groups, but this is not so. The youth ministers giving the lowest evaluations of youth ownership are those serving groups that number less than 40. The highest evaluations are found with youth ministers serving youth groups with over 101 participants. It may well be that youth are most likely to invite their friends to join them when their youth group is growing and large enough to evoke interest.

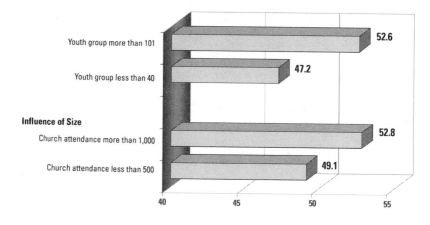

Figure 6.8—Degree youth ownership is achieved, by youth group size and church attendence

For some strange reason numbers are important also with respect to size of congregation. It is in churches where the number of people attending a Sunday morning service is largest that one is more likely to find youth accepting ownership of their program.

This is likely because larger churches are able to hire more experienced or gifted youth ministers, who in turn are better able to achieve this desired outcome. One finds encouragement for this hypothesis in the fact that evaluations are consistently higher for youth ministers who have been in the business for 16 years or more and work in a large city.

One characteristic of national organizations such as Young Life and Youth for Christ is their strong accent on charismatic leaders. This is an important quality of leadership for them because their club leaders must attract youth to their programs. They do not begin with young people who are a captive audience due to their membership in a congregation. Rather they must attract youth from the community who are either unchurched or members of a congregation.

This may help to explain why youth ministers from the national youth organizations (Young Life and Youth for Christ) score lowest on this measure. Their clubs are leader-led. Their youth carry very little responsibility for launching or maintaining the club's program. They have to be attracted and this usually means luring them through entertaining activities. The initiative comes from the leader and not the youth.

The small sample of Episcopal youth ministers (N=71) does excel in the way their youth accept ownership for their youth ministry.

Adjuncts to Youth Ownership

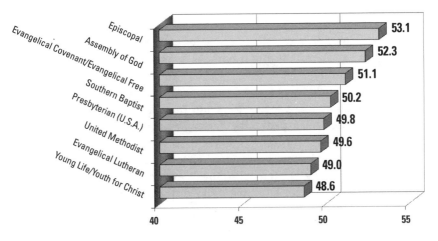

Figure 6.9—Youth ownership achievement

A helpful commentary is available regarding what often follows when youth assume responsibility for their program. The commentary is provided by the clusters correlating significantly with "Youth Ownership."

They tell us that when youth ministers have achieved a degree of youth ownership, one usually finds youth who treat one another with respect, participate in the life of the congregation, actively give public witness of their faith, grow in their commitment to Christ, and demonstrate interest and motivation. One can be impressed with byproducts such as these knowing that they tend to follow the goal of achieving "Youth Ownership."

Achievement
Strengthened Family Relationships

An aspect of youth ministry that has emerged recently in the life of the church is a ministry to the entire family with a focus on parents. This is a necessary development for a number of reasons, not least the importance of parents in the spiritual development of their children and youths. Increasingly, there is awareness that faith is best ignited in the home and that parents are best situated to shape the faith lives of their children.

Mark DeVries, Associate Pastor for Youths and Their Families at First Presbyterian Church, underscores the importance of this desired outcome in his book, Family-Based Youth Ministry. He poses the issue being faced by youth ministers everywhere.

> Without question the most damaging isolation that teenagers in our culture experience is from their own families. American parents spend less time with their children than do parents of any other country in the world, according to Harvard psychiatrist Armand Nicholi. Fifty years ago families worked and ate together by necessity. Teenagers and parents spent hours and hours together; in the process, young people could not avoid observing and listening in on the adult world. These experiences laid a natural track for adolescents to enter adulthood.
>
> It might be hoped that churches would stand in the gap and provide an environment in which children and youths could dialogue and collaborate with adults. But sadly enough, for many teenagers, the place they are the most segregated from the world of adults is their church. And churches with the more "successful" youth program seem to particularly exacerbate this problem.
>
> Most "successful" youth ministries have their own youth Sunday school, youth mission, youth small groups, youth evangelism teams, youth worship, youth budget, youth interns, youth committees, youth offering, youth Bible studies, youth "elders" (never understand that one), youth centers, youth choir, youth rooms, youth discipleship programs, youth conferences, youth retreats, youth fundraisers, and (my personal favorite) youth ministers.[7]

He poses the issue well. Youth raised in the church can come to the time of high school graduation without having entered into the intergenerational life of a congregation. As such, they feel little loyalty to their congregation, little involvement in her mission, and little feeling of obligation to support its work. For many congregations it can be said that little has been done to strengthen family relationships and bring parents, children and youth together for significant faith experiences.

Marjorie Thompson, in *Family: The Forming Center,* raises the all-important question, "What if the family were not merely an object of the church's teaching mission, but one of the most basic units of the church's mission to the world?" Her answer: "What I am suggesting is that the communal church and the domestic church need to recapture a vision of the Christian family as a sacred community. This will require an awareness of the 'sacred' in the 'secular' of God in the flesh of human life."[8]

The Youth and Family Institute at Augsburg College is intent on introducing this concept of a partnership between family and church. Through its conferences, training events, and resources it is attempting to shift people's thinking from the old paradigm of a church-centered, home-supported congregation to a home-centered, home supported congregation. It is seeking to alter the concept young and old hold of the church, namely, that it is a "God-box".

In a subtle and unspoken way, people have come to think that faith is nurtured only in the church and that faith is best taught by its professionals. Therefore they bring their children and youth to church in hopes that there they will find a faith. Some parents think they have fulfilled their obligation when they do no more than drive them to church, drop them off, and then leave. The end result of this thinking is an institutionalization of faith.

Today there are congregations wanting to change that paradigm. They have even changed their mission statement to indicate their intent of making the Christian home the primary agency for faith formation. This point of view is presented as the central thesis in *Passing on the Faith: A Radical New Model for Youth and Family Ministry.* The authors, Merton Strommen and Richard Hardel, demonstrate with research documentation that a youth ministry is most successful when carried out in the context of a partnership between church and home.

Roland Martinson, professor of pastoral care at Luther Seminary, helped develop a vision of a "communal" and "domestic" church partnership between church and family, introduced through an approach called "The Child in Our Hands." He describes it in this way:

A female/male home visitation team meets with children and their families on the occasion of

twelve rites of passage, or milestones, during a
child's journey from birth to graduation from high
school. During the visit the team prepares the family and child for the coming milestone by presenting
the information on baptismal grace, child-develop-
ment, and faith-informed child rearing. In addition
they present ideas and resources for maintaining
the life of faith in the household. During this visit a
FaithChest and a FaithLife in the Home Resource
Guide are provided.

The FaithLife in the Home Resource Guide identifies resources such as musical tapes, Bible and
faith-in-daily life story books, puppets, and games
they can use at bedtime, cartime, laptime, sicktime,
mealtime, and other significant family "touch-
points" to communicate faith across the life cycle.

Each of the twelve passages, or milestones, are
celebrated in a congregational festival worship service followed by a reception for the child and family
members. These worship celebrations and all other
worship services are intentionally child friendly as
well as intriguing to youths and adults.[9]

Significantly, the component "Improving Family Relationships,"
emerges in this study of youth ministers as an outcome to be sought.
The items that clustered together describe a need they feel, namely, that
of helping parents strengthen relationships in their families. They recognize that this will require parental involvement in their youth ministry,
providing opportunities for teens and parents to interact, assisting in
times of conflict and helping parents cope with nontraditional family
issues. Without question this outcome—if pursued—will require giving
greater recognition to the family as God's domestic church.

Verses in Deuteronomy, among the most quoted in the Bible, under-
score the importance of the parents' role in the spiritual development of
their children.

Love the Lord your God with all your heart and with
all your soul and with all your strength. These com-
mandments that I give you today are to be upon
your hearts. Impress them on your children. Talk
about them when you sit at home and when you
walk down the road, when you lie down and when
you get up. (Deuteronomy 6: 5-7)

An effort to revive this kind of participation by parents is reflected in the items that follow. The eight items form a tight cluster that can qualify as a highly reliable (r =.86) measure.

CLUSTER
Helping parents improve family relationships

- Strengthening family relationships
- Helping parents become more involved in the lives of their children.
- Helping parents recognize and adopt wise methods of discipline
- Providing opportunities for teens and parents to interact.
- Giving special assistance to parents coping with nontraditional family issues.
- Gaining parental involvement in the ministry.
- Helping youth and their parents deal with conflict.
- Encouraging families to teach service as a way of life through their involvement in helping activities.

Though many youth ministers did identify these items as "very important", they evaluated their achievement of these as lowest of the seven desired outcomes. A fair estimate of how limited is their perceived achievement of these items can be seen in their response to the following item (one that gained the most responses):

How well are you achieving in your youth ministry the Strengthening of Family Relationships?

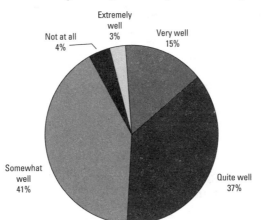

Figure 6.10—Percent helping parents strengthen family relationships

The way these percentages lean toward the bottom of the ratings makes it very clear that this aspect of ministry needs developing. Unfortunately, it is presently receiving little more than a pioneering effort.

That is exactly how a youth minister describes his recent efforts to minister to parents and families. What he writes illustrates how this aspect of ministry often starts small and slow.

> **Our youth ministry has recently started to see ministry to the families of our students as one of our primary goals. (I'm not sure why it took us so long). We began with the simple sharing of information about youth ministry events through newsletters and quarterly meetings.**
>
> **The attendance at our meetings was quite dismal, so we began offering help for parents. We brought in seminars (attendance was still dismal) but those who attended were enthusiastic and thankful. We then began to involve parents in various aspects of our ministry, giving them opportunities to connect with their kids in more substantial ways. We're still learning a lot, but we're convinced that we're on a path that will lead to a richer, more effective ministry.**

Consider the following chart that shows the actual ratings of achievement for each of the eight items compared to their perceived importance. You will note that there are some notable gaps between importance and achievement on several of the items.

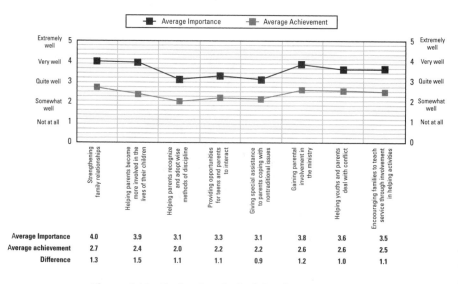

Figure 6.11—Evaluating desired family outcomes

Where this ministry is emphasized most

Youth ministers in the Southern Baptist Convention are seemingly the most focused on providing assistance to parents. Their evaluations of what is being achieved are the highest, while evaluations are lowest for those serving a national youth organization (Young Life and Youth for Christ). Their low score is understandable. Both parachurch organizations function outside the context of a congregation. Their focus is on reaching youths through their clubs and not on working with families. Parents are involved only tangentially as for instance when their help is needed for fundraisers.

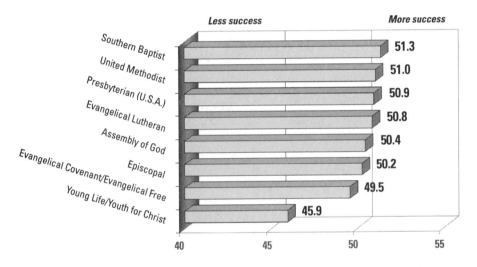

Figure 6.12—Achievement in strengthening family relationships, by theological orientation

This difference of five standard scores calls attention to the fact that there is notable difference in what is being emphasized by youth ministers in the top and bottom groups.

Groups showing notable differences

Two comparisons worthy of note relate to the *youth ministers' tenure* and how they *approach ministry*.

One might surmise that youth ministers intent on protecting their youth would be among the first to involve parents in a variety of ways. It is understandable also, that those in the business of youth ministry for a number of years will be more conscious of the importance of strengthening family relationships.

Lest a protection approach be singled out as more commendable and one to be recommended, the limitation of the sample available for this group of youth ministers needs to be mentioned. Only 42 youth ministers identified themselves with the approach described below.

Just as the Bible asks us to be separate from the world, I try to arrange youth events so that my youth are kept as far as possible from the temptations that come from such things as movies, dances, wrong books, and magazines.

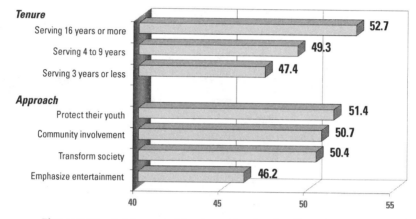

Figure 6.13—Achievement in strengthening family relationships, by tenure and approach

A sample of 42 youth ministers means that results are based on the evaluations of a few. Nevertheless, we include their results because they provide the only information we have for this approach to youth ministry. Obviously, these youth ministers do take their ministry seriously and do work closely with their youth. As a result they appear on a number of measures to be having greater success in achieving desirable outcomes than those using other approaches.

Aside from the comparisons presented above, little else can be presented from our analyses. Most of the differences found in comparisons, which use a range of criteria, are too small to be of practical significance. In general, they point in the following directions: achievement with respect to a ministry to family is greater when youth groups are larger that 101, located in the Atlantic region, are led by youth ministers over 40 years of age, trained past college or university, and whose theological orientation is liberal.

Strengthening the congregation's sense of family

Roland Martinson draws attention to the fact that intergenerational approaches to nurturing faith in children, youth, and adults stand in long traditions of evangelizing and instructing the young and recent converts to the faith. These classic traditions reach back through colonial America, the Reformation and medieval times, to the church fathers, In each of these periods, Christian leaders recognized that faith was communicated and molded in the familial and communal intersections of the Christian community.

Bringing the generations together creates an environment in which the gifts of each generation can be given to the other. Intergenerational instruction is by nature experiential and relational. More often than not, it is interactive and utilizes most of the sense. Each participant brings something to the learning experience and enhances the result with his or her contribution.[10]

Drawing on James White's book *Intergenerational Religious Education,* Martinson summarizes the four ways intergenerational learning is frequently organized.

In-common learning experiences bring persons of different ages or generations to do the same thing together. These experiences are usually more active, less verbal occasions when all participants take in information such as viewing a film or doing a project. Following the event, participants share or respond to what they have been through together. In-common learning provides the generations immediate, concrete experiences that engage each at their own level and result in shared response.

Parallel learning separates people according to age or generations to work on the same project or topic simultaneously. Later these people either intentionally or informally come together to speak about or act out their common focus. Parallel learning permits all ages to engage a common issue or topic in their own unique way. The study of biblical stories and life skills are examples of intergenerational learning accomplished well in parallel learning.

Contributive occasions often follow parallel learning activities where each generation shares what they have learned or developed in their respective setting. These moments create a "right here among us" experience and often generate an educational occasion where the whole is larger than the sum of the parts.

Interactive sharing is a pattern in which groups of various ages work toward preparing something for interpersonal exchange. A story, an art piece, a skit. or a solution worked out by a particular person or age group is shared with the rest. Case studies and problem-solving situations are good examples of this kind of learning.

The parables of Jesus surprise, confront, and heal as they become frames within which the generations find themselves. Personal stories are often intentionally or spontaneously the most meaningful teaching/learning moments in intergenerational education. At one level, intergenerational instruction is primarily storytelling.[11]

Summary

This chapter has presented the evaluations that youth ministers gave to three important outcomes: the spiritual development of youth, youth ownership of their ministry, and strengthened family relationships.

We noticed considerable variation in their perceived achievement of spiritual development. Membership in certain denominations or youth organizations considerably influences how well spiritual development is seen as being achieved. The same is true for theological orientation.

Generally, males give higher ratings than females to their achievement of spiritual development in their youths. The highest scores appear for those serving in large cities. Females, though more modest in their ratings, show the highest scores for those serving in large congregations.

Youth's ownership of their youth ministry varies predictably—higher for groups over 101 and for groups in churches where attendance on Sunday is over 1,000. Strengthened family relationships, though a highly desired outcome, is yet to be achieved. Considerable distance appeared in the evaluations between the importance accorded eight items evaluating family outcomes and the degree to which they are seen as being achieved.

Here again, those serving 16 years or more in youth ministry draw the highest evaluations in their ability to help parents strengthen family relationships. Those new to the profession do the poorest.

1. How do you explain the "strange effect of size" (larger youth groups and larger congregations are more likely to realize spiritual development of youth than smaller size groups/congregations)?

2. What explanations would you offer for the contrast between the profile of female and male youth ministers most likely to achieve spiritual development with teens?

3. Why *should* youth ownership be important to youth ministers? See if you can come up with theological as well as practical pros and cons.

4. Brainstorm some ways that Young Life and Youth for Christ could help bring about stronger family relationships without compromising their particular youth ministry mission.

5. What sorts of outcomes are being realized in your particular denomination/ organization relative to those in other youth ministries? Which findings are the most difficult to accept? to explain?

Notes 6

1. Merton Strommen, *Five Cries of Youth* (San Francisco: HarperCollins, 1988), 133.

2. Doug Fields, *Purpose-Driven Youth Ministry* (Grand Rapids, Michigan: Zondervan Publishing House, 1998), 108-109.

3. Rick Chromey, *Youth Ministry in Small Churches* (Loveland, Colorado: Group Books, 1990), 14-30.

4. Christian Schwarz, *Natural Church Development: A Guide to Eight Essential Qualities for Healthy Churches* (Emmelsbull, Germany: C & P Publishing, 1998; Published in USA by Carol Stream, Illinois: ChurchSmart Resources, 1996), 46-48.

5. Bo Boshers, *Student Ministry for the 21st Century* (Grand Rapids, Michigan: Zondervan Publishing House, 1997), 253.

6. Boshers, 140.

7. Mark DeVries, *Family-Based Youth Ministry* (Downers Grove, Illinois: InterVarsity Press, 1994), 40-41.

8. Marjorie Thompson, *Family: The Forming Center* (Nashville: Upper Room Books, 1989), 24-26.

9. Roland Martinson, "The Role of the Family in the Faith and Value Formation of Children" in Dr. David Anderson *Leadership Manual* (Youth and Family Institute of Augsburg College: 1998), 79.

10. Roland Martinson, "Learning across Generations," in Dr. David Anderson *Leadership Manual*, 102.

11. Martinson, 103-104.

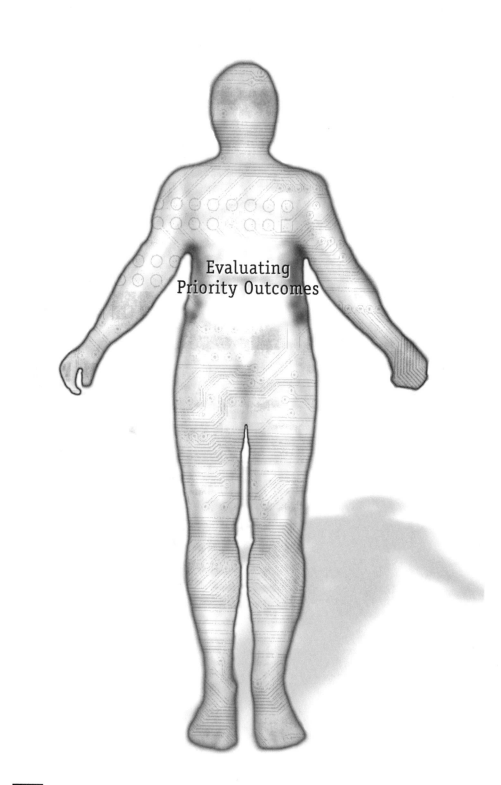

Evaluating
Priority Outcomes

Chapter 7

Evaluating Priority Outcomes: Youth Response and Witness

Merton Strommen

In the previous chapter we considered what today's youth ministries have achieved. We made a concerted effort to present their evaluations of priority outcomes. The focus was on the youth minister's perception of how well they were achieving three important aspects of ministry: youth's spiritual development, their sense of ownership, and the strengthening of family relationships. It was an evaluation of current youth ministries.

In this chapter we continue our consideration of this aspect of the conceptual model by noting the youth minister's evaluations of their youth's response—their attitudes, their demonstration of interest, the involvement in serving activities, and their missionary response. Though both chapters deal with perceived outcomes, and for that reason are linked, this one focuses on youth's response, namely, what is visually apparent.

The four clusters of items that provide the focus for this chapter are these:

Four clusters: Youth response and interest
- Joyous Attitudes of Respect and Love
- Interested Youth
- Youth Serving Church and Community
- Youth Active in Public Witness and Ministry

Evaluation
Joyous Attitudes of Respect and Love

We at Search Institute became aware of the shaping power of attitudes in a youth group when we carried out a national study involving the adults who work with youths in five youth serving organizations: The National Catholic Educational Association, 4-H Extension, The American Lutheran Church, the United Methodist Church, and Campfire Inc. The study, funded by the National Institute of Mental Health, was designed to determine why it is so hard to introduce needed change in organizations. In doing so, it identified both what facilitates and hinders change.

Five shaping forces were identified, one of which was the atmosphere of a group—its sense of openness, freedom, and warmth. Where the attitudes of youth establish this kind of atmosphere, the following characteristics are apparent in those youth groups.

- Larger numbers of volunteer leaders in the youth program.
- The youth exhibit a concern for people.
- The youth group is referred to as a caring community.
- Larger numbers of youth in the youth group.
- Efforts being made to encourage youth in the practice of daily devotions.

Each of these characteristics identified through the study is unlikely to have occurred by chance. On the contrary they emerged for those youth groups because a joyous, warm attitude characterized both the youth and their leaders. The study demonstrated that there is a shaping power in the emotional atmosphere of a group.[1]

Fortunately, this facet of youth ministry, namely the attitudes of youth, draws a relatively high evaluation from the youth ministers. Here we refer to the positive attitudes that establish a joyous atmosphere. Note how the items listed below include attitudes of respect, love, joy, faithfulness, and a sense of responsibility. They resemble in part the attitudes the apostle Paul covets for his young associate, Timothy: "Don't let anyone look down on you because you are young but set an example for the believers in speech, in life, in love, in faith, and in purity" (1 Timothy 4:12).

CLUSTER
Joyous Attitudes of Respect and Love
- Acting respectful of people in authority.
- Reflecting positive, loving attitudes toward each other.
- Establishing a joyous atmosphere at youth meetings.
- Attending our youth meetings in high percentages.
- Taking responsibility for some aspect of their youth ministry.

When the youth ministers considered how true these attitudes are of their youth, their evaluations fell half way between "often true" and "sometimes true." Another estimate of how well they evaluate this important outcome is found in the item gaining the highest percentage response:

Acting respectful of people in authority. How true of your youths?

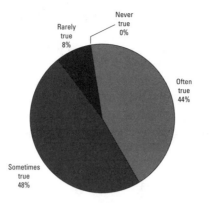

Figure 7.1—Extent youth show respect

These are remarkably high percentages. It speaks well of how youth in congregations and clubs around the country are being seen as relating to people in authority.

The significance of these positive attitudes

These percentages show that church youth do indeed differ from general public youth. This difference is seen in bold relief in the findings of 1997 national study (quoted earlier) entitled "Kids These Days: What Americans Think about the Next Generation". When the 2,000 randomly selected adults were asked to describe today's teenagers, two-thirds gave as their first response the words *rude, wild,* and *irresponsible.*[2]

In a day when American youth are being characterized as disrespectful and rude, one can applaud what youth ministers report. Without question, the gospel shapes positive attitudes and creates a people who stand in marked contrast with a significant number of American youths.

Additional insight is gained into what youth are often like who show attitudes of respect and love. We see it in two clusters of items that correlate significantly with "Attitudes of Respect and Love". One cluster identifies youth that feel a sense of ownership in their youth program and the other identifies those who are interested and motivated. Both describe attitudes youth ministers love to see in their young people.

Clusters correlating with Respect/Love	Correlation
Youth Ownership of Their Youth Program	.52
Interested and Motivated Youth	.54

Groups showing differences in their evaluations

Size of youth group is also associated here with varying evaluations of youth's attitudes. One might think that when youth ministers work with smaller numbers of youth, more would know each other and, through relationships that are established, reflect more positive attitudes. But the data shows otherwise. It also shows that the desired attitudes are more likely to be present when youth ministers are more experienced.

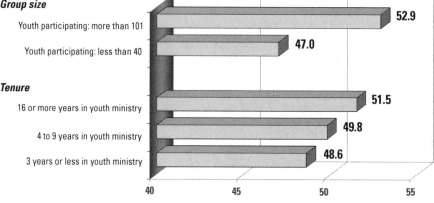

Figure 7.2—Evaluation of youth attitudes of respect

It is likely that those who have more experience in a youth ministry have larger numbers of youth in their program. If so, that would partially account for the rather consistent differences that appear between large and small youth groups. One can assume that when larger congregations hire people, they seek to hire the best, recognizing that they must pay the best.

Denominational youth ministers differ in how they evaluate their youth's attitudes of respect and love. The ones giving lowest evaluations are Lutheran youth ministers and those who are working in a national youth organization (Youth for Christ and Young Life). The ones giving highest evaluations come from the small sample (n = .71) of youth ministers of the Episcopal Church.

It may be that because Young Life and Youth for Christ reach more unchurched youth, fewer of their youth are going to reflect attitudes of love and respect. Or it may mean that those youth that attend only for reasons of entertainment and fun do not feel obligated or moved to show love and respect.

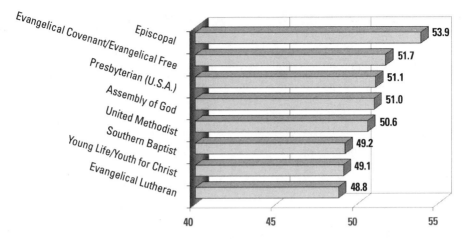

Figure 7.3—Evaluation of youth's attitudes of respect, by denomination

It should be noted that, with respect to "Attitudes of Love and Respect", Lutheran youth ministers evaluate their youths lowest and Episcopal youth ministers highest. This is not a chance statistic. We see the scores of these two groups reversed on measures of concern—concern over seeing negative attitudes of disinterest in one's youth. On this measure of "Disinterested Youth", Lutherans express the most concern and Episcopal youth ministers the least. Apparently Lutherans are not as successful in gaining the response they want from their youths.

Evaluation
Interested and Motivated Youths

This outcome of a youth ministry is most interesting. Its items, previously discussed under the title of "Disinterested Youths", correlate negatively with the six outcomes discussed here in chapters 6 and 7. A negative correlation means that wherever the other six outcomes are being realized, one is likely to find interested and motivated youth, as reflected in this cluster:

CLUSTER
Interested and Motivated Youth
- The youths show much interest in church or their youth ministry.
- I find it easy to motivate my youth.
- Our youth ministry is primarily youth-led.
- I believe my youth ministry is successful.
- I am seeing results from my ministry.

In a sense these items get at the core of evaluation. If the youth are interested and motivated, almost anything will succeed. Their attitudes will have an energizing effect on the youth minister's morale as well as on the morale of volunteer adults who assist with youth leadership.

The added power of positive youth' attitudes is seen in the dimensions that correlate with them. Where these are found one will often find interested and motivated youth.

Clusters correlating with Interested Youth	Correlation
Youth Treating Others with Respect and Love	.53
Youth Actively Involved in Public Witnessing	.51

Evaluation
Youths Serving Church and Community

An outcome one is pleased to find in a youth group relates to service. It can involve a variety of activities carried out in the church and community.

In a way not previously known, service activities generate both a sense of ownership in one's congregation and a greater faith life within the lives of youth.

The major study "Effective Christian Education", carried out by Search Institute, found this to be true. Three thousand youth involved in the study, randomly selected from six major Protestant denominations, responded to 38 items that assessed evidences of faith. The surprise finding was that youth involved in service activities for church or community registered significantly higher faith scores.

When adults who also participated in this study responded to the same items about service activities, the same results appeared. Those who remembered being involved in service activities when they were in high school, scored significantly higher on evidences of faith than did nonparticipants The evidence strongly suggests that something profound happens when people live beyond their own interests and seek to meet needs of others.

There is another significant outcome from service activities. It is bonding to one's church that comes as a result of giving service to a community through one's congregation. The same study ("Effective Christian Education") showed that as the number of hours increase that youth give to "helping people in one's town or city," the percentages increased of those strongly agreeing that "their church means a great deal to them."[3]

This and other studies carried out by Search Institute show that the more time youth give in service to the community through their congregation, the greater their loyalty and bonding to the church. Which means that as young people experience meaningful service and the resulting impact on their faith life, they become more loyal to the organization providing the opportunity.

The seven items given below represent a fair sampling of the kinds of activities that characterize youth who are service motivated.

CLUSTER
Youth Serving Church and Community

- Involved in activities to better their community.
- Involved in serving others.
- Assuming leadership in some aspect of congregational life beyond youth ministry.
- Reaching out to lonely and hurting peers.
- Going out of their way to welcome persons from different ethnic backgrounds.
- Taking public stands on moral issues.
- Taking responsibility for some aspect of their youth ministry.

One wonders how many youth ministers give a high evaluation of their youth's response to this rich array of service activities. An estimate is found in their answer to the item drawing the highest response:

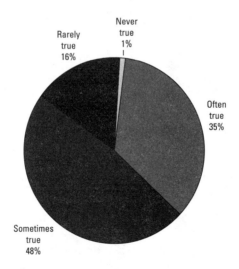

Figure 7.4—Degree youth are serving others

As is evident from this item, many young people in the denominations and youth organizations participating in this study are involved in some form of service activity. There is, however, considerable variation in which groups are encouraging such service activities.

Sources of greatest contrast in service involvement

Denominational differences pose the greatest contrast in how well this desired outcome is evaluated. The differences range from a high for the Episcopal youth ministers to a low for those serving a national youth organization (Young Life/Youth for Christ). Given below are their scores.

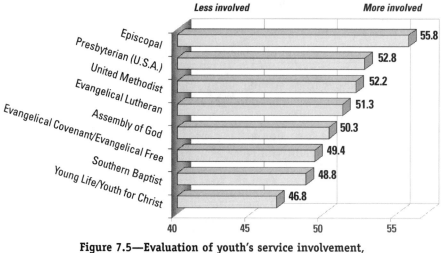

Figure 7.5—Evaluation of youth's service involvement, by denomination/organization

Inasmuch as the primary aim of Young Life and Youth for Christ is evangelism, it is understandable that less attention would be given to the kinds of service activities being described by items in this measure. But it does point up the weakness in their limited objective, especially when these organizations lack success in integrating youth they have reached back into a congregation.

Four other contrasting groups

Tenure of youth minister and size of youth group again emerge as causing significant differences in how well youths are involved in service. To these two can be added the youth minister's theology and approach to youth work. All four factors are significant in their ability to involve youth in service activities. The contrasts in evaluation are upwards of five standard scores—a contrast that could not have happened by chance.

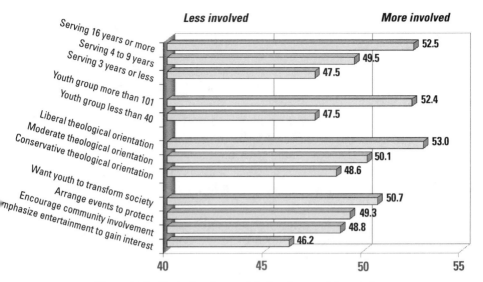

Figure 7.6—Variation in youth's involvement in service

These contrasts are provocative. They certainly indicate that it is in the larger youth groups, served by experienced youth ministers whose theology is liberal and whose approach is to transform society, that one can expect youth to be the most involved in service activities.

It is also noteworthy that here we see a contrast created on the basis of theology. It indicates there is a connection between what a youth minister believes and what he or she emphasizes.

Characteristics of service-oriented youth groups

We gain added insight into the kinds of youth groups who volunteer to help by noting which clusters correlate significantly with this measure of "Youth Serving Church and Community". It is clear that service tends to flourish where there is youth ownership and interested, motivated youths.

Clusters correlating with Service	Correlation
Youth Have a Sense of Ownership for Their Program	.52
Youth Are Interested and Motivated	.47

These correlating clusters make sense. It is in groups where such attitudes exist towards one another that youths are most likely to volunteer their services to meet a need.

Evaluation
Youth Active in Public Witness And Ministry

I was impressed by the sense of mission that motivated a small youth group in Silverton, Oregon. Though lacking a youth director or a pastor who was particularly good with youth, the 15 or so Lutheran youth reflected a strong sense of mission gained presumably from their homes. Their witness activities included visits to hospitals, nursing homes, and churches. When they graduated from high school and moved on to college, several of them brought a strong sense of mission to the campus of Willamette University. Here they helped form a group that viewed the campus, including faculty, as their mission field.

Their first focus was a popular political science professor who had been challenging them to be open to various political viewpoints. They adopted his stance by challenging him to be open to the claims of the Christian faith. He accepted their challenge by responding to their invitation to attend their Bible studies. Through attendance at these Bible studies, this political science professor, Mark Hatfield, became a Christian. Later, as a distinguished U.S. senator from Oregon, Hatfield publicly acknowledged that this group of mission-oriented young people were responsible for his conversion.

This outcome of a youth ministry has to do with youth becoming Godbearers. It relates to their participation in public prayer, witness, educational, and ministry opportunities. It has to do with their sense of vocation as evidenced by the number who decide to enter into a full time ministry. It has to do with evangelistic zeal.

One of the clear voices calling for evangelistic commitment comes from the youth leader Doug Fields. He emphasizes the importance of an evangelistic youth ministry in his book, *Purpose-Driven Youth Ministry*, by saying,

> **The majority of teenagers I've worked with did not jump for joy when they learned about their responsibility to evangelize. Most would rather not do it. They are comfortable with the friends they have at church and don't feel an inherent need to reach the lost. But when they see evangelism modeled by their leaders and diligently taught from Scripture, they gradually understand its purpose and make it a priority.[4]**

Items describing this evangelistic stance of youth are given below. They identify young people who are truly serious about the faith and willing to become ambassadors for their Lord. They describe a wide range of activities that have a common focus on witnessing to a faith personally held.

CLUSTER
Youth Active in Public Witness and Ministry

- Witnessing publicly about their faith.
- Meeting to pray for other youth not in the faith.
- Deciding to enter full time ministry.
- Taking part in public prayer.
- Involved in witness groups (e.g., singing, instrumental, drama).
- Taking advantage of Bible-study opportunities.
- Coming to know Jesus Christ as their Savior and Lord.
- Taking advantage of ministry training opportunities.

Evaluations given these items prove to among the lowest given for all seven outcomes. considered in this chapter and chapter six. Note how the youth ministers evaluated the following item—an item which drew the highest response of all those listed above.

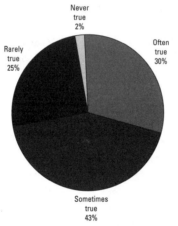

Never true 2%

Often true 30%

Rarely true 25%

Sometimes true 43%

Figure 7.7—Looking at my ministry, I see youth taking part in public prayer

One cannot but be impressed with what some youth ministers see as characterizing the youth they serve. It means that a substantial number of young people are indeed identifying themselves with the Christian faith and a life of discipleship. Their participation as teenagers is preparing them for leadership in the church.

Striking contrasts in evaluations

Great differences appear when the sample is divided on the basis of denomination, size of youth group, approach to youth work, and tenure. We find that the youth involved most in sharing their faith are

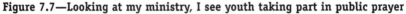

found in Assembly of God churches. Those drawing the lowest evaluation with respect to this outcome are Presbyterians.

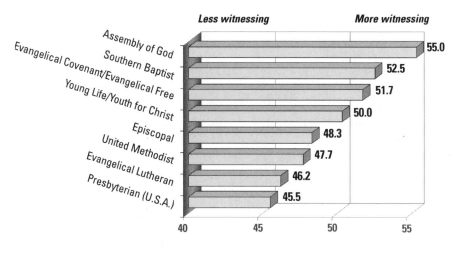

Figure 7.8—Evaluation of youth in public witness

The distance between the high and low scores is 10 standard scores, a remarkably great distance. Clearly, there are denominational differences in the degree to which evangelism is emphasized and practiced. The two denominations which rank lowest on this measure—Evangelical Lutherans and Presbyterian (U.S.A.)—also rank lowest in their being motivated by God's calling (figure 9.18 on page 251) and in being theologically grounded (figure 9.19 on page 251).

Similar contrasts appear when other comparisons are made. A greater evangelistic zeal is evidenced by those in youth groups of 101 members or more, in churches where the youth approach is to provide protection, and where the youth minister has been serving for 16 years or more. (A more detailed interpretation of this information is given in chapter 9.)

Note how the number of youth participating in a public witness declines as the size of their youth group declines and increases with the number of years their youth minister has been involved in ministry. These contrasts in scores are certainly provocative with regard to their implication. But there are still some surprises.

Lesser contrasts that also warrant consideration

For some reason the number of people attending a Sunday morning service is related to differences in how many youths witness publicly to

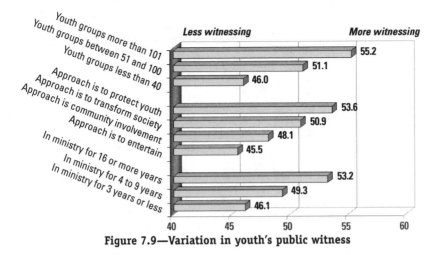

Youth groups more than 101

Youth groups between 51 and 100

Youth groups less than 40

Approach is to protect youth

Approach is to transform society

Approach is community involvement

Approach is to entertain

In ministry for 16 or more years

In ministry for 4 to 9 years

In ministry for 3 years or less

55.2

51.1

46.0

53.6

50.9

48.1

45.5

53.2

49.3

46.1

40   45   50   55   60

Figure 7.9—Variation in youth's public witness

their faith. Congregations reporting over 1,000 attendees see far more of their youths involved this type of public witness. This may mean that churches which emphasize evangelism are the ones that average over 1,000 in attendance on Sundays.

A notable difference also appears when a division is made on the basis of how the youth ministers classify themselves theologically. A public witness by youth occurs more often for those whose youth ministers claim to be conservative and less often for those identifying themselves as liberal.

It is interesting that seminary training does not pose significant differences in the degree to which this outcome is being achieved. Youth ministers lacking seminary training seem to be as effective in modeling a mission concern as those with this training. The advantage of a seminary education for youth ministers shows in more confident leadership, more competent job performance, and being more theologically grounded (see figure 9.12 on page 242).

Characteristics of youth involved in public witness

Youth who identify strongly with the "Faith and Mission of their Church" are often ones who have a sense of ownership in their program and who are interested and motivated. This fact is seen in the way the following clusters correlate with "Public Witness":

Clusters correlating with *Public Witness*	Correlation
Youth Have Ownership of Their Youth Program	.49
Youth Are Interested and Motivated	.51

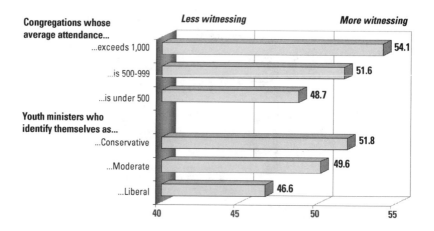

Less witnessing   More witnessing

Congregations whose
average attendance...
...exceeds 1,000   54.1
...is 500-999   51.6
...is under 500   48.7

Youth ministers who
identify themselves as...
...Conservative   51.8
...Moderate   49.6
...Liberal   46.6

40   45   50   55

Figure 7.10—Variation by group in public witness

No doubt it is the youth minister's quality of leadership that gives the young people the confidence they need to participate publicly in sharing their faith. A youth leader is far more influential than commonly realized in being able to convey a contagious spirit and attitude.

Summary

This chapter completes our attention to an aspect of the conceptual model identified as "Evaluating Priority Outcomes". The focus has been upon the response and witness of youth as evidenced by—
- Their joyous attitudes of respect and love
- The interest they show in their youth ministry
- The extent to which they are serving their church and community
- Their active involvement in a public witness and ministry

We observe here again that attitudes of respect typically come from those participating in larger youth groups, under the direction of youth ministers who have been in the business for 16 years or more.

Youth are more likely to be involved in service if their youth minister is a member of a mainline denomination, who classifies self as a liberal in theology, who wants youth to transform society, who has served for 16 years or more, and who heads a youth group of 101 or more youths. These are all factors especially associated with a service involvement.

When it comes to making a public witness or reaching out in some form of ministry, it is the youth served by youth ministers in evangelical churches that take center stage. The Assembly of God, Southern Baptist, Evangelical Covenant, and Evangelical Free Churches show a far greater involvement in this aspect of missionating than do youth from mainline denominations. It is youth served by youth ministers with a conservative theology, employed by churches that draw over 1,000 people on Sunday that one will find the greatest involvement of youth in a public witness.

THINK IT OVER, TALK IT THROUGH

1. If you could only be guaranteed of realizing two of the four results among young people, which two would you choose? Given what you learn from this chapter, what would be the greatest predictors of these two outcomes?

2. What's missing from this chapter? That is, what additional outcomes among young people would you hope might be reported if a similar study were conducted ten years from now?

3. What do you find most surprising in this chapter?

4. How do the findings about youth-related outcomes from your own denomination or organization align with your own ministry experience?

Notes 7

1. Merton Strommen and Shelby Andress, *Five Shaping Forces: Using Organizational Dynamics to Do More with Less* (Minneapolis: Search Institute, 1980), 19.

2. Steve Farcas and Jean Johnson, *Kids These Days: What Americans Really Think about the Next Generation* (New York: Public Agenda,1997), 8-9.

3. Peter Benson and Eugene Roehlkepartain, *Beyond Leaf Raking: Learning to Serve / Serving to Learn* (Nashville: Abingdon Press,1993), 27.

4. Doug Fields, *Purpose-Driven Youth Ministry* (Grand Rapids, Michigan: Zondervan Publishing House, 1998), 109.

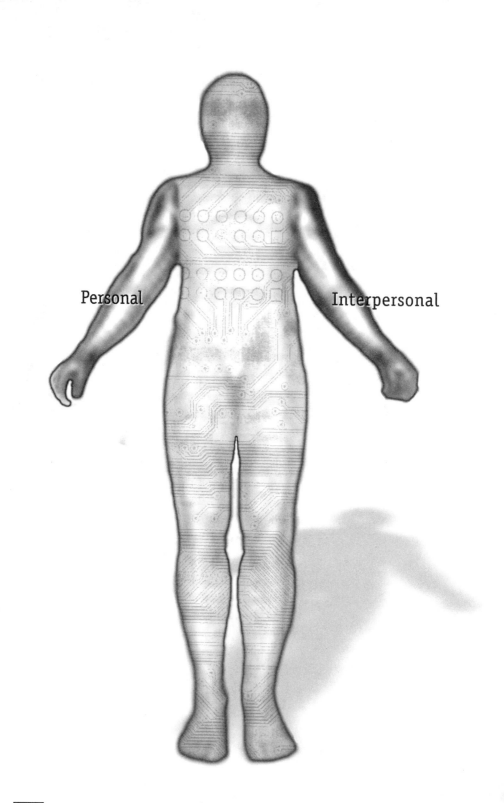

Personal

Interpersonal

Chapter 8

Setting Ministry Goals: Personal and Interpersonal
Karen E. Jones

This chapter explores the degree to which youth ministers accomplish critical vocational ministry goals. As illustrated by the outstretched arms in the conceptual model, there are two distinct aspects of these professional goals—personal and interpersonal—reaching out and reaching in. The accomplishment of personal goals is directly related to the value youth ministers place on them and the amount of personal effort they expend to meet these goals. Interpersonal goals require valuing and investment on the part of the youth minister if they are to be accomplished, as well, but they also rely on the ability of the minister to live in community, to both offer and receive support.

Importance of Ministry Goals

Reflecting on his search for life's meaning, the author of Ecclesiastes writes of the power of work in the life of an individual, its potential to infuse life with pleasure and purpose.

> **The best thing we can do is to enjoy eating and drinking, and working. I believe these are God's gifts to us.**
> **What do we gain by all our hard work? I have seen what difficult things God demands of us. God makes everything happen at the right time. Yet none of us can ever fully understand all he has done, and he puts questions in our minds about the past and the future. I know the best thing we can do is to always enjoy life, because God's gift to us is the happiness we get from our food and drink and from the work we do. (Ecclesiastes 2:24; 3:9-13, CEV)**

The privilege of ministering with youth is a gift of God that brings profound joy and a sense of fulfillment to those who faithfully carry out the mission. It embodies something of the mysterious, as seeds are scattered onto a variety of soils, often carried by the winds of culture. The sower/youth minister is never quite sure where the seeds have landed, whether or not they are germinating, or if growth will ensue from their planting. Questions abound and discouragement can infiltrate the mind and soul of the worker, as the uncertain future looms ahead, with the power to affirm or invalidate the minister's efforts. Yet, while youth ministers experience these self-doubts and concerns over various issues and aspects of their chosen profession, they also experience deep feelings of personal satisfaction from their work.

This sense of joy is the by product of specific fulfilled ministry goals, related both to the areas of personal/professional growth and interpersonal relationships. Mike Nygren, director of Student Leadership Ministries, tells about his experience of finally setting goals for leadership growth after being in leadership positions for many years.

> I started to wrestle with the role of leadership in youth ministry for my own life. I was faced with a Sunday School class of 100 teens and adults committed to the quest of biblical leadership. How wonderful!
>
> The inquiry I faced was internal. I had held leadership positions for twenty-five years prior to this upcoming 13-week course, and yet I still felt completely unprepared to direct this group.
>
> My self-realization was that leadership growth had never before been a deliberate goal with any of my leadership roles. I became even more cognizant that no one had ever challenged me to be a critical thinker as it related to my own leadership.
>
> One Sunday morning I changed the process of our youth ministry by making it an intentional goal to integrate leadership into our discipleship and mission emphasis. I decided to make leadership teaching one of the principal responsibilities of our leadership staff.
>
> Integrating leadership into discipleship caused great spiritual maturity as well as numerical growth within our ministry. By being personally committed to lead by my actions more than my words, I reassessed the use of my own time. Much of my time spent with students in traditional youth ministry activities soon shifted to providing adults and teens, leadership and discipleship training.[1]

Because Mike identified a specific need within his ministry and set a personal goal to see the need met, he was able to realize fulfillment, not only of the goal, but of personal needs.

Identifying goals and developing strategies to bring the goals to fruition can mean the difference between a satisfactory job and personal satisfaction *in* a job. Our study identified ministry goals involving attitudes, actions, and characteristics, which lead to ministry satisfaction. These 48 aspects of youth ministry form ten cohesive item clusters, which give us a clear indication of what is embodied in each goal. Our data shows the degree to which each of these goals is accomplished by the respondents, and more specifically, which groups of youth ministers are most likely to possess each of the characteristics. To facilitate a discussion of the data, these ten clusters, or personal goals, have been organized into two separate categories: "Personal Growth" and "Interpersonal Relationships."

Ministry goals
PERSONAL GROWTH

Here is how the responses of the 2,416 respondents clustered with respect to their personal ministry goals. To what extent do these five clusters correspond to you own ministry goals?

Five clusters that reflect personal ministry goals
- Competent Job Performance
- Confident Leadership
- Creative Response to Youth Culture
- Theological Grounding
- Commitment to Specialized Ministry Training

Before reading the results of the national study, take this informal inventory of your personal ministry. Complete the following questionnaire as a means of comparing yourself to the responses of the 2,400+ full-time youth ministers who participated in the research.

Personal growth self-check

Respond to each of the following statements with one of the following:

SA	Strongly agree
A	Agree
MA	Mildly agree
MD	Mildly disagree
D	Disagree
SD	Strongly disagree

Competent Job Performance

____ 1. I feel I make good decisions in my ministry.
____ 2. I am a good organizer.
____ 3. I feel competent in my job.
____ 4. I am an effective youth minister.
____ 5. I know why I do what I do.
____ 6. I have a philosophy of youth ministry.

Confident Leadership

____ 7. I feel that my leadership style produces good leaders.
____ 8. I am a good delegator.
____ 9. I find it easy to recruit volunteers.
____ 10. I feel competent to train adult volunteers.
____ 11. I'm an effective model to volunteers of how to do youth ministry.
____ 12. Being an effective leader is a key aspect of my ministry.
____ 13. Goals are regularly accomplished under my leadership.
____ 14. I regularly assess the effectiveness of my work.

Creative Response to Youth Culture

____ 15. I keep up with changes in the youth culture.
____ 16. I try to do things in new and creative ways.
____ 17. I have made changes in my methodology based on new insights from youth culture.
____ 18. I am involved in efforts to improve the effectiveness of our youth ministry.

Theological Grounding

____ 19. I have a good grasp of theological concepts.
____ 20. I am confident in my knowledge of Scripture.
____ 21. I read the Bible regularly.
____ 22. My youth ministry is theologically based.
____ 23. My youth ministry is shaped more by youth culture than theology.

Specialized Training

____ 24. I take advantage of formal education opportunities related to my field.
____ 25. I have had specialized training in some aspect of youth ministry.
____ 26. I am certified/licensed as a youth minister.

As you study each of the areas of personal growth that follow in this chapter, compare the results with your own responses to the survey items in that cluster. You might want to take note of those areas in which you differ from the majority of respondents. Consider the implications of those differences. Are they your personal strengths, or are they deficiencies that keep you from experiencing greater satisfaction in your ministry?

Competent job performance

In the early 1950s William James, one of the first to deal with the issue of self-esteem, taught that one's accomplishments and abilities were directly linked to his/her sense of self.[2] Psychologists and educators since that time have consistently addressed the relationship between competence, confidence, and self-worth; experiencing success in any given task increases an individual's confidence level and feelings of personal satisfaction, providing the motivation for increased efforts at related tasks. Given this understanding, it is not surprising that our first item cluster represents a priority ministry goal, one that strongly contributes to the youth minister's sense of satisfaction when it is successfully achieved.

Specific aspects of competent job performance assessed by this cluster are listed below, including the percentage of respondents who indicate agreement or disagreement on varying levels.

Survey Item	Percentage of youth ministers who responded "strongly agree"	Percentage of youth ministers who responded "agree"	Percentage of youth ministers who responded "mildly agree"	Percentage of youth ministers who responded "mildly disagree"	Percentage of youth ministers who responded "disagree"	Percentage of youth ministers who responded "strongly disagree"
1. I feel I make good decisions in my ministry.	28	57	13	2	0	0
2. I am a good organizer.	31	31	23	10	4	1
3. I feel competent in my job.	34	48	13	4	1	0
4. I am an effective youth minister.	24	52	21	3	0	0
5. I know why I do what I do.	51	40	8	1	0	0
6. I have a philosophy of youth ministry.	51	34	12	2	0	0

Figure 8.1—Percent agreeing they are competent in job performance

Having a sense of mission, a clear sense of direction and purpose, is key to experiencing personal fulfillment in any task. I asked a young youth minister who was in his first year of ministry out of college about his philosophy of ministry. He wasn't sure what I was asking. Thinking the word *philosophy* might have made him shy, I asked him if he had a mission statement—if one existed for the youth ministry. He knew the term from reading Covey, but said he had never found the time to write out one of those formal statements with all of the identified values and visions—he was too busy doing ministry.

"Well," I finally asked, "what is it you *do* in your ministry and *why* do you do it? What is your *purpose*? Why does this church *have* a youth ministry? What are you trying to *accomplish*? What do you want a seventh-grader to *know* and *be* and *do* when he leaves here after six years? How will he be different than he was when he came into your ministry? How do you make decisions about how you invest your time and other resources? What makes you *different* from the Boy Scouts or Junior Firefighters? Why are *you* here anyway, when you could be making more money at almost any other job in town?"

I'll admit, I was exasperated and probably overreacted—yet the reason we were having a conversation in the first place is because he had been experiencing a tremendous amount of frustration and disillusionment, and the church had also been experiencing frustration and disillusionment. I stumbled upon the heart of the problem before I even got warmed up to make the assessment. There was no philosophy, there was no written mission statement, but most importantly, there was absolutely no sense of direction, clear or otherwise. This young youth minister had absolutely no idea what it was he thought he was called to do, let alone how to do it.

Youth group does not equal youth ministry
Youth ministries can appear successful from the outside, even without a well-thought-out purpose statement. They can draw large crowds and win the accolades of onlookers and participants alike. But to be authentic ministry, young people must be continuously and intentionally drawn closer to Jesus Christ.[3] If this isn't happening, then it may be a youth group, but it isn't a youth ministry.

Without a guiding philosophy or goals to strive for, one can never be sure that success has been attained. It is greatly encouraging that youth ministers do have this sense of mission, that they plan intentionally (item 5 in figure 8.1) and trust themselves to make decisions that will enhance their ministries (item 1). (One caution needs to be issued: *Having* a philosophy and purpose statement should not be equated with actually *implementing* that philosophy or purpose statement. Even *having* a mission statement or philosophy and *using it* to guide the ministry may not guarantee ministry satisfaction. It is entirely possible to buy into a philosophy that is unbiblical or unorthodox.)

It is important to note that less than two-thirds of the youth ministers in the study indicate high levels of confidence in their organizational abilities (item 2). While only 5 percent view this as a *serious* deficit, increased efforts at organization could assist ministers in accomplishing their goals and carrying out their plans more effectively. Besides saving time and increasing efficiency, organizational skills can go a long way toward winning the respect of the congregation; it gives the appearance of professionalism. How many other professionals in the "outside world" could survive without some level of administrative or organizational acumen?

A notable negative correlation (-.51) exists between competent job performance and a concern over the lack of training needed to feel qualified. Obviously, youth ministers who harbor the greatest doubts over their own personal training and qualifications for ministry will be those who express the least amount of satisfaction in their own job performance. While cause and effect relationships cannot be ascertained from this study, the assumption can be made from this negative correlation that as youth ministers are able to receive increased training, they will begin to view themselves as more effective, better organizers, and more competent at making decisions.

Confident Leadership

True leadership is vital to ministry, and those youth ministers who possess confidence in their own leadership abilities experience greater satisfaction from their work than those who harbor self-doubts.

Survey Item	Percentage of youth ministers who responded "strongly agree"	Percentage of youth ministers who responded "agree"	Percentage of youth ministers who responded "mildly agree"	Percentage of youth ministers who responded "mildly disagree"	Percentage of youth ministers who responded "disagree"	Percentage of youth ministers who responded "strongly disagree"
1. I feel that my leadership style produces other leaders.	16	38	33	11	2	0
2. I am a good delegator.	12	30	34	16	7	1
3. I find it easy to recruit volunteers.	7	21	31	21	15	5
4. I feel competent to train adult volunteers.	19	44	25	9	3	0

5. I'm an effective model to volunteers of how to do youth ministry.	18	48	26	7	1	0
6. Being an effective leader is a key aspect of my ministry.	26	47	23	3	1	0
7. Goals are regularly accomplished under my leadership.	12	51	30	5	2	0
8. I regularly assess the effectiveness of my work.	19	44	27	9	1	0

Figure 8.2—Percent agreeing they are confident leaders

Ministry is multiplied when it is shared, and this multiplication is a necessary ingredient of effective leadership. If satisfaction and feelings of competency about one's leadership are to be realized, then the youth minister must employ strategies for involving other adults. These need to be ones who are willing and capable of taking on leadership roles and who are ready to assist in carrying out the mission.

It is somewhat disconcerting to realize that most youth ministers view themselves as effective leaders (item 6 in figure 8.2), but only slightly more than half report great success at producing other leaders (item 1). This is not surprising, however, when it is discovered that less than half believe themselves to possess strong skills of delegation (item 2) and less than one-third enjoy regular success at recruiting volunteers (item 3). Regardless of these statistics, approximately two-thirds of the ministers in the study view themselves as good models for volunteer leaders (item 5). One wonders whether this modeling is only for show, or if the volunteers are ever allowed to actually participate in leadership tasks! If ministry tasks are not delegated, volunteers will not have the opportunity to develop into leaders.

Even more troubling than the low numbers who find it easy to recruit volunteers is the fact that one out of five find it very difficult to do so (item 3). There is much talk about the need for volunteers in ministry, but apparently few know how to go about making it happen. This is a key area that needs to be strengthened, and for which future ministers need to be trained. Delegation is another essential ministry skill that must be developed if youth ministers are to experience continued satisfaction from their work. Even those skilled in leadership often find it hard to delegate. Eight percent of the respondents have difficulty delegating tasks, and less than half are confident in their ability to delegate (item 2).

Though Moses was a powerful and effective leader, his father-in-law, Jethro, observed that he was spending too much time and effort trying to handle issues alone.

What you are doing is not good. You and these people who come to you will only wear yourselves out. The work is too heavy for you; you cannot handle it alone. Listen now to me and I will give you some advice, and may God be with you. You must be the people's representative before God and bring their disputes to him. Teach them the decrees and laws, and show them the way to live and the duties they are to perform. But select capable men from all the people—men who fear God, trustworthy men who hate dishonest gain—and appoint them as officials over thousands, hundreds, fifties and tens. Have them serve as judges for the people at all times, but have them bring every difficult case to you; the simple cases they can decide themselves. That will make your load lighter, because they will share it with you. If you do this and God so commands, you will be able to stand the strain, and all these people will go home satisfied. (Exodus 18: 17b-23).

This same principle is observed by the most effective youth ministers. They share the ministry and lighten their own loads by delegating to volunteers those tasks that can be delegated. This reduction in time and emotional and mental strain frees them to experience the joy that comes from a greater sense of accomplishment.

Creative Response to Youth Culture

Culture is a popular topic of conversation in Christian and academic circles, but exactly what is it that is being discussed? I cannot begin to count the number of professional meetings I have attended in which culture was a major player on the agenda. I often have the feeling that no one knows just exactly what it is they are all talking about; everyone is just agitated about something out there affecting youth, so they call it culture and begin to vent. The following discussion of culture, from *Passing on the Faith* by Strommen and Hardel, is useful both for normalizing our understanding of the concept and for helping us understand why cultural views are so important in youth ministry.

Culture is a way of living that has become normative for a group of human beings. Culture includes music, art, media, and intellectual stimuli that contain and communicate norms and values.

But cultures whose basic norms and values are life enriching and are a source of enjoyment and blessing can be misrepresented and eroded by the media that communicates them. Media that encourage self-gratification, individualism, anti-authoritarianism, and the like are powerful shapers of the attitudes and values not only of young people but also of families, communities, and the culture itself.[4]

Those who are students of culture know that effective youth ministry can no longer mirror society, holding events that reflect the latest trends with an added Christian twist. If there is no difference between youth ministry gatherings and school or other social functions, why should youths make them a scheduling priority? Ministers who seek to understand the world in which their youths live find the greatest sense of satisfaction from their work. They are not content to merely change the date on their calendars and recycle the previous year's agenda and events, but they constantly seek to improve their ministry effectiveness, employing new strategies based on the insights they have gained from their study of culture. The following items were used to assess the youth minister's cultural responsiveness.

Survey Item	Percentage of youth ministers who responded "strongly agree"	Percentage of youth ministers who responded "agree"	Percentage of youth ministers who responded "mildly agree"	Percentage of youth ministers who responded "mildly disagree"	Percentage of youth ministers who responded "disagree"	Percentage of youth ministers who responded "strongly disagree"
1. I keep up with the changes in youth culture.	26	48	22	3	1	0
2. I try to do things in new and creative ways.	30	47	19	4	0	0
3. I have made changes in my methodology based on new insights from culture.	18	46	26	6	3	1
4. I am involved in efforts to improve the effectiveness of our youth ministry.	54	40	5	1	0	0

Figure 8.3—Percent agreeing to creative response to youth culture

Ministers who seek to separate their youths from the evils in the world, creating an alternative environment which is more protected and more "spiritual," report significantly higher levels (3.8 standard scores) of cultural responsiveness than those who persist in merely attempting to capture the interest of youth by making use of popular culture in their ministries. This is not an endorsement for a cultural retreat on the part of youth ministry, but simply an insight gained from the study. Apparently, greater awareness of youth culture and resulting attempts at ministry effectiveness are made by ministry isolationists than by those who bless and baptize the latest trends.

Theologically Grounded

Properly understood, youth ministry is a theological endeavor, with theology informing not only its content, but also its practice. The way we prioritize and relate and administrate and teach all reflect our understanding of who God is and where and how we have allowed him to enter our lives. A very high percentage of youth ministers indicate that their ministry is theologically based (item 4 in figure 8.4, page 210). This may surprise a lot of other theologians who have systematically looked down upon the profession of youth ministry, but it is long-awaited tangible proof that youth ministers are *not* shallow entertainers or pied pipers. It is the *good* news. The *bad* news is that 10 percent of the respondents agreed with the statement "My youth ministry is shaped more by youth culture than theology" (item 5) and only 46 percent of the ministers disagreed with this statement with any conviction ("agree" or "strongly agree"). (Because this item was scored in the reverse, it has been reworded in figure 8.4 for purposes of clarity.) In effect, many youth ministers apparently have one foot firmly planted on a theological base and another firmly planted on a cultural base. It seems to be a very precarious position. An *understanding* of contemporary popular culture is necessary for effective youth ministry, but should never be the foundation upon which it is built.

This item cluster also measures the degree to which youth ministers perceive their ministry to be based on a solid knowledge of theology and Scripture, and how frequently they read the Bible. Participants in the study report high levels of confidence in their own theological understanding (item 1), yet less than three-fourths of them possess a great deal of confidence in their scriptural knowledge (item 2), and approximately one-fourth of the ministers in this study cannot emphatically state that they read their Bible on a regular basis (item 3). See figure 8.4 below.

Survey Item	Percentage of youth ministers who responded "strongly agree"	Percentage of youth ministers who responded "agree"	Percentage of youth ministers who responded "mildly agree"	Percentage of youth ministers who responded "mildly disagree"	Percentage of youth ministers who responded "disagree"	Percentage of youth ministers who responded "strongly disagree"
1. I have a good grasp of theological concepts.	30	48	17	4	1	0
2. I am confident in my knowledge of scripture.	25	45	22	5	3	0
3. I read the Bible regularly.	38	38	17	5	2	0
4. My youth ministry is theologically based.	45	41	12	2	1	0
*5. My youth ministry is shaped more by theology than by youth culture.	14	32	27	17	8	2

* This item was originally worded "My youth ministry is shaped more by youth culture than by theology." and was scored in the reverse. For purposes of clarity for the reader, it is reworded in this table with scores reflecting the change.

Figure 8.4—Percent agreeing they are theologically grounded

There are significant differences in theological grounding between youth ministers who hold one of four positions regarding youth and culture. These dramatic differences are illustrated here:

Approach to Youth Culture	Theological Grounding Standard Scores
Believe in arranging events to protect youth from the temptations of the world.	53.9
Seek ways for youth to influence social conditions in an effort to help them live out the gospel.	50.6
Want youth to feel responsibility for both kingdom of God and kingdom of humans, encourages compartmentalizing.	48.5
Emphasis on entertainment and building relationships without turning them off with too much of the "religious."	46.3

Figure 8.5—Standard scores for theological grounding, by approach to culture

Those whose philosophical commitment is to protect their youth from negative cultural influences by planning events which will keep them isolated from it, are more confident about their own theological grounding than youth ministers with any other cultural philosophy toward ministry. Those ministers who plan events to attract and entertain youth, often mimicking popular cultural trends, are the least likely to have strong theological foundations.

Specialized Training and Certification

For several years professors of youth ministry in the national organization Youth Ministry Educators have formally discussed and debated licensing and/or certification for youth ministers, but was eventually dropped from their agenda in 1999 when it became clear that it was a divisive issue over which no consensus was forthcoming. Figure 8.6 demonstrates how our survey participants responded to this cluster.

Survey Item	Percentage of youth ministers who responded "strongly agree"	Percentage of youth ministers who responded "agree"	Percentage of youth ministers who responded "mildly agree"	Percentage of youth ministers who responded "mildly disagree"	Percentage of youth ministers who responded "disagree"	Percentage of youth ministers who responded "strongly disagree"
1. Youth ministers should undergo formal education related to the field.	24	32	26	11	5	2
2. Youth ministers should receive specialized training in order to serve in church.	32	37	20	6	4	1
3. Youth ministers should be certified/licensed.	29	28	22	10	8	3

Figure 8.6—Percent agreeing they should have specialized training

While some denominations and youth ministry organizations do have specific qualifications that ministers must meet in order to serve as a minister with youth, many do not. Even though 69 percent of those in this study believe that youth ministers should receive specialized training in order to serve in a church, just over half see formal training, certification, or licensing to be important (items 2 and 3). More than 10 percent strongly object to the idea of requiring certification or licensing for youth ministers—which may explain why the issue was so divisive for Youth Ministry Educators.

INTERPERSONAL RELATIONSHIPS

In addition to striving for competence in areas of leadership, youth ministers seek meaningful involvement in the lives of others. Ministry is relational if it is biblical. The belief that God has called and equipped us for ministry is affirmed as we are able to establish and develop authentic relationships with youth, volunteers, parents and peers. It matters little how organized we are, how adept we are at delegating, how sharply focused is our mission statement or how orthodox our theology, if we are not living out our calling by allowing God's love to flow through us. We minister not only by giving and being a blessing, but also by freely receiving the blessing from others, allowing others to fulfill their calling by ministering to us.

The last five professional ministry goal clusters in our study are related to interpersonal relationships in youth ministry:

Five clusters that reflect interpersonal relationship goals
- Motivated by God's Calling
- Effective Youth Relationships
- Relates Well to Parents/Adults
- Achievement: Developing Adult Volunteers
- Peer Involvement

To what extent do these relational ministry goals correspond with your own ministry goals? Before reading the results of the national study, I suggest you take another informal inventory of your personal ministry. Complete the following questionnaire as a means of comparing yourself to the responses of the 2,400-plus full-time youth ministers who participated in the research.

INTERPERSONAL RELATIONSHIPS SELF-CHECK
Respond to each of the following statements with one of the following:

SA	Strongly agree
A	Agree
MA	Mildly agree
MD	Mildly disagree
D	Disagree
SD	Strongly disagree

Motivated by God's Calling
____ 1. God called me to youth ministry.
____ 2. God's call is my primary motivation for doing youth ministry.
____ 3. I enjoy my work.
____ 4. I want to be involved in the lives of youth.
____ 5. Youth ministry should not be viewed as a stepping stone profession.

Effective Youth Relationships
____ 6. Young people open up to me easily.
____ 7. My youth enjoy spending time with me.
____ 8. It is easy for me to build relationships with youth.
____ 9. I am a good counselor of youth.
____ 10. I am able to motivate youth to follow my leadership.
____ 11. Youth affirm me often.
____ 12. I know how to nurture youth's spiritual walk.

Relates Well to Parents/Adults
____ 13. Working with parents is an important part of my work.
____ 14. I feel valued and loved by the parents of youth.
____ 15. I feel equipped to prepare parents for youth ministry leadership.
____ 16. I relate well to parents of youth.
____ 17. I feel respected by the members of my congregation.

Achievement: Developing Adult Volunteers
____ 18. I am able to successfully recruit adults for one-to-one mentoring with youth.
____ 19. I have a systematic plan for training volunteer youth workers.
____ 20. I have equipped adult volunteers to lead small groups.

Peer Involvement
____ 21. I am using peers to meet my need for fellowship.
____ 22. I am using peers to meet my need for accountability.
____ 23. I am using peers to provide ongoing training.

As you study each of these relational ministry goals, compare your responses to each of the items with those of the participants in this study. Take note of those areas in which you differ from the majority of respondents and thoughtfully consider the implications of your differences. Are the differences indications of your personal strengths, or do they signal deficiencies which keep you from experiencing greater satisfaction in your ministry?

Motivated by God's Calling

It is often said that, in ministry, all one has to hang onto in times of difficulty is the assurance of God's call. This call of God and the desire to minister with youth is strongly evident in the lives of youth ministers (item 1). Inversely related to this sense of calling is the belief that youth ministry is merely a stop on the way to a more important or prestigious position. Overwhelmingly, youth ministers reject the idea that their vocation is a stepping stone, a place to serve while they wait for the pastorate (item 5 in figure 8.7). This is encouraging news, that men and women who serve as full-time professional youth ministers throughout these various denominations and ministries view themselves as called by God to minister with youth—for life. The following items were used to assess this characteristic. (It is important to note that the first two statements listed in the figure, relating specifically to God's calling, possess the strongest correlations to the cluster, with coefficients of .78 and .66, respectively.)

Survey Item	Percentage of youth ministers who responded "strongly agree"	Percentage of youth ministers who responded "agree"	Percentage of youth ministers who responded "mildly agree"	Percentage of youth ministers who responded "mildly disagree"	Percentage of youth ministers who responded "disagree"	Percentage of youth ministers who responded "strongly disagree"
1. God called me to youth ministry.	67	22	8	2	1	0
2. God's call is my primary motivation for doing youth ministry.	63	27	7	2	1	0
3. I enjoy my work.	45	42	10	2	1	0
4. I want to be involved in the lives of youth.	56	37	6	1	0	0
*5. Youth ministry should not be viewed as a stepping-stone position.	57	29	9	3	2	0

* This item was originally worded "My youth ministry should be viewed as a stepping-stone position." and was scored in the reverse. For purposes for clarity of the reader, it is reworded in this table with scores reflecting the change.

Figure 8.7—Percent motivated by God's calling

A striking difference exists between youth ministers who advocate two different approaches or philosophies of ministry. Those youth ministers who were previously described as desiring to separate their youth from the negative influences and temptations of the world report a much stronger (3.54 standard scores) awareness of, or belief in, God's calling than do youth ministers who advocate a dual kingdom approach to life. Ministers who advocate dual kingdom ministry do not seek to protect their youths from the world, but neither do they attempt to infiltrate and transform the surrounding culture.

> **The youth minister with this understanding will see to it that teenagers receive the proper religious instruction without bothering too much with outside concerns. Insuring that the youths passes through the fixed stations of faith is the church's interest. What happens the other six days is mostly irrelevant and beyond the sphere of the rather aloof youth leader in any case.[5]**

This understanding of the dual kingdom approach helps us understand why youth ministers advocating this philosophical response to culture have a lesser sense of the divine call to minister. They do not have a grasp on the enormity of the task they are seeking to undertake. There are, however, other more theologically acceptable interpretations of this cultural approach. Leonard Sweet's terminology for this position is *incultural*:

> **The aim of the incultural church is an incarnation process first demonstrated in Jesus' own incarnation. The doctrine of the incarnation is this: if our Savior joins us where we are, not where we ought to be, what excuse do we have not to join people where they are, not where they ought to be? If Jesus descended into hell and founded his church at the very "gates of hell," what hells need we fear?**
> **Incarnation is not enculturation or acculturation. It begins with Christ and then moves to a host cultural context, not the other way around. . . .**
> **Jesus himself set forth some cultural principles for his disciples to follow and demonstrated the incultural method at work: Jesus told the seventy to "stay in that house, eating and drinking whatever they give you" (Luke 10:7), adding, "When you enter a town and are welcomed, eat what is set before you." (Luke 10:8). Earlier, when Jesus sent out his disciples, he gave them the freedom to stay—"search for some worthy person. . . and stay at his house until you leave." (Matthew 10:11)**
> **The incultural Christian realizes that the gospel travels through time not in some ideal form, but**

from one inculturated form to another. . . . What missiologists call "the culturally indigenous church" is the aim of the incultural church.[6]

This interpretation of the dual kingdom approach to youth ministry does not appear to be the one adopted by the youth ministers in this study. How could one advocate being in the world as a missiological function and not do so out of a sense of God's leading?

Effective Youth Relationships

God created us for relationship, both with himself and with others. God's love for his creation resulted in the very personal sacrifice of Christ, so that his relationship with us, broken through sin, might be restored. Being created in God's image, humans also have the need for relationship, not only with their Creator, but also with one another. From the beginning, God determined that it was not good for man to be alone. Even those without a belief in God recognize that one of the most critical needs for all human beings is to feel loved and valued by at least one other person. In youth ministry, one of the greatest joys is a feeling of love and acceptance by the youth we serve. The following seven items indicate the degree to which respondents enjoy positive relationships with the members of their youth groups.

Survey Item	Percentage of youth ministers who responded "strongly agree"	Percentage of youth ministers who responded "agree"	Percentage of youth ministers who responded "mildly agree"	Percentage of youth ministers who responded "mildly disagree"	Percentage of youth ministers who responded "disagree"	Percentage of youth ministers who responded "strongly disagree"
1. Young people open up to me easily.	23	45	26	5	1	0
2. My youth enjoy spending time with me.	36	55	9	0	0	0
3. It is easy for me to build relationships with youth.	39	43	14	3	1	0
4. I am a good counselor of youth.	22	48	25	4	1	0
5. I am able to motivate youth to follow my leadership.	17	53	26	3	1	0
6. Youth affirm me often.	17	39	31	9	3	1
7. I know how to nurture the spiritual walk of my youth.	15	51	28	5	1	0

Figure 8.8—Percent agreeing they have effective youth relationships

Youth ministers find it easy to relate to youth (item 3) and believe that their presence is valued by them (item 2), even though affirmation is overtly experienced by only slightly more than half of those in this study (item 6). There are high levels of confidence on the part of youth ministers related to communication and counseling skills (items 1 and 4), including the aspect of spiritual nurture (item 7).

Relates Well to Parents/Adults

Youth ministers can develop close bonds with their youth and experience great amounts of personal satisfaction in their own ability to attract, influence, and relate to young people, but if they fail to build bonds with youth parents, their ministry effectiveness will always be limited. Regardless of popular opinion, parents remain the single most influential persons in the lives of teenagers. It is presumptuous of youth ministers to think that their ministry, apart from the family, will be sufficient to foster radical commitment and transformation in the lives of teens. While this does occur, it is most likely the exception and not the rule. Unfortunately, we cannot cite statistics to verify this position. While we *can* cite cases in which teens have been reached for Christ without familial support or inclusion, it would be *impossible* to count the numbers of teens who have been unreached because their families were *not* included in the ministry. Contemporary theory in counseling and psychology reminds us that the problems which plague youth were not created in a vacuum; there are systemic explanations for their occurrence which need to be identified and treated if healing is to occur. This whole-family approach to ministry is one which is gaining popular support, because it is biblical and it is also logical. An excellent source for implementing this type of youth ministry model is *Passing on the Faith: A Radical New Model for Youth and Family Ministry* by Merton P. Strommen and Richard A. Hardel (Saint Mary's Press, 2000).

The following items were used to assess the youth ministers' perceptions of relationships with parents and other adults in the congregation.

Respect and appreciation by parents and other congregational members is experienced in high levels by ministers with youth (item 2 and 5), possibly because of the high value these same ministers place on developing these relationships and involving them in the ministry (item 1). Regardless of the importance youth ministers place on ministering with parents, as well as their teens, there is a definite need for further education as to how parents can best be equipped. Less than half of those in the study believe themselves adequately prepared to carry out this important role (item 3).

Survey Item	Percentage of youth ministers who responded "strongly agree"	Percentage of youth ministers who responded "agree"	Percentage of youth ministers who responded "mildly agree"	Percentage of youth ministers who responded "mildly disagree"	Percentage of youth ministers who responded "disagree"	Percentage of youth ministers who responded "strongly disagree"
1. Working with parents is an important part of my work.	22	44	26	6	2	0
2. I feel valued and loved by the parents of youth.	18	45	29	6	2	0
3. I feel equipped to prepare parents for youth ministry leadership.	10	35	32	17	5	1
4. I relate well to the parents of youth.	25	56	16	3	0	0
5. I feel respected by the members of my congregation.	36	46	14	3	1	0

Figure 8.9—Percent agreeing that they relate well to parents/adults

Dr. Philip Briggs, distinguished professor of student ministry and youth education at Southwestern Seminary, offers the following very basic and practical steps to beginning a ministry with parents:

- Ask yourself why you want a parent ministry.
- Plan with parents, not for them.
- Survey the needs of parents and youth.
- Coordinate and communicate parent needs with the pastor and church staff.
- Work through the existing church organizations.
- Do thorough calendar planning. Events are best when both parents andyouths are involved.
- Budget for parent ministry.
- Secure a parent council for planning and suggestions.
- Pray about parent ministry.
- Learn what other youth ministers are doing in their parent ministries.[7]

Taking even these basic first steps will allow youth ministers to begin connecting with parents in ways that communicate concern for their needs, as well as for their youth.

The youth minister's approach to cultural interaction also impacts the quality of relationships the minister enjoys with parents of youth and with other adults. Significantly more positive relationships, (3.76 standard scores) are reported by those who practice an incarnational ministry model, seeking to assist youth in entering the world as transforming instruments of God's love, than by those whose ministry focus

youth ministry that transforms

is on entertainment and recreation. In his book *Called to Care* Stevens describes this transformational view:

> This approach . . . does not deny that culture needs to be changed, but it does not flinch from engagement. Youth ministry, according to this theory, will be interested in every facet of the kids' lives. The minister will enter their world with every intention of being an instrument of God's transforming love. He or she is more than willing to work within the cultural system but reserves the right to challenge practices contrary to the well-being of adolescents. . . . . We are compelled to exhibit both pessimism and optimism. We are realistic about human nature and its predilection for waywardness.   Yet we cannot be robbed of a hope that dares to believe that redemption is always a possibility (it is not for us to make final judgments.) Because of Christ's work in the world and in us, we are enabled to make a difference in the lives of young people we meet.[8]

The high-profile acts of violence propagated by, and directed toward, youth during the decade of the nineties has caused parents to become more sensitized to the need for substantive ministries which address real issues. The consumer/protector mentality of parents during the last part of the century was once satisfied with ministry which sponsored events to keep their children entertained and out of trouble. The reality about the world which teenagers face every day, from rural America to the inner city, can no longer be ignored by parents. Youth ministers who actively seek to enter this world with an optimistic view toward the transformation which only Christ can bring, win the respect of parents and other adults in the church and enjoy positive, satisfying relationships as a result.

Analysis of the data identified five other item clusters strongly related to positive relationships with parents and other adults in the congregation. The strength of these correlations is outlined below.

Clusters correlating with Relates Well to Parents/Adults	*Correlation coefficient*
Congregation's Personal Support	.74
Confident Leadership	.60
Competent Job Performance	.55
Effective Youth Relationships	.53
Achievement: Helping Parents Minister to Their Youth	.51

Achievement: Developing Adult Volunteers

The ability to recruit and train volunteers to assist with youth ministry, though not an important value historically, is a critical need today, as the ministry has developed a sharper focus and sense of mission. One person acting alone cannot adequately fulfill the purpose of any given ministry, regardless of size. Even youth ministers who are able to recruit the needed volunteers desperately need help in knowing how to develop and equip them for effective ministry. Less than one-fourth of the ministers in the study are able to do this successfully (items 2 and 3 in figure 8.10), and approximately half report little or no success at all in the task. Recruiting volunteers for one-to-one mentoring is the greatest deficiency in the development of adult volunteers (item 1).

Perhaps this is because person-to-person mentoring in youth ministry is a relatively new trend in the field. Several resources now exist for assisting youth ministers in recruiting and training mentors for their youth, but few models are available which exemplify a successful attempt at this ministry approach. In fact, long-time practitioners and youth ministry educators hold differing viewpoints on the merits of incorporating formal mentoring relationships into a ministerial framework. While mentoring is a biblical concept, some believe that the most effective mentoring relationships occur naturally, when youth and adults select each other informally. I was reminded of this recently when a prospective student asked me if we had a mentoring program in our educational ministries department. After I explained our approach to this process, he confessed that he did not want to be placed in a situation in which he was assigned a mentor, but felt that true mentoring took place naturally. He wanted to seek out a suitable spiritual mentor on his own.

Survey Item	Percentage of youth ministers who responded "extremely well"	Percentage of youth ministers who responded "very well"	Percentage of youth ministers who responded "quite well"	Percentage of youth ministers who responded "somewhat well"	Percentage of youth ministers who responded "not well"
1. Recruiting adults for one-to-one mentoring with youth.	4	9	15	37	35
2. Developing a systematic plan for training volunteer youth workers.	7	16	24	36	17
3. Equipping adult volunteers who lead small groups.	6	17	28	34	15

Figure 8.10—Percent agreeing that they develop adult volunteers

Whether it is a philosophical resistance to recruiting for one-to-one mentoring or the inability to successfully locate willing adults, there is a desperate need for teenagers to be able to connect with at least one spiritually mature adult in a significant way. This area of volunteer development is overwhelmingly the most neglected by youth ministers (item 1). There are many good resources available to help youth ministers more clearly understand the need for mentoring and how they can make sure that it is not being neglected in their ministries. Figure 8.10 above includes the percentage responses for each of the items in this cluster.

Peer Involvement

The importance of networking in youth ministry is advocated by those in positions of leadership throughout the profession, and opportunities now exist for ministers to meet with others in the field, across denominational and organizational lines. With the technological advances in recent years, there is no excuse for youth ministers, regardless of where they serve, to isolate themselves from their ministry peers. Even if location prevents them from face-to-face meetings on a regular basis, electronic messaging can provide them with daily opportunities to interact with others in the profession. Responses for each of the items in this cluster are found in figure 8.11 below.

Survey Item	Percentage of youth ministers who responded "strongly agree"	Percentage of youth ministers who responded "agree"	Percentage of youth ministers who responded "mildly agree"	Percentage of youth ministers who responded "mildly disagree"	Percentage of youth ministers who responded "disagree"	Percentage of youth ministers who responded "strongly disagree"
1. I am using peers to meet my need for fellowship.	16	41	24	11	6	2
2. I am using peers to meet my need for accountability.	15	33	25	13	11	3
3. I am using peers to provide ongoing training.	9	28	30	18	13	2

Figure 8.11—Percent agreeing that they are involved with peers

The need for peer accountability is an issue repeatedly addressed in professional publications and meetings, but our study indicates that this is still a largely neglected activity. More than half of all youth ministers meet with their peers for fellowship purposes (item 1), but less than half are in professional accountability relationships or take advantage of opportunities to learn from their peers (items 2 and 3).

Taking time out for meaningful peer relationships is not just a good idea, it is a biblical imperative. Throughout the book of Proverbs, especially, we are taught the importance of friendships for encouragement, wise counsel, sharing burdens, prayer support, and simple laughter. The potential for greater satisfaction in youth ministry can be realized through greater peer involvement.

Summary

Our study paints a relatively healthy picture of the profession of youth ministry, indicating high levels of satisfaction which result from competence in job performance, confidence in leadership, positive relationships with youth and adults, a healthy understanding and responsiveness to culture, strong theological foundations, and an undeniable belief in ministering out of a sense of God's calling. Increased involvement with other youth ministers and a better understanding of how to develop volunteer leaders would add to the joy which comes from ministry with youth. These two areas should continue to be emphasized by national organizations, denominations, and educational institutions which desire to increase ministry effectiveness.

Youth ministers' views of cultural interaction affect the degree to which they achieve each of these ministry goals. What other factors impact youth ministers' responses to these items? There are a number of these significant goal modifiers, and chapter 9 provides a detailed analysis of which youth ministers are the most likely to achieve each of the personal and interpersonal goals described in this chapter.

1. How do your own goals related to personal and professional growth compare to those of other youth ministers around the country?

2. How would you advise someone who wants to develop a greater degree of confidence in his or her own leadership ability?

3. What disciplines are you engaged in that help you to stay in touch with the youth culture?

4. What are the conditions in youth ministry that trigger the felt need for greater theological grounding?

5. What specialized training has been missing in your own youth ministry preparation?

6. How do your own goals related to interpersonal relationships compare to those of other youth ministers around the country?

7. What are some of the various ways that persons experience God's calling to youth ministry?

8. From the data presented, it seems that most youth ministers would agree that they need to develop strong relationships with young people. There doesn't seem to be the same universal support for the goal of developing strong adult and parental relationships. How do you explain this? What is at stake with these goals?

9. How do you balance your relationships between adults and young people?

Notes 8

1. Mike Nygren, "On the Road to Spiritual Maturity," electronic newsletter, Dec. 6, 1999.

2. William James, *The Principles of Psychology*, 1890. Great Books of the Western World (Chicago: Encyclopedia Britannica, 1952), 200.

3. See Senter's second axiom of youth ministry in Mark H. Senter III and Richard R. Dunn (eds.), *Reaching a Generation for Christ* (Chicago: Moody Press, 1997), 125.

4. Merton P. Strommen and Richard A. Hardel, *Passing on the Faith: A Radical New Model for Youth and Family Ministry* (Winona, Minnesota: Saint Mary's Press, 2000), 257.

5. James, 94, 95.

6. Leonard Sweet, "Living an Ancient Future Faith," *At-Risk Youth, At-Risk Church: What Jesus Christ and American Teenagers Are Saying to the Mainline Church*, The 1997 Princeton Lectures on Youth, Church, and Culture (Princeton, New Jersey: Institute of Youth Ministry, Princeton Theological Seminary), 111-12.

7. Phil Briggs, "Building a Healthy Parent Ministry," Student Ministry. *Zip: The Electronic Newsletter for the Student Minister on the Cutting Edge*, May 2000, 13 (LifeWay Christian Resources).

8. Doug Stevens, *Called to Care: Youth Ministry for the Church* (Grand Rapids, Michigan: Zondervan Publishing House, 1985), 95-6.

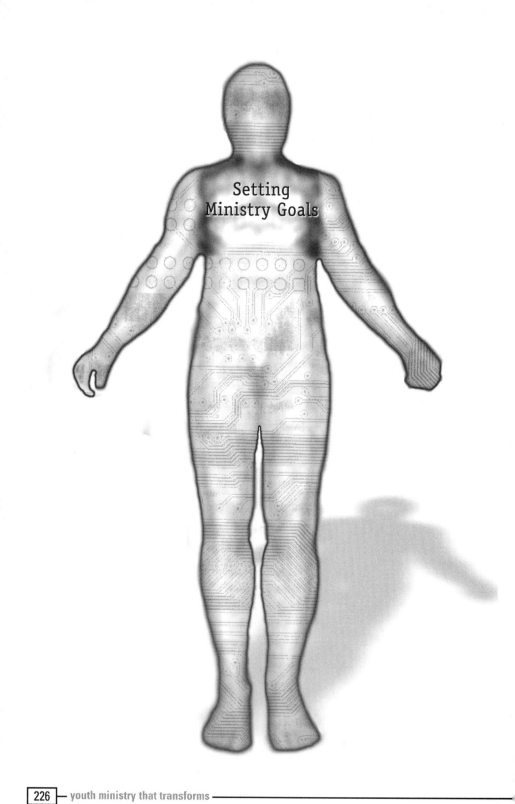

Setting
Ministry Goals

Chapter 9

Setting Ministry Goals: Significant Goal Modifiers
Karen E. Jones

This chapter continues an exploration of the importance of setting ministry goals. It is distinguished from the previous chapter in that it focuses on those highly significant differences between groups of youth ministers for each of the components of personal and interpersonal goals. It answers questions such as: "Which youth ministers are most effective at building relationships with parents? Are younger youth ministers able to more effectively relate to youth? Do some youth ministers place more importance on theology than others? Is formal ministry training a distinguishing factor in the realization of ministry goals?"

Significant differences

More than a decade ago, Search Institute initiated a significant study, "Effective Christian Education: A National Study of Protestant Congregations" which examined the faith, loyalty, and congregational life of six different denominations. The summary report of their findings, published in 1990, revealed significant differences between groups, especially when such variables as gender, denomination, age, and experience were considered.[1] An awareness of these differences is critical for Christian educators desiring to initiate change in their local congregations which will result in significant spiritual growth for their members. Similarly, there are significant differences among groups and between variables for youth ministers participating in our study. An awareness of these differences can provide youth ministers, local congregations, and youth ministry educators with the information they need to implement changes that may increase the effectiveness of ministry with youth.

Many of the most noteworthy differences are highlighted throughout the book, however; there are several variables that emerge as significant factors throughout the study. These factors deserve a more thorough examination due to their persistent recurrence. Figure 9.1 illustrates the number of clusters in which each of these variables measures statistically significant differences.

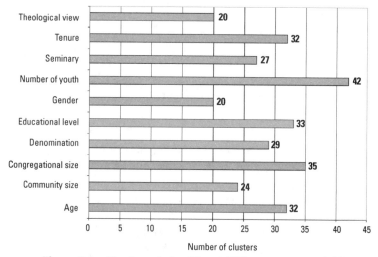

Figure 9.1—Number of significant differences per variable

This information is more than interesting trivia; it has important implications for youth ministers looking for peers who can understand what they are experiencing in ministry.

Consider Jodi's situation, for example. She has finally arrived at a gathering of several thousand youth ministers for a conference in a distant city where she will spend the next three days. Jodi has looked forward to this time away from her small youth group for many months. Even though her modest-sized congregation could not afford to pay her expenses, they allowed her to take time away from her local church to attend. She needs to be renewed, to recapture a vision for her ministry, and to be recharged spiritually.

Jodi is 32 years old, but has been a youth minister for only the last two years. After graduating from college, she taught in a public school for nine years before responding to God's call to vocational ministry. She finds personal fulfillment most of the time in her small midwestern church, but often experiences frustration over her inability to find volunteers. Sometimes she even feels like the youth parents don't really trust her to lead their teenagers. Jodi needs to find some other youth ministers to talk with, some who can understand what she is going through.

Given this information about Jodi and what we have discovered about the differences between groups of youth ministers, what are the most important characteristics Jodi should be looking for if she wants to find a support group? That is, which youth ministers will have the most in common with Jodi? Other females? Ministers from other small cities in the midwest? Those who share her own theological views? None of these characteristics should be Jodi's primary concerns. Her top priorities should be to find other youth ministers who—

- Have youth groups which are approximately the same size.
- Come from congregations of a similar size.
- Have the same type of educational preparation, as opposed to seminary or other post-collegiate studies.
- Are about the same age and have the same amount of experience in youth ministry. (If she has to choose between the two, experience is more important than age, as you will discover in this chapter.)

While not all of the differences shown in figure 9.1 are as large as three standard scores or more (the level we have selected for reporting on significant findings), the fact that certain variables repeatedly impact youth ministers' responses alerts us to their level of influence on the profession. For example, females and males differ significantly on 20 of the 48 clusters, but these differences are less than three standard scores in all but five of the clusters. Therefore, gender differences are not referenced very often in our study, though there are statistically significant gender differences in 42 percent of the clusters. These differences are simply not as pronounced as some might have thought.

It is very possible, however, that these gender differences, such as on measures of confident leadership, motivation by calling, or theological grounding are due less to gender than they are to other factors which typify female or male youth ministers.[2] Understanding more about the descriptive characteristics of these youth ministers may shed more light on their differences. The following figures (see figures 9.2 and 9.3) provide some additional information about the males and females in this study.

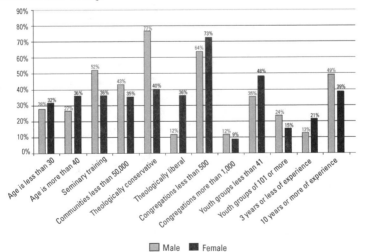

Figure 9.2—Percentage of all females and all males, by each variable category

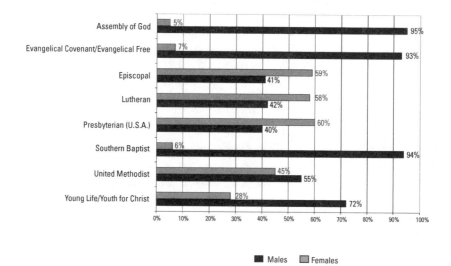

Figure 9.3—Percentage of females and males, by denomination/organization

As you study figures 9.2 and 9.3, think about which of these characteristics have the most potential to cause females and males to respond differently to items in our study. (Look back at figure 9.1 to see how often each characteristic impacts the responses of the participants. For example, the responses of ministers with large youth groups are almost always very different than the responses of those with small youth groups. Differences between how females and males respond are not nearly as frequent.)

There are certain variables, such as size of congregation and youth group, which greatly and repeatedly affect the minister's sense of accomplishment and satisfaction. Which of these are most important in terms of the impact they have on the minister's professional ministry goals? On what measures are the most pronounced differences found? This chapter answers these questions, focusing on the most significant modifiers of the ministry goals described in chapter eight.

Age and experience

The stereotypical youth minister is young—congregations look for young youth ministers whom they believe will more naturally relate to their teens. Youth ministers themselves may begin to question their continued effectiveness in the profession as they age. This may, however, be less true for those with years of experience in full-time ministry (our sample) than for those who are volunteers or serve part-time. I frequently hear volunteers or bi-vocational ministers commenting on their advancing age, as if it is something to be ashamed of or feared. They seem to be apologizing for the fact that they are no longer young, even soliciting affirmation for their continued dedication to youth. But those whose primary life vocation has been to minister with youth seem to understand that their calling does not expire when they reach middle age.

Those who hire or even supervise youth ministers often reveal the most bias against aging ministers. Take Jerry's situation, for instance. He served effectively as a minister to youth for several decades, acting as mentor to dozens of youth ministers who are serving today. His wisdom was much in demand by others, and he was frequently invited to lead training workshops and teach courses in professional educational settings. Scores of youth made life-changing decisions while part of Jerry's ministry, and many of them are involved in vocational ministry today as a result. In Jerry's last youth ministry position, where he led a large, growing ministry in an influential suburban church in a major metropolitan area, he was promoted to another staff position—though against his wishes. It was move up or move out, and Jerry moved up. Why? He was no longer young. His youth group could have been his grandchildren; the perception of the senior pastor and those in power was that Jerry was too old for a position in youth ministry.

Similarly, Eric directed a specialized segment of youth ministry at a denominational level. His entire life had been devoted to reaching and teaching youth, with a special passion for discipleship. When Eric passed 50, however, the denominational leadership asked him to move out of youth ministry. The asking was essentially a telling. These arbitrary decisions are unfortunate. Instead of viewing age as a detriment, those in power should have viewed the years of experience as an asset.

Relates Well to Parents/Adults

The only noteworthy difference in the areas of personal growth and interpersonal relationships based on age is in the area of relating to parents and other adults in the ministry. Age is a non-factor in predicting the responses of youth ministers for any of the other nine ministry goals. When it comes to relating to parents and adults, however, youth ministers 40 years of age or older rank 3.5 standard scores higher than those 29 or younger. Age is an asset, and understandably so, since these ministers are typically of the same generation as the parents and most have children of their own. It is difficult for younger youth ministers to fully comprehend the life issues facing the parents of teenagers and, all too often, these ministers do not fully understand the need to develop relationships with parents and other adults in the church. Their focus is on the youth group.

Even when younger ministers do understand the importance of relating to parents and adults, their efforts may not always be well received. The perception by parents that the minister is too young to understand their life situations may prevent these younger ministers from being successful in their efforts to relate. For parents, the credibility of youth ministers and the trust they place in them are exponentially tied to age, and even more strongly to experience. Pam, a veteran youth minister, tells about leading a conference to help parents understand their teenagers. Even though she has years of experience working with youth, when it was discovered that she has no children of her own, several parents left her conference. Her lack of experience as a parent devalued her credibility on the topic, and it is hard to overcome a credibility gap. However, those who remained did so out of a recognition of her many years of experience working with teenagers. If she has been a youth minister for more than 15 years, they reasoned, then she must know something about relating to teenagers.

When considering the relationship between age and relating to parents/adults in the congregation, it is interesting to note the age and experience demographics for youth ministers of various denominations and youth organizations (see figure 9.4).

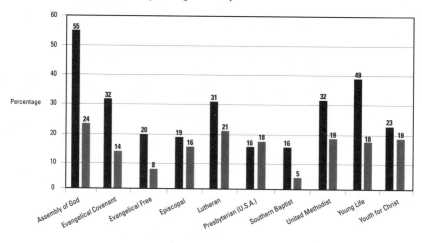

Figure 9.4—Percentage of youth ministers who are among the youngest and least experienced, by denominaton/organization

The youngest and least experienced youth ministers in the study are found in Assembly of God churches. They also rank next to last in their ability to positively relate to youth parents, second only to the Young Life and Youth for Christ staff (no statistically significant difference between these groups and Assembly of God youth ministers), which have historically viewed their mission as focusing on youth outside the local church, and not their parents. (Notice also that Young Life ministers are the second youngest group in the sample.) The oldest and most experienced group of youth ministers in the study is found in Southern Baptist churches. They rank at the top in experiencing the love and respect of youth parents and other adults in the congregation. This is a difference of more than four standard scores between Southern Baptist youth ministers and those serving with Young Life or Youth for Christ, and more than three standard scores between Southern Baptist and Assembly of God youth ministers—as you can see here:

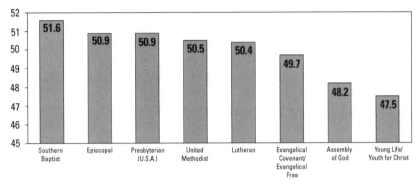

Figure. 9.5—Standard scores for relating well to parents/adults, by denomination

These denominational findings clearly reinforce the relationship between age, experience, and the ability to relate to youth parents. The youngest and least experienced have the greatest difficulty in this area. (These are the same youth ministers who are the most vulnerable to issues troubling those in the profession. See chapter 3.) It is important to re-emphasize the greater influence of experience over age in relating to parents. There are significant differences between each level of age and experience for this item cluster ("Relates Well to Parents/Adults"), but the differences are much greater for experience than for age:

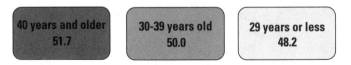

Figure 9.6—Standard scores for relating well to parents/adults, by age

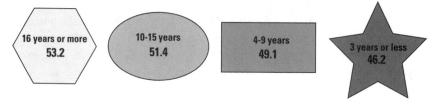

Figure 9.7—Standard scores for relating well to parents/adults,
by years of experience

When it comes to enjoying satisfying relationships with parents, there is a much larger difference in scores between those with the most and least experience than between the oldest and youngest youth ministers. Experience is a powerful contributor to the quality of interaction ministers experience with youth parents and other adults in the congregation. It appears to be a more powerful factor than age. For example, a youth minister who is 26 years old might have served for five years, if not longer. The standard score one might expect for this item cluster, based on age, is only 48.2, but when the five years of experience are used as a measure, the standard score could be expected to rise to 49.1. Or consider a youth minister who is 44 years of age and has been in youth ministry for 16 years or more. The standard score one might expect on this cluster for a 44-year-old youth minister is 51.7, but the expected standard score based on 16 or more years of experience rises to 53.2.

In what other areas of personal growth and interpersonal relationships does experience prove to be a highly significant goal modifier? The answer is found in the following list of item clusters, which are listed in the order of how greatly they are impacted by the youth minister's experience:

Seven clusters in which experience is highly significant goal modifier
- Competent Job Performance
- Confident Leadership
- Effective Youth Relationships
- Theological Grounding
- Achieving the Development of Adult Volunteers
- Motivated by God's Calling
- Creative Response to Youth Culture

Standard score differences and a brief discussion of the first three clusters follows, with standard scores on the remaining item clusters reported in the endnotes.

Competent Job Performance

The percentages are high for all areas of competent job performance in the entire sample, but significant differences do exist between those with the most and least experience in youth ministry. This is not particularly surprising, since competence for any task is gained with experience, or practice. What is highly significant is the difference of more than four standard scores between how those with 16-plus years of experience and those with nine or less years of experience view their own job performance. As seen below, there is a difference of more than eight standard scores between the most and least experienced youth ministers.

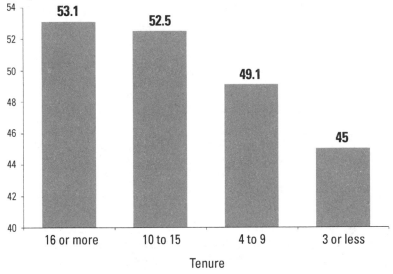

Figure 9.8—Standard scores for competent job performance, by years of service

One of the items in this cluster which clearly illustrates the contrast in competent job performance between youth ministers with varying years of experience is in the area of decision-making. Item 1: "I feel I make good decisions in my ministry." Wise decision-making is a necessary skill for the competent minister, but the ability to do so is a perceptual skill and not a psychomotor skill. This means that understanding and insight are required in decision-making, as opposed to the mastery of specific steps or techniques. One can very quickly learn the process of decision making by memorizing a series of action steps, and while it is helpful to follow such a process for making important ministry decisions, there can be no substitute for the wisdom which comes in the form of spiritual direction, insight gained through prayer and while in the trenches.

Confident decision-making is especially important in times of crisis. Inexperienced youth ministers may have an arsenal of emergency and contingency plans, but until they have actually come face-to-face with true crises, their plans are merely hypothetical; they may or may not be able to pull them off in "real life". Veteran youth ministers who have already encountered various and sundry youth ministry emergencies not only have plans, but have had practice putting those plans into action. They are confident that their plans work; they have learned from past decisions and are able to think on their feet when crisis hits.

On this particular item in the cluster, only 13 percent of the least experienced ministers (3 years or less) are able to strongly agree that their decision-making skills are good. This percentage rises to 32 percent for those with four or more years in youth ministry. Closely related to feelings of competence are confidence in leadership and a sense of effectiveness in relating with youth, two additional areas in which experience impacts youth ministers' self-evaluations.

Confident Leadership and Effective Youth Relationships

The ability to nurture the spiritual walk of adolescents is an important indicator of how successfully ministers are able to connect with their youth. Item 7 in the cluster "Effective Youth Relationships" (figure 8.8, page 216) addresses this very specifically: I know how to nurture youth's spiritual walk. Those with three years experience or less rate themselves considerably lower on this item than those with four or more years in the ministry. Only 48 percent indicate agreement or strong agreement with this statement, as opposed to 70 percent for those with more experience. It makes sense that those who have been involved in ministering with youth the longest are the ones who have best figured out how to impact them for Christ. However, the most statistically influential item in this "relating"cluster does not specifically address spiritual issues, but assesses the degree to which the minister is able to make youth feel comfortable enough to self-disclose—Item 1: "Young people open up to me easily."[3]

It would be natural to assume that young ministers might win youth's confidences easier than those old enough to represent parental authorities in their lives, but this is not supported in the study. Age is not a significant modifier for realizing meaningful youth relationships, however; experience is. Those with the most experience are the most effective in connecting with and influencing youth. This is likely due to the trust and confidence that are established over time. Though not specifically addressed in the data, it is reasonable to speculate that ministers who serve multiple years in the same location would enjoy the greatest levels of trust on the part of their youth. Standard scores for this item cluster are found in figure 9.9 below. Notice the difference of four standard scores between those with three and ten years of experience.

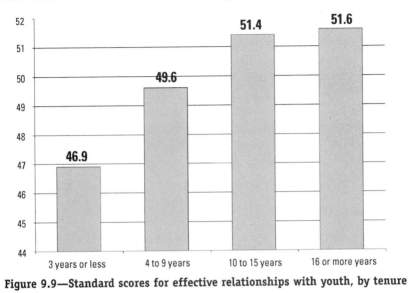

Figure 9.9—Standard scores for effective relationships with youth, by tenure

It takes time to build one's confidence in leadership. This cluster measures behaviors which are only evident after the fact, such as the ability to reproduce leaders, successfully recruit and train volunteers, achieve goals, and assess effectiveness. (See chapter 8 for a review of the items in this cluster.) It is not surprising, then, that experience is a major contributor to the minister's leadership confidence. Standard scores for this item cluster are reported in figure 9.10 below.

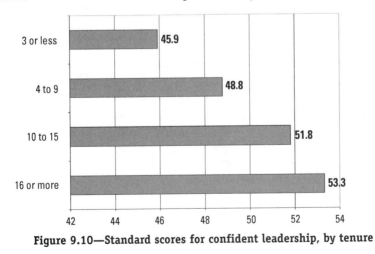

Figure 9.10—Standard scores for confident leadership, by tenure

The variance of more than four standard scores between youth ministers with 16 and nine years of experience rises to more than seven standard scores between those with the most and least amount of time in the profession. (Additional standard scores impacted by experience are included in the endnotes.[4])

After serving more than 16 years in full-time youth ministry, Glen Procopio wrote a devotional book based on his own experiences in order to inspire and encourage other youth ministers to keep at the task.[5] That is also one of the admonishments of this study; persevere. The longer you minister with youth, the more goals you will see accomplished, the more competent and confident you will feel, the more satisfaction you will derive from your relationships with youth and their parents, and the stronger will be your sense of purpose and confidence in God and his Word.

Education and Training

If perseverance is such an important factor in assisting youth ministers to realize their professional ministry goals, why invest the resources of time, money, and energy in a formal education? Even without the benefit of this study, there are many who would argue this point. It is a question I was asked repeatedly when my husband and I made the decision to move our family from Missouri to Texas so that I could attend Southwestern Baptist Theological Seminary in Fort Worth. I had been in youth ministry for more than nine years when we felt called to make the transition. Many peers attempted to convince me that seminary would do nothing to improve my ministry abilities. In addition to seeing youth come to know Christ and commit their lives to ministry, I was enjoying success as a curriculum writer and conference speaker.

So what more was I hoping to achieve by earning a seminary degree? Reflecting on that decision today, my first response is that I sensed God's calling supernaturally, and secondly, God used influential mentors in my life to convey that call. Other than the blessings which accompany obedience, were there practical benefits gained from my seminary education? The words of my academic advisor and professor, Dr. Wesley O. Black, very succinctly sum up what was, perhaps, the greatest value of those years. Whenever students questioned assignments or complained about schedules he would often respond with, "It builds character!" Although I hated those words at the time, I believe that my seminary experience did just that—it built character, confidence, competence, theological grounding, assurance of God's call, and perseverance.

I encourage my undergraduate youth ministry majors to continually learn after they receive their degrees, and to pursue further formal educational studies after they gain several years of experience. The findings of this study reinforce my intuitive beliefs about the value of this specialized training for youth ministry.[6]

Education is a significant factor in the satisfaction youth ministers realize in their personal growth and interpersonal relationships. While a seminary degree is one form of education included in the variable level of education, we have also chosen to examine its impact as a separate category. For both of these variables, there are several distinguishing benefits, but seminary training appears to have the greatest impact on professional ministry goals. Understanding the importance of other significant variables in the study, such as age, ministry setting, and experience, may be helpful to us in attempting to comprehend why seminary is such a significant goal modifier. Consider the following descriptive characteristics of seminary trained ministers in the study. (These facts are even more insightful when one considers that 52 percent of the participants in this study do not have seminary training.)

Descriptive characteristics of participants with seminary training

- 53 percent of youth ministers with four or more years of experience have received seminary training; only 24 percent of those with three years of experience or less have attended seminary

- 53 percent of those 30 and over have seminary training; only 21 percent of those under 30 have received similar training

- 59 percent of youth ministers serving groups with 40 or fewer youth have not had seminary training; only 41 percent of these smallest youth groups have seminary-trained ministers

- 36 percent of the females are seminary-trained and 52 percent of the males have seminary training

- 25 percent of seminary-trained youth ministers serve groups larger than 100; only 18 percent of non-seminary-trained youth ministers serve groups this large

- 40 percent of seminary-educated youth ministers serve congregations of 500 or larger; only 27 percent of those without seminary training serve in congregations this large

Another significant goal modifier is denomination (organization), and there are some interesting relationships between this variable and seminary training. The percentage of seminary-trained youth ministers in each denomination/organization is included in figure 9.11 below.

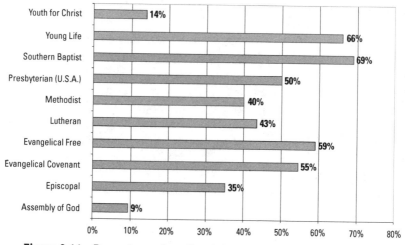

Figure 9.11—Percentage of youth ministers with seminary education

The Southern Baptist denomination has the largest percentage of seminary-educated youth ministers; this is not surprising, given the fact that they have six seminaries associated with and partially supported by their Convention, as well as several others with denominational ties or leanings. Youth ministers have long been recognized as credible professionals in Southern Baptist life. Southwestern Seminary hired the first full-time professor of youth education, Philip B. Harris, before the mid-century mark of the 20th century, indicating their commitment to the formal education of those committed to ministry with youth.[7]

What is remarkable is that the group with the second highest percentage of seminary-educated ministers is the Young Life parachurch organization. They outrank their Youth for Christ counterparts by 52 percent in this area. This is especially intriguing given the fact that the Young Life organization has a much higher percentage of young youth ministers than Youth for Christ. Mike O'Leary, vice president of recruiting, training, and deploying for Young Life, clarified this phenomenon. Most Young Life recruits come straight out of college; however, they are given the opportunity to immediately begin earning seminary credit while involved in their required intensive ministry training. This is made possible due to the partnership relationships Young Life enjoys with seven different seminaries. During their two-year internship period, Young Life ministers may earn several hours of seminary course credit. In addition, because of the partnerships, these ministers are able to continue their seminary education at a reduced rate after their required Young Life training is completed, and they are encouraged to do so.[8]

Four distinct item clusters are significantly affected by both of the variables of educational level and seminary training: theological grounding, specialized training, competent job performance, and relationships with parents/adults. Seminary training also significantly impacts one additional cluster, confident leadership. A brief discussion of each of these areas follows.

Theological Grounding

The area in which education appears to have the strongest influence on the minister's professional goals is related to confidence in and knowledge of Scripture: theological grounding. Those with a post-collegiate education score 3.8 standard scores higher than ministers with a college or university degree on this measure. Seminary graduates outrank non-seminary graduates by 5.3 standard scores. One item in particular characterizes this cluster: Item 4, My youth ministry is theologically based. Participants were asked to respond to this statement on the basis of a six-point Likert scale, from strongly disagree to strongly agree. Of those with seminary training, 53 percent strongly agreed to having a theological foundation to their ministry, but only 38 percent of those without seminary strongly agreed to the statement.

Theological grounding is one of the clusters which is most susceptible to differences between variables. Statistical differences were found on this item cluster for ten of the 11 variables used in the analysis. Because this is such an important aspect of youth ministry, an Automatic Interaction Detection analysis was performed to determine which of these variables most significantly contributes to the youth minister's theological grounding. The analysis reveals the overwhelming importance of seminary for this foundational youth ministry prerequisite. It is the key factor predicting high or low scores on this dimension. The standard score of .50 jumps to 52.6 for those with seminary and falls to 48.3 for those without. Beyond seminary, what are the additional factors that contribute to greater or lesser scores in theological grounding? They are illustrated in figure 9.12 below.

For seminary-trained youth ministers, the second most important predictor of theological grounding is the minister's approach to culture. Those who a) seek to protect their youth from negative cultural influences, b) view culture as another competing kingdom their youth must accept or reject to some degree, or c) believe their youth should become transforming agents in the world, all outscore youth ministers who hold to an entertainment philosophy. In basic terms, this means that when youth ministers begin to read their Bibles on a regular basis and become confident in their knowledge of Scripture, when they begin to grasp theological concepts and use them to shape their ministry, then they reject the fun and games, Coke-and-a-joke approach to youth ministry. They understand that their mission has eternal consequences and time can't be squandered.

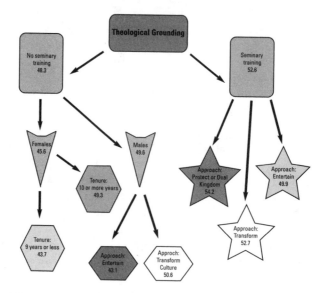

Figure 9.12—Factors effecting theological grounding

For those without seminary training, gender is the second greatest predictor of theological grounding, with males scoring three standard scores higher than females. Beyond gender, cultural approach is the next most significant predictor of theological grounding for males. Once again, we are reminded that those who practice "youth ministry light" are those who do not have a solid theological background and who do not place high value on Scripture. (Notice the difference in standard scores between male youth ministers preferring an entertainment approach and those who believe that youth ministry should seek to transform culture: 7.5 standard scores.)

The third greatest predictor of theological grounding for female youth ministers without seminary training is tenure. There is a difference of more than five standard scores between female youth ministers with 10 or more years of experience and those with less.

Notice that, while seminary training is the key predictor of the minister's theological grounding, educational level does not emerge as a factor in this highly complex analysis. This helps us to understand that post-collegiate degrees from institutions other than theological seminaries are not as successful in grounding a youth minister theologically.

Specialized training

I once served in a state youth ministry organization with someone who greatly discouraged young ministers from attending seminary. The surprising thing about his attitude was that he already had a degree from a seminary. I was never quite sure whether his admonition was due to a negative experience he had in school or whether he thought these youth ministers honestly didn't need further education because of their experience and superior performance record. The more typical scenario is for those with the most training to encourage others to follow in their footsteps. Not surprisingly, that is what we discovered through the data.

Those groups which are most favorable to advocating specialized training and certification or licensing for youth ministers are those which probably have already met any requirements which would likely be proposed. Youth ministers with a post-collegiate education rate the value of specialized training more than three standard scores higher than those with only a college or university degree, and youth ministers with seminary training outscore non-seminary ministers on this item cluster by more than four standard scores. (Standard scores are reported in the endnotes.)[9]

Competent Job Performance and Confident Leadership

One of the advantages of education for the youth minister is a heightened sense of job competence:

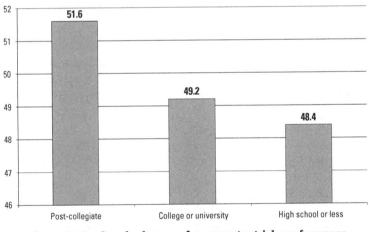

Figure 9.13—Standard scores for competent job performance, by educational level

There is a difference of more than three standard scores on competent job performance ratings between those with some form of post-collegiate education and those who have never attended college or university. Similarly, youth ministers with seminary training view their sense of competence much higher than their peers who have not attended seminary classes. One additional benefit of a seminary education is the increase in leadership confidence:

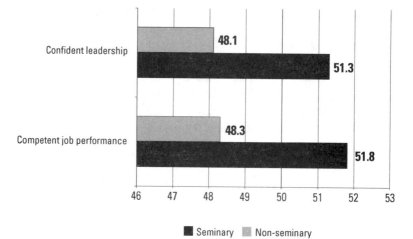

Figure 9.14—Standard scores for competent job performance and confident leadership, by seminary training

We know that youth ministers with post-collegiate or seminary training are also the oldest and most experienced, two other factors also known to positively impact competence and confidence scores. (These related characteristics may also explain why youth ministers with seminary training enjoy more satisfactory relationships with parents/adults. Standard scores for this cluster are found in the endnotes.)[10] This is probably not the only reason that the most highly trained ministers experience the greatest satisfaction and fulfillment of professional ministry goals, however. It just makes sense that the more training one has received for a task or profession, the more qualified that person will feel. It is disconcerting to attempt to fulfill a role for which no training has been given. Until one has navigated through the requirements of any job and successfully learned the ropes, there is an undercurrent of stress and self-doubt.

As already mentioned, I served as a youth minister for several years before attending seminary. Whenever I was in meetings with my peers, I was inevitably asked where I had attended seminary. The question was innocent enough; it was more small talk than interrogation. Still, I always felt slightly inferior when I had to respond that I had never been to seminary. Despite the untold training seminars I had attended, sponsored by my denomination and various youth ministry resource organizations, I felt as if I were less competent than those other ministers who had received a seminary degree. This self-assessment was not based on my actual ministry practices, but only on my lack of formal training. I can now say that those feelings were totally unjustified, but they were my reality at the time. Besides strengthening my theological grounding, seminary retro-validated my ministry, increasing my self-confidence and sense of accomplishment. It is likely that these same misplaced feelings of inferiority plague many of the youth ministers in our study who do not have college or seminary degrees. The very fact that one has pursued formal education may be, in itself, enough to raise competence and confidence levels.

Size of Community, Congregation, and Youth Group

Most of the youth ministry resources made available in the past decade have been targeted at larger churches, and most of these churches are found in the largest cities. Even when national training seminars offer special sessions focusing on youth ministry in smaller churches or designed for those in rural communities or smaller towns, interested youth ministers typically must travel to major urban areas to access them. Sometimes the financial realities of ministry in small churches or communities rule out these possibilities altogether. This is unfortunate, for these are the youth ministers who appear to have the greatest need for training and encouragement.

As the body of Christ, we have rejected the notion that worth is tied to size; we have looked disparagingly on the slogan "Bigger is better." However, bigger may translate to better for the youth minister who wants to realize key professional ministry goals; size is positively associated with satisfaction for several item clusters. Notice the differences in standard scores between youth ministers in communities and congregations of varying size for each of the item clusters included in the following charts. (See figures 9.15 and 9.16.)

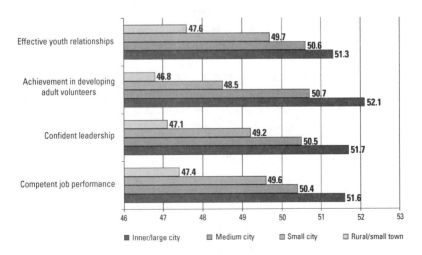

Figure 9.15—Standard scores for significant professional ministry goals, by community size

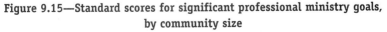

Youth ministers in the largest urban areas (over 250,000 population) report significantly higher standard scores than those in the smallest communities (under 10,000) on four of the 10 professional ministry goal item clusters: "Competent Job Performance", "Confident Leadership", "Achievement of Developing Adult Volunteers", and "Effective Youth Relationships". In addition, their ability to successfully develop volunteer leaders is much higher than that of youth ministers in small cities (population 10,000-49,000). The difficulty for those in smaller communities to be able to recruit and train adequate numbers of volunteers is not difficult to understand; the fewer the people, the fewer available and/or qualified as volunteers. However, the significantly lower scores for confidence, competence, and ability to develop effective youth relationships are more difficult to understand. What else do we know about these ministers which might bring some clarity to the situation?[11]

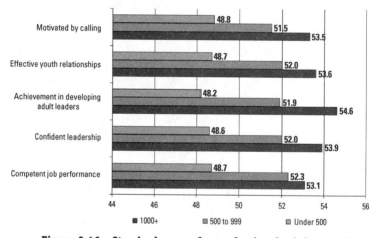

Figure 9.16—Standard scores for professional ministry goals, by congregational size

Undoubtedly, the low percentage of seminary-trained ministers in small towns certainly contributes to their significantly lower scores for competent job performance and confident leadership. The last two descriptors, however, are also important in helping us understand why they are less able to accomplish certain professional ministry goals than their peers in larger communities.

Youth ministers in congregations with an average Sunday attendance of less than 500 are less successful than those in larger churches in their ability to develop adult volunteers and build effective relationships with youth. They also feel less competent in their job performance and less confident in their leadership abilities and are less likely to minister out of a primary sense of God's calling. (See figure 9.16.) Congregations of this size are found everywhere, not just in small communities, but the fact that almost all of the congregations in these communities are small certainly impacts their standard scores for all of these item clusters.[12]

The major impact of size is evident when comparisons are made by the average number of youth participating in the ministry. Significant differences were found between small and large groups on eight of the ten professional ministry goal clusters for this variable. For the item clusters "Competent Job Performance", "Confident Leadership", and "Developing Adult Volunteers", significant differences exist between groups of each size: small (40 and under), medium (41-100), and large (101 and over). Standard scores for all eight clusters are reported in figure 9.17 below.

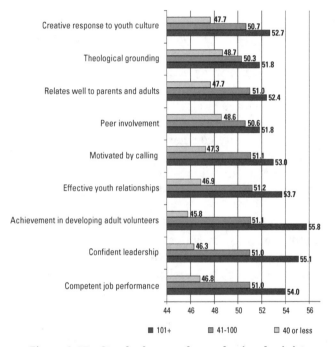

Figure 9.17—Standard scores for professional ministry goals, by number of youth

Is youth ministry better in larger churches? Yes and no. Clearly, this is the present reality, based on the self-assessments of those ministering in the smallest settings. No, youth ministry is not inherently better in larger churches, when one understands the true measure of ministry success. Consider the words of youth evangelist Jonathan Hewett as he addresses this issue:

> • **Professional success in youth ministry doesn't have to do with going through a succession of**

churches to an ever-larger church with an ever-larger budget and an ever-larger group of youth. But, many of us act as if we're measured by the size of our churches. That would be true if we worked in the secular job market.

• "Evaluating ministers by secular standards of success," according to Richard Ross, "is like using a gallon jug to count railroad ties. It is simply a standard of measure that doesn't apply."

• The corner office on the top floor is the goal in the secular world, but our Boss evaluates us differently when it comes to success.[13]

If size is not a measure of effective ministry, why is it that those in the smallest churches with the smallest youth groups rate themselves so much lower on these evaluative characteristics? (Size is a major factor on nearly every aspect of the study. Refer back to figure 9.1 for an overview of the number of total item clusters significantly impacted by size.) One possible explanation is offered by Rich Grassel, Assistant Professor of Student Ministry at Geneva College: The youth ministers may be suffering from an inferiority complex. Grassel experienced these feelings himself after making the transition from ministering in a large church to a small one after enrolling in seminary. He identifies three sources of frustration which contributed to those feelings:

Lack of resources. This includes a lack of media equipment, vehicles for transportation, finances for conferences and seminars and to subsidize student trips, and less money to purchase miscellaneous materials which can be used to enhance creativity.

The comparison game. Youth ministers engage in this constantly, and it can be demoralizing when other ministries have more "toys" and more students. Playing this game can result in feelings of resentment toward other ministries or personal insignificance.

Green apples to bell peppers. This is even more complex than comparing apples to oranges. Apples and oranges don't look a thing alike—one is orange and the other is red, green, or yellow. One is textured, the other has smooth skin. Green apples and bell peppers, however, are close in color and texture; they look similar on the outside. But when you bite into them, you immediately notice their differences.

> **Large and small youth groups can often appear
> very similar; one is just a bigger or smaller version
> of the other, right? Wrong! When you examine them
> more than superficially you will discover that their
> underlying dynamics are surprisingly different.[14]**

Is it possible, then, that youth ministers with fewer youth are ministering just as effectively as the majority of ministers in larger settings, but are simply feeling less competent and confident? Before answering this, keep in mind that youth ministers were not asked to rate their level of ministry competence or even asked to assess their feelings of confidence. The scores reported in our study are based on ministers' personal assessments of some very concrete outcomes which have labeled competent job performance and confident leadership. (Refer back to chapter 8 for a list of individual items included in each of these item clusters.)

Regardless of the reasons, and however unpalatable it may be, reality says there are profound differences between youth ministers in small and large ministries, and these are more than differences of group dynamics or strategies or cultural climate.

Given the relational nature of ministry, it would seem that smaller groups would actually be preferable to those which are larger. Schwarz concluded this in his church growth studies; Senter suggests this in his 15 youth ministry axioms, "propositions regarding self-evident truths."[15] Axiom 8 states, "Most youth groups reach peak effectiveness when attendance reaches twenty to thirty high school students."[16] This axiom is supported by Cromer, long-time professor of Christian education at Southern Baptist Theological Seminary in Louisville, Kentucky, who offers the following assets of small youth groups:

- Youth in small groups tend to be more closely identified with their families, and there is more of a familial sense in the congregation.
- Leaders of small groups tend to be more open to training and feel a stronger sense of responsibility for their ministry.
- There are more opportunities for youth to use their talents and develop their personal gifts in a smaller congregation. When they do so, they are permitted to fail with a minimal risk of embarrassment.
- It is easier for ministers of small youth groups to connect and communicate with the parents of their youth.
- Youth have a greater opportunity to know their senior pastor on a personal level, building feelings of trust and friendship which ca create bridges for ministry in times of need at present or in the future

- Small groups are better able to provide a feeling of community. It is easier to detect when a youth is suffering from a personal hurt, is absent, or is beginning to withdraw. This ability to discover problems when they arise enhances the likelihood that youth concerns will be addressed and they will be nurtured back to spiritual health.
- The needs of all of the group members can be considered when shaping the ministry.
- All youth can have the opportunity to serve in leadership positions. The youth group is more likely to serve as a reference group, in which value choices and beliefs are shaped.
- There is a more uniform school identity, which facilitates more effective outreach, enables the ministry to be more identified with its community, and allows leaders greater opportunity to participate in school events.
- The intimate contact and interaction in these small groups can lead to greater comfort and confidence in evangelism.[17]

According to our research, these potential benefits of small youth groups are not being realized. With all of the possibilities of a more personal, fruitful ministry with smaller groups, why are these ministers significantly less satisfied than those with larger numbers? Is it possible that they have simply failed to take advantage of their unique opportunities and have, instead, wasted energy and resources attempting to imitate larger ministries? Whatever the causes for this discrepancy between potential and reality, youth ministers in smaller communities and congregations must begin to capitalize on their assets. Denominations and youth ministry organizations must begin to address this issue, allocating more resources to help these ministers begin to understand how to minister more effectively in their unique settings.

Denomination and Theological View

Two final professional ministry goal modifiers worthy of discussion are closely related: denomination and theological view. There are two key areas in which both of these variables reveal significant differences—"Motivated by God's Calling" and "Theological Grounding". Standard scores for these item clusters based on denomination/organization are found below in figures 9.18 and 9.19.

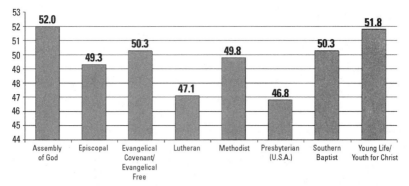

Figure 9.18—Standard scores for calling, by denomination/organization

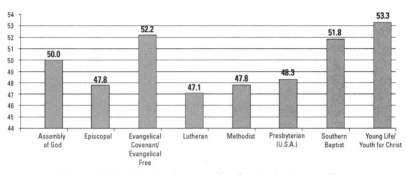

Figure 9.19—Standard scores for theological grounding,
by denomination/organization

Youth for Christ/Young Life

These two clusters are both inherently tied to one's theological interpretations, so it is not surprising that significant differences exist
between groups. For both of these clusters, the differences are clearly
split between ministers in traditionally evangelical and mainline churches.

The parachurch organizations score significantly higher in theological grounding than all of the mainline denominations, with a difference
of more than six standard scores over the lowest-scoring Lutheran youth
ministers. Ministers in Episcopal, Methodist, and Lutheran churches
score significantly lower than those in all other groups.

One important observation needs to be made at this point, in light
of the fact that Youth for Christ and Young Life rank higher than any of
the denominations in theological grounding. As you will recall from the
introduction, Youth for Christ and Young Life were combined into one
group and their responses tabulated together for the purposes of this
study. However, because we are able to examine some characteristics of
the two groups separately, we know that 66 percent of the Young Life
ministers have seminary-training, but only 14 percent of those serving

with Youth for Christ have similar training. Why is this important? As discussed earlier in the chapter, the most significant predictor of theological grounding is seminary training. (See figure 9.12 on page 242) It is very understandable, then, that Young Life youth ministers would score at or near the top in theological grounding, because of their high percentage of seminary-educated ministers. On the other hand, it is just as unlikely that Youth for Christ ministers would score at or near the top on this item cluster, due to their extremely low levels of seminary training. Clearly, Youth for Christ has benefitted from being partnered with Young Life on this item cluster, and this score should not be interpreted as an affirmation of strong theological grounding.

One of the individual items used to assess theological grounding is Item 2: "I am confident in my knowledge of Scripture." A percentage of youth ministers from each denomination/organization strongly agrees to this statement. Notice that a higher percentage of Evangelical Covenant and Evangelical Free youth ministers are able without reservation to express confidence in their own scriptural understanding than any other group—17 percent more than Episcopal youth ministers and 12 percent more than those with Youth for Christ and Young Life.

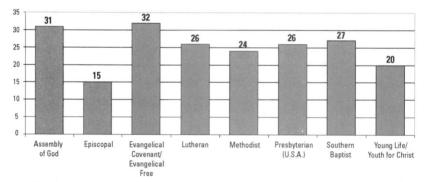

Figure 9.20—Standard scores for confidence in Scripture knowledge, by denomination/organization

Theology as a determiner of Theological Grounding and Calling

Theology also influences the way youth ministers explain their motivation to serve. Those from mainline denominations are less likely to feel that God has called them to a specific ministry with youth; they are more likely to be motivated by other factors other than a call from God, such as using youth ministry to gain the experience necessary to serve in another ministry position (as you can see in the chart below). The only highly significant differences for this item cluster, however, are between Assembly of God/Youth for Christ/Young Life ministers and those from Lutheran and Presbyterian churches. This difference is more than five standard scores between Assembly of God and Presbyterian ministers.

When these same issues, "Theological Grounding" and "Motivated by God's Calling", are analyzed along theological lines—from conservative to liberal—the differences are even more acute:

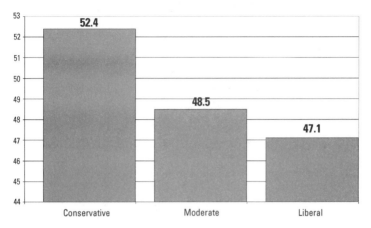

Figure 9.21—Standard scores for theological grounding, by theological view

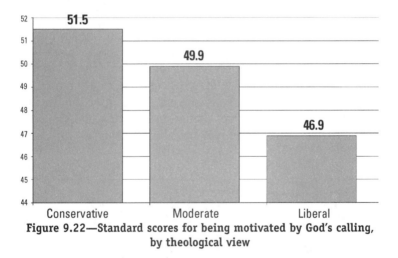

Figure 9.22—Standard scores for being motivated by God's calling, by theological view

Theologically conservative youth ministers evaluate their grasp of theological concepts, their Scripture knowledge and confidence, and their faithfulness in Bible study more than five standard scores higher than self-described liberals. The motivation for being in youth ministry is also related to youth ministers' theological views. Conservatives and moderates do not differ that much on their sense of calling, but both of these groups place much more importance on God's call to youth ministry than those who call themselves liberals. The responses to two key items illustrate the theological differences between these three groups of youth ministers:

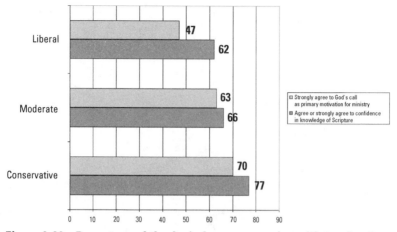

Figure 9.23—Percentage of theological groups agreeing with two key items

There are three more key differences between ministers in various denominations/organizations, all of them focusing on interpersonal relationships. Differences in how each of these youth ministry groups relate to parents has already been discussed earlier in the chapter. (See figure 9.5 on page 233). Two other measures of relationship are the ability to effectively relate with teenagers and the ability to successfully recruit, train, and develop volunteer leaders (see charts below). Notice that for both of these relational clusters, most of the denominations and organizations have very similar results; only one group is significantly different than all the rest on each item cluster.

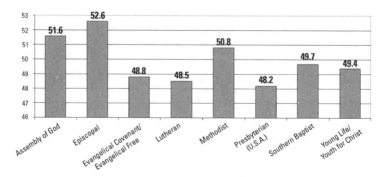

Figure 9.24—Standard scores for effective youth relationships,
by denomination/organization

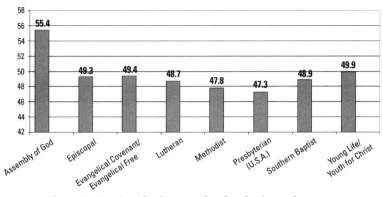

Figure 9.25—Standard scores for developing volunteers, by denomination/organization

When it comes to building open, friendly relationships with youth, Episcopal ministers are much more confident of their abilities than their counterparts in Evangelical Covenant, Evangelical Free, Lutheran, and Presbyterian congregations. In the area of volunteer development, Assembly of God youth ministers appear to be much more accomplished than any other group in equipping adults to lead small groups and serve as mentors for youth. They rate their achievement of this task more than five standard scores higher than Youth for Christ and Young Life youth ministers who rank second in volunteer development. They outscore Presbyterian youth ministers on this cluster by more than eight standard scores.

Summary

How many hundreds of times have generalizations been made about youth ministers? They believe, they act, they think, they don't, they do, they want, they refuse... Stereotypes are never wise to buy into, but occasionally they really do appear to be "one size fits all" in their utility. This is not one of those times!

There are major differences between groups of youth ministers on almost all measures of professional ministry goals, and these differences center around a few key variables, with three being the most influential: experience, education, and size of youth group. Those who commit themselves to long-term ministry with youth are among the most satisfied youth ministers. They don't give up during those difficult early years; they allow God to direct them as they wander through that wilderness because they know the promised land is out there. The most personally fulfilled youth ministers don't ever take the attitude that they know all there is to know about youth ministry. They take every opportunity to keep learning and studying, to grow deeper theological roots. They understand that there is more to youth ministry preparation than clever ideas and poignant illustrations. They know the value of studying foundational philosophical disciplines. The most satisfied youth ministers are those who are blessed with more and more youth. They believe the Great Commission and the Great Commandment have a message for them, and they respond in obedience by equipping and evangelizing and loving and worshiping. They don't rely upon numerical growth goals; they simply serve God faithfully, and he brings forth the increase.

THINK IT OVER, TALK IT THROUGH

1. What significant hurdles have you jumped as you've gained experience in youth ministry? How do you see more experience helping you to reach an even greater degree of goal fulfillment?

2. In what ways has your formal education and training been most helpful in youth ministry? To what educational opportunities do you wish you had access?

3. Which do you think is the better explanation of one of the findings of this chapter? "A competent youth minister will build a large youth group" OR "A large youth ministry will help to develop competent youth ministers".

4. How does the denomination/organization with which you are most familiar compare to others in the pursuit of the particular goals rep resented in the last two chapters?

The People Who Brought You this Book...

invite you to discover MORE valuable youth ministry resources.

Youth Specialities has three decades of experience working alongside Christian youth workers of just about every denomination and youth-serving organization. We're here to help you, whether you're brand new to youth ministry or a veteran, whether you're a volunteer or a career youth pastor. Each year we serve over 100,000 youth workers worldwide through our training seminars, conventions, magazines, resource products, and internet Web site (www.YouthSpecialties.com).

For FREE information about ways YS can help your youth ministry, complete and return this card.

Are you: ☐ A paid youth worker ☐ A volunteer S=480001

Name_____

Church/Org. _____

Address ☐ Church or ☐ Home _____

City _____ State _____ Zip _____

Daytime Phone Number (_____) _____

E-Mail _____

Denomination _____ Average Weekly Church Attendance _____

The People Who Brought You this Book...

invite you to discover MORE valuable youth ministry resources.

Youth Specialities has three decades of experience working alongside Christian youth workers of just about every denomination and youth-serving organization. We're here to help you, whether you're brand new to youth ministry or a veteran, whether you're a volunteer or a career youth pastor. Each year we serve over 100,000 youth workers worldwide through our training seminars, conventions, magazines, resource products, and internet Web site (www.YouthSpecialties.com).

For FREE information about ways YS can help your youth ministry, complete and return this card.

Are you: ☐ A paid youth worker ☐ A volunteer S=480001

Name_____

Church/Org. _____

Address ☐ Church or ☐ Home _____

City _____ State _____ Zip _____

Daytime Phone Number (_____) _____

E-Mail _____

Denomination _____ Average Weekly Church Attendance _____

BUSINESS REPLY MAIL

FIRST-CLASS MAIL   PERMIT 268   HOLMES PA

POSTAGE WILL BE PAID BY ADDRESSEE

YOUTH SPECIALTIES
P.O. BOX 668
HOLMES, PA 19043-0668

BUSINESS REPLY MAIL

FIRST-CLASS MAIL   PERMIT 268   HOLMES PA

POSTAGE WILL BE PAID BY ADDRESSEE

YOUTH SPECIALTIES
P.O. BOX 668
HOLMES, PA 19043-0668

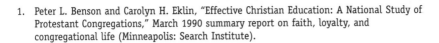

1. Peter L. Benson and Carolyn H. Eklin, "Effective Christian Education: A National Study of Protestant Congregations," March 1990 summary report on faith, loyalty, and congregational life (Minneapolis: Search Institute).

2. With the exception of theological grounding, there are less than two standard score differences between females and males for every item cluster in the area of professional ministry goals. On this measure, males score 51.1, almost four standard scores higher than females.

3. Item correlation to total cluster is $r = .71$.

4. The following lists of standard scores are reported by item cluster, as based on tenure (number of years).

   Theological Grounding
16+	52.4
10-15	51.5
4-9	49.3
3 or less	47.0

   Achieving Development of Adult Volunteers
16+	52.0
10-15	50.9
4-9	49.4
3 or less	47.2

   Motivated by God's Calling
16+	51.0
10-15	51.2
4-9	50.0
3 or less	47.7

   (Though the standard score is higher for 10-15 years than for 16 or more, it is not statistically significant.)

   Creative Response to Youth Culture
16+	51.1
10-15	51.1
4-9	49.7
3 or less	47.9

5. Glenn Procopio, *So That's Why I Keep Doing This!* (El Cajon, California: Youth Specialties), 1998.

6. The ability of educational training to increase youth ministers' accomplishment of personal growth goals and development of significant interpersonal relationships is not significantly impacted by the baccalaureate degree. Post-collegiate and seminary education are the only educational factors which stand out as predictors for any of the ten item clusters in this area. Though this may be disconcerting to undergraduate youth ministry educators, it is important to carefully consider the following:

   • The data does not specify the participant's major course of study at the college or university level.

   • Formal youth ministry educational programs at the undergraduate level are a relatively recent phenomenon, many created in the nineties. It is unlikely that a majority of the respondents were enrolled in such a program of study. (The first professional organization for Youth Ministry Educators just held its first meeting in 1994.)

7. Richard Ross, *The Work of the Minister of Youth* (Nashville: Convention Press, 1989), 14.

8. This is based on a personal conversation with Mike O'Leary, vice-president of Young Life's recruiting, training, and deploying, at a meeting of National Network's Youth Ministry executive council on May 3, 2000, in Washington, DC.

9. Standard scores for the item cluster Specialized Training:
    Seminary   52.4
    Non-seminary   48.0
    Post-collegiate   51.9
    High school or less   48.9
    College/university   48.8

10. Standard scores for the item cluster Relates Well to Parents/Adults:
    Seminary   51.6
    Non-seminary   48.4
    Post-collegiate   51.8
    College/university   48.7
    High school or less   48.7

11. Of the youth ministers in the study, 20 percent serve in communities with a population less than 10,000. The characteristics listed are descriptive only of those in small towns which have a population between 2,500 and 9,999. Due to the fact that only 8 percent of the total sample serve in smaller communities, it did not seem necessary to include an additional list of descriptors. Those ministering in the very smallest towns and those serving in rural or open country do not differ significantly from their peers in small towns.

12. Sixty-six percent of the congregations represented in the study have an average Sunday morning attendance of less than 500; 23 percent have between 500 and 999 in attendance per Sunday.

13. Jonathan Hewett, "Pleasing People or Pleasing God? Evaluating Youth Ministry Success," *The Minister's Family* (Winter 1998-99), 27-28.

14. Rich Grassel, "The Purple Zero Syndrome: On Thriving in Small-Church Youth Ministry," *Youthworker* (May/June 2000), 45.

15. Mark H. Senter III, "Axioms of Youth Ministry: The Context," in Richard R. Dunn and Mark H. Senter III (eds.), *Reaching a Generation for Christ* (Chicago: Moody Press, 1997), 122.

16. Senter, 142.

17. William R. Cromer, Jr., "Ministering to Youth in Small Churches," Richard Ross (ed.), *Big Help for Small Youth Groups* (Nashville: Convention Press, 1990), 10-14.

Gaining Broad Support

Chapter 10

Gaining Broad Support: Organizational Climate
Karen E. Jones

If youth ministers are to gain support for their ministries, they must be able to both envision a goal and then impart that vision to others. The next two chapters explore youth ministers' ability to gain support from their congregations, supervisors, and youths. They are represented on our conceptual model by the face. The human face contains eyes, ears, and mouth—for seeing, listening, and communicating—all of which are necessary actions for garnering support.

This chapter explores very specific organizational issues related to ministry support. It answers such questions as—

- To what degree do youth ministers feel the support of their supervisors or senior pastors?
- Are youth ministers content where they serve or do they feel taken for granted?
- Do youth ministers sense freedom in their positions or do they feel constrained by the red tape of their organizational policies?

Organizational climate matters

There are a variety of youth ministry models in operation, each with distinct philosophical beliefs about the degree to which the youth group is to be related to and involved with the total life of the church. Even ministries that take the total isolationist approach and only rarely interface with the adults and children in the church *still* need the support of the entire congregation. This support may come in the form of finances, material supplies, volunteer leaders, or verbal/written affirmation—but should *always* be given in the form of prayer. The body of Christ has not been cloned; it is *one*, and youth ministry is *one* part of that *one* body. It does not happen in a vacuum; it is impacted and shaped by the entire congregation or the organization in which it exists. Effective, innovative ministry will occur only when it is encouraged, emphasized, and valued by the congregation. Because of the shaping influence leaders have on their respective ministries, they also require encouragement and support if their ministry is to produce lasting spiritual fruit.

Think of this principle in terms of life in a fish bowl (not a foreign analogy for those in ministry). The water in the bowl literally affects the life or death of the fish swimming in it. If you place a perfectly healthy goldfish in a bowl of polluted water it may very well go belly-up before you even notice there's a problem. Even if the water appears clean, hidden contaminants can prevent the fish from thriving, or even surviving. Sometimes you are able to detect the problem before it destroys the goldfish; you may notice it floundering and scoop it out before it succumbs to the hidden pollutants. You analyze the water, discover the problem, add or remove whatever needs to be changed, replace the fish, and it swims along without a care in the world, doing whatever goldfish like to do in fish bowls. It is also possible, however, that the dangers lurking in the water won't be detected until they have already damaged the fish; one day you peer into the bowl and notice your goldfish is no longer gold at all, but a dingy white or greenish-brown.

The youth minister's fish bowl is the church or organization in which the minister serves, and the item clusters in this portion of the study are those unseen ingredients in the water which affect the minister's health and performance, which, in turn, impact the ministry itself. This portion of the study is an assessment of the water quality in the fish bowl more than it is an evaluation of the minister who is swimming there. What is it, then, which needs to be analyzed?

Dynamics that influence change

Five distinct constructs contributing to group innovation were identified by Search Institute in their study "Five Shaping Forces," addressing the organizational dynamics which hinder or facilitate change. Those constructs are: commitment to change, supportive leadership, innovative atmosphere, sense of team, and organizational pride.[1] Elements of each of these five constructs are embedded in our study and are reflected in the four item clusters we used to assess youth ministers' perceptions of the levels of support they receive from their respective churches or organizations. Youth ministers were asked to: 1) evaluate the level of support they receive from their senior pastors/supervisors, 2) evaluate the support they receive from their congregations, 3) assess the overall climate of their churches or organizations, and 4) indicate the degree to which roadblocks in their ministry settings prevent them from realizing greater satisfaction or success in their work.

How do youth ministers' churches and organizations measure up in terms of the amount of support they provide for their youth ministers? If this were a medical exam, the doctor would probably say, "Well, everything checks out okay, but I am going to prescribe some vitamins, put you on a strict diet, recommend you increase your daily intake of water, and suggest that you begin a regiment of rigorous exercise in order to reduce your cholesterol level and help you drop that extra weight. Otherwise, you could be staring in the face of some serious health problems down the road!" In other words, the water in the fish bowl is polluted, but the goldfish is still swimming.

A more concrete evaluation of the support youth ministers experience may be helpful. Using the methodology of determining grade point averages, percentage grades were tabulated for every item in each item cluster. Those percentage grades were then averaged to arrive at an evaluative grade for each component of support, and finally, those grades were averaged to arrive at an overall letter grade.[2] This is the organizational report card:

Positive Organizational Climate	C- (73%)
Supervisor's Personal Support	B- (83%)
Congregation's Personal Support	C+ (79%)
Freedom from Ministry Roadblocks	D+ (69%)
CUMULATIVE GRADE:	**C+**

Receiving group grades is never popular; there are always some members of a team which contribute more or less to a particular project. This is also true when assessing the level of support churches and congregations offer their youth ministers. The groups in which ministers serve significantly impact their perception of support on three of the four item clusters. The size of the youth group is a significant factor for two of the clusters, community and congregational size alter the standard scores in one of the four support categories, and tenure is a significant factor for a single item cluster. All of these differences are described in the remaining portion of this chapter, along with a general description and summary report for each of the four categories of support.

CLUSTER

Organizational Climate Is Positive and Stimulating

Throughout my years in youth ministry, I have met men and women from all parts of the country whose lives have been committed to ministry with youths. From these encounters I have discovered that churches, like individual ministers, have personalities, and that their personalities are reflected in their adult leaders and in their youths. Those who find their own personalities in conflict with that of their churches don't often serve in those locations for very long. The ministers who *do* choose to remain in a mismatched environment out of a sense of calling or commitment to their youth often undergo a personality change or experience deep discouragement or even depression. I am not referring here to relational conflicts, but to more deeply rooted fundamental value differences between ministers and their congregations, such as attitudes toward those from differing ethnic, racial, or social groups; relational styles of aloofness or warmth; degrees of thirst for knowledge; optimistic or pessimistic views of the future; strategies for addressing cultural problems; or attitudes toward evangelism or missions. These characteristics are all components of the organizational climate.

Another way of describing a *positive* organizational climate is as a close, loving family. Not only does such an atmosphere of love and concern benefit the youth minister, but those congregations which exhibit the strongest sense of family are the most effective in promoting faith and loyalty among their members, according to a study conducted by Search Institute. The eight factors that contribute to this family atmosphere are—

1. A Hospitable Climate
2. Inspirational Worship
3. A Caring Environment
4. A Thinking Climate
5. Families Who Help Families
6. An Emphasis on Prayer
7. Intergenerational Service Efforts
8. A Sense of Mission[3]

Aspects of each of these factors are included in the nine items used to assess the organizational climate in which youth ministers serve. Those items and youth ministers' responses are recorded here:

Survey Item	Percentage of youth ministers who responded "strongly agree"	Percentage of youth ministers who responded "agree"	Percentage of youth ministers who responded "mildly agree"	Percentage of youth ministers who responded "mildly disagree"	Percentage of youth ministers who responded "disagree"	Percentage of youth ministers who responded "strongly disagree"
1. I learn a lot from the church I attend.	20	38	23	11	6	2
2. My church or organization is innovative.	20	30	27	12	8	3
3. The church or organization I serve expects people to think.	26	43	19	8	3	1
4. People who are different are valued in my church or organization.	16	35	28	13	6	2
5. My church is friendly.	29	44	20	5	2	0
6. My leaders encourage me to ask questions.	20	39	23	11	5	2
7. I am happy with the way things are going in my congregation or organization.	13	37	27	12	7	4
8. My church is not boring.*	28	31	16	15	7	3
9. Most of the staff of my church or organization want to be challenged about religious issues and ideas.	7	26	28	20	15	4

* This item was orginally worded "My church is boring." and was scored in reverse. For purposes of clarity to the reader, it is reworded in this table with scores reflecting the change.

Figure 10.1—Percent agreeing to positive organizational climate

Notice the low percentage of youth ministers who are able to emphatically agree to each of these measures of a positive organizational climate; none of them received "strong agreement" from even one-third of the participants. However, when the responses are totaled for both levels of "strong agreement" and "agreement" the results are more encouraging; at least one half of the youth ministers are able to indicate a positive response at this level to all of the items, with one exception—item 9 (see figure 10.1 on page 264). "Most of the staff of my church or organization want to be challenged about religious issues and ideas" receives the lowest levels of agreement (33 percent). This could be due to interpretation of the item; the word *challenge* may be a stumbling block. If ministers interpret this to mean a questioning or mistrust of the staff's theological views or interpretations, then it is understandable that they would not register strong agreement.

Even with this interpretation, however, the low scores are troubling. Challenges to one's theology should not be interpreted as negative. In fact, they are necessary encounters for mature faith, for both interrogator and interrogated alike. Christ received challenges to his teachings on a regular basis; he welcomed them and used them as opportunities to clarify truth. He instigated many a challenge himself, causing religious leaders and even faithful followers to examine what they believed, to attempt to defend their positions so their faith might be strengthened or their unorthodox beliefs exposed. Untested theological beliefs are those which have been embedded into our lives over time, but which may or may not be biblically sound. We believe them to be true just because we have *always* believed them to be true. Deliberative theology is what emerges from the ashes of a scorching examination of our beliefs; it is the gold, those nuggets of truth which endure the refiner's fire.

The pain of questioning one's beliefs

Deliberating upon one's theological beliefs can be a painful and frightening process. There is a greater sense of security when our beliefs are never challenged. In a sense, clinging to an embedded theological position and refusing to enter into a deliberate process of reflection is like putting a deadbolt on a cardboard shack. It may make us *feel* secure, but at anytime our house could be reduced to a pile of ashes or blown over in a sudden storm; the lock provides a sense of false security. The difference between embedded and deliberated theology has much in common with the manner in which the two builders selected the sites for their new homes, an incident related by Jesus.[4] The wise man builds his house upon a solid foundation, the Truth of the gospel, Jesus Christ. How does he *know* he is building on solid rock? He tests the soil to make sure, instead of merely assuming that it will hold. An embedded theology may very well prove to be based on a solid foundation, but the wise minister (Christian) will welcome a soil test!

It may be helpful to interpret youth ministers' understanding of item 9 ("Most of the staff of my church or organization want to be challenged about religious issues and ideas") in light of their responses to item 3, "The church or organization I serve expects people to think" (69 percent agree or strongly agree) and item 6, "My leaders encourage me to ask questions" (59 percent agree or strongly agree). The higher level of agreement to these statements suggests that ministers and congregants aren't expected to blindly accept dogma or policy which has been propagated from the top; reflection *is* valued, if not at the level of "challenge."

Significant differences

Significant differences exist between groups on their assessment of organizational climate. Figure 10.2 below shows how youth ministers from each of the denominations and parachurch groups evaluate the atmosphere surrounding their ministries. Receiving the highest marks are Assembly of God congregations, with youth ministers rating them significantly higher than Methodist, Lutheran, and Southern Baptist churches. Episcopal churches also receive significantly higher scores than these same three denominational groups. Without participating in the congregational life of each of these denominational groups, no valid assessment of these differences is feasible, nor would it be wise to speculate. It is strongly recommended, however, that each of these groups seek to discover a denominational entry point into which they might begin to address these perceptions about the climate surrounding their churches' ministries.

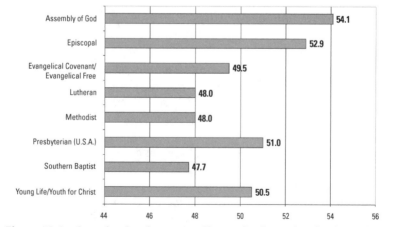

Figure 10.2—Organizational support climate, by denomination/organization

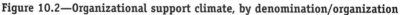

Size is another predictor of organizational climate: size of community, size of congregation, and size of youth group. The nostalgic view that the small country church is much warmer, friendlier, and more sincere than the big megachurch in the city is discredited by this study. Youth ministers in the largest congregations, with the largest youth groups, located in the largest cities, give their churches the highest ratings on the characteristics associated with a positive and stimulating organizational climate. Perhaps it is the negative organizational climate, the desire to do things the same old way, the resistance to change, that keeps these small churches and youth groups from attracting more members. (See figures 10.3, 10.4, and 10.5.)

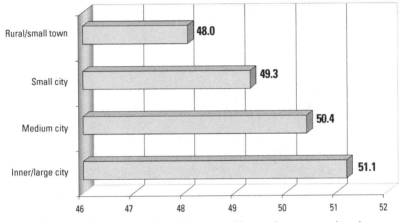

Figure 10.3—Organizational support climate, by community size

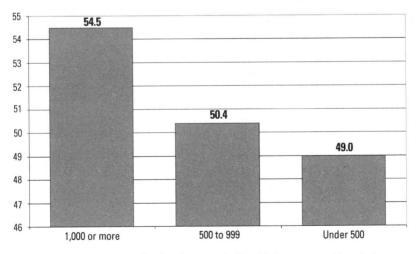

Figure 10.4—Organizational support climate, by congregational size

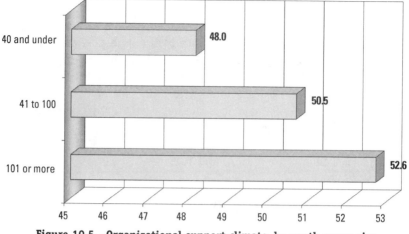

Figure 10.5—Organizational support climate, by youth group size

Community size is a significant predictor of a positive organizational climate. When comparing congregations, those found in inner/large cities receive higher standard scores than those in rural areas or towns. Even more important than community size, however, is the size of the youth group. Youth ministers with 101 or more students rate their congregations' organizational climate more favorably than those with 40 or fewer students. The greatest differences in standard scores are related to average Sunday morning attendance. Congregations of 1,000 or more receive scores that are higher than those with fewer than 500 in attendance. These findings are consistent with the "Five Shaping Forces" research, in which a sense of team (including a concern for people) was found to increase "with the number of youths and volunteer adult leaders in a group."[5]

Which of these variables is the greatest predictor of organizational climate? To gain a clearer understanding of the dynamics that have the most influence on this important item cluster, an Automatic Interaction Detection analysis was performed. As you will notice in figure 10.5, the results are fairly complicated, but they provide some excellent insight into those factors that are the greatest contributors to and detractors from positive organizational atmosphere.

The size of a congregation's youth group is the greatest predictor of its overall climate. The standard score for youth groups with more than 40 members is 51.3, compared to only 48 for those with 40 or fewer members. The larger the youth group, the more likely it is that the church is innovative and vibrant, open and accepting. Beyond youth group size, what other factors are the most important predictors of an organization's climate? Denomination or organization.

Youth for Christ and Young Life ministers with groups of 40 students or less are more likely to experience a positive organizational climate

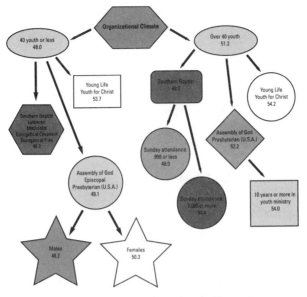

Figure 10.6—Organizational climate

than those in denominational youth groups. Their standard score rises from 48.0 to 53.7. Similarly, these same parachurch staff members have a higher standard score than denominational youth ministers when their youth groups are larger. It must be mentioned, at this point, that this item cluster "Positive Organizational Climate" is one for which distinctions between youth ministers in denominations and para-organizations is troublesome. (Refer to figure 10.1 on page 264) Three of the ten items in this cluster ask ministers to evaluate their church, and the remaining six call for an evaluation of church *or* organization. On other measures of support, we find the parachurch organizations to be very healthy, so there is no reason to believe that their organizational climates are *not* the most positive. It is just not a clean comparison for this particular item cluster. More important are the denominational differences.

Notice that, regardless of youth group size, Southern Baptist youth ministers find themselves among the least satisfied with the climate in their churches. This takes an interesting twist, however, when these ministers are serving in large churches. Southern Baptist youth ministers with large youth groups who *also* serve in large churches believe their churches to be intellectually challenging, innovative, and warm. Assembly of God and Presbyterian youth ministers who enjoy a tenure of ten or more years are also quite satisfied with their churches' character.

Another interesting observation can be made from youth ministers with small youth groups. For those in Assembly of God, Episcopal, and Presbyterian churches, female youth ministers report greater contentment in their churches.

The most important predictor of organizational climate is youth group size, and denomination/organization is a strong second.

Friendly churches?

A large portion of the youth ministers in this study view their churches as friendly (item 5, 73 percent responding either agree or strongly agree). This is heartening, but it is also somewhat puzzling. Consider the fact that only 51 percent (agree or strongly agree) say their church or organization values people who are different (item 4). One is left to wonder, *Friendly churches? Friendly to whom?*

Three other items in this assessment of organizational climate register lower percentages of agreement than item 4, but they are not nearly as disconcerting as these results. I believe this to be one of the most, if not *the* most, disturbing findings in the entire study. Why? Take a moment to consider what the church is called *to be* and *to do* by reading the Great Commission and the Great Commandment.[6] We are not given the freedom to select our own particular target audience or to narrowly define our church's demographic scope. We are called to imitate Christ, who was born, crucified, and resurrected for *all* people.

Picking and choosing based on an arbitrary standard is discrimination, and it is forbidden.

> **You are all sons of God through faith in Christ Jesus, for all of you who were baptized into Christ have clothed yourselves with Christ. There is neither Jew nor Greek, slave nor free, male nor female, for you are all one in Christ Jesus. (Galatians 3:8)**

> **My brothers, as believers in our glorious Lord Jesus Christ, don't show favoritism. Suppose a man comes into your meeting wearing a gold ring and fine clothes, and a poor man in shabby clothes also comes in. If you show special attention to the man wearing fine clothes and say "Here's a good seat for you," but say to the poor man, "You stand there" or "Sit on the floor by my feet," have you not discriminated among yourselves and become judges with evil thoughts? . . . If you really keep the royal law found in Scripture, "Love your neighbor as yourself," you are doing right. But if you show favoritism, you sin and are convicted by the law as lawbreakers. (James 2:1-4, 8-9)**

Could it be that nearly half of the churches and organizations in which our youth ministers serve do not keep the royal law, to love their neighbors as they love themselves? To gain a clearer understanding of how youth ministers responded to this item, percentage responses are shown by denomination and congregational size in figures 10.7 and 10.8 below. These two variables were selected because of their significant differences in standard scores on this item cluster.

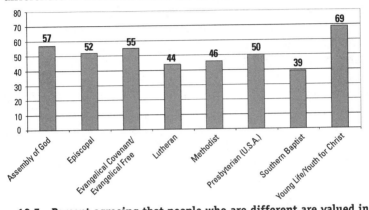

Figure 10.7—Percent agreeing that people who are different are valued in my church or organization, by denomination/organization

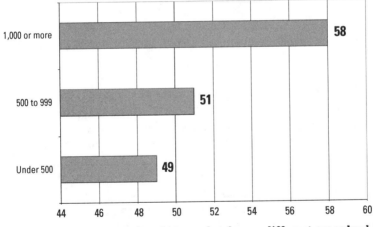

Figure 10.8—Percent agreeing that people who are different are valued in my church or organization, by congregational size

Of all the groups in the sample, the parachurch organizations appear to be the most accepting. It would be surprising if this were not the case, given their strong and narrowly focused evangelistic mission. Even with their percentage score higher than the sample mean, it is still disturbing that more than 30 percent of these respondents do not view their organizations as ones which value those who are "different." Notice the four denominations which fall below the mean percentage score of

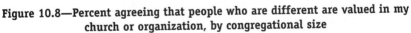

51: Presbyterians (50 percent), Methodists (45 percent), Lutherans (44 percent), and Southern Baptists (39 percent). If our churches and organizations are not modeling unconditional love, is it even conceivable that we might expect this Christ-like acceptance out of our students?

The 9 percent gap between the perceptions of youth ministers in the largest and smallest congregations is also very troubling. Congregations with fewer than 500 members account for approximately 66 percent of those in our sample, and only 49 percent of their youth ministers believe that these churches or organizations value those who are different. Think about the implications of this: *Most of our congregations are not modeling the love of Christ.* This could be one reason why these congregations *are* small, according to a comprehensive study on the causes of church growth by the Institute for Natural Church Development. From their research (1000 churches, 32 countries, six continents), universally applicable principles of church growth success were identified. One of the eight essential quality characteristics of healthy, growing congregations is the presence of loving relationships. This "research indicates that there is a highly significant relationship between the ability of a church to demonstrate love and its long-term growth potential."[7] Regardless of whether their efforts would or would not result in growth, these congregations need to seriously consider their treatment of one another, and the witness of their actions to the non-Christian world.

In the words of Roland Martinson, professor of pastoral theology and ministry at Luther Seminary, churches and Christian organizations need to be reminded that

> **The value of a relationship is not based on strength, skin color, denomination, or social class. It is based on the fact that we are all *imago dei*—created in the image of God. The purpose of these relationships is certainly to experience individual freedom and satisfaction. The purpose of these relationships is also to bring the generations together in such a way that they can care for one another. In doing so, the biggest challenge is going to be to allow the oldest among us and the youngest among us to give their gifts to one another.[8]**

CLUSTER
Supervisor's Personal Support

The relationship between the youth minister and the senior pastor is one of the most critically important measures of a ministry climate; it has the power to impact a young youth minister's success like nothing else. (This may be less true for parachurch youth ministers, who typical-ly operate with greater individual freedom in their ministries and whose ministry sites are generally not housed in the same location as their administrative offices.) Despite the common perception that senior pas-tors look down upon youth ministers and feel the need to constantly look over their shoulders, this is not at all supported by our data; their relationships appear to be very healthy:

Survey Item	Percentage of youth ministers who responded "strongly agree"	Percentage of youth ministers who responded "agree"	Percentage of youth ministers who responded "mildly agree"	Percentage of youth ministers who responded "mildly disagree"	Percentage of youth ministers who responded "disagree"	Percentage of youth ministers who responded "strongly disagree"
1. My senior pastor or supervisor shows an interest in what I am doing.	43	33	16	4	3	1
2. I feel trusted by my senior minister or supervisor.	48	36	9	4	2	1
3. Doing things in new and creative ways is appreciated by my senior pastor or supervisor.	33	39	18	5	4	1

Figure 10.9—Percent agreeing to supervisor's personal support

These percentages are representative of the entire sample, but sig-nificant differences do exist between denominations and organizations. Once again, Southern Baptist youth ministers rank at the bottom of the list, scoring significantly lower than those in Episcopal churches. (See figure 10.10 below.)

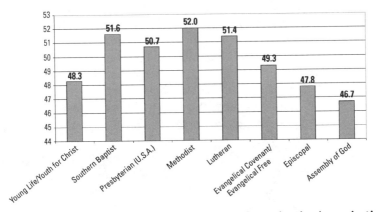

Figure 10.10—Supervisor's personal support, by denomination/organization

The good news is that regardless of age, gender, tenure, or size of community, congregation, or youth group, this level of support does not vary significantly. Youth ministers perceive high levels of interest and trust from their senior pastors and supervisors.

CLUSTER
Congregation's Personal Support

Youth ministry is one part of the body of Christ and needs the emotional, financial, and prayerful support of the rest of the body. Not only does this bless the youth ministry, but:

> **The gifts and support given to the youth ministry also fulfill needs the members of the congregations have in their own lives. People in all congregations want to be needed, and they love to be able to give what has been given to them. Getting the congregation involved and excited is a shared blessing for everyone.**[9]

How can congregations provide support for youth ministers?

- Lift up your youth ministers in prayer, and make them aware of your continued prayer support.
- Provide adequate financial compensation and benefits so they do not have the added stress of wondering how they will meet their obligations or provide for their family's needs.
- Treat them with the same level of respect you give to other adults instead of looking upon them as youth.
- Recognize that they are humans and that they will fail. Allow them to fail and offer forgiveness freely when they do.
- Do not place unrealistic expectations on their spouses or family members.
- Offer encouragement through phone calls, email messages, cards, or letters.
- Publicly recognize their accomplishments; affirm them often.
- Open your homes to them and offer them your friendship.
- Volunteer to assist them with the ministry, using the resources God has given you.
- Recognize their need for recreation and renewal and provide them with the time they need to refresh their souls.
- Provide a sabbatical, when appropriate, to allow them to study and grow personally and professionally.
- Treat them as you would like to be treated, if you were the youth minister.

As seen in figure 10.11, most youth ministers receive support and respect from their congregations (item 1). When the congregation is more narrowly focused on parents of youth, however, their sense of being valued and loved drops off (item 2), though 63 percent *do* indicate receiving this needed affirmation ("strongly agree" or "agree").

Survey Item	Percentage of youth ministers who responded "strongly agree"	Percentage of youth ministers who responded "agree"	Percentage of youth ministers who responded "mildly agree"	Percentage of youth ministers who responded "mildly disagree"	Percentage of youth ministers who responded "disagree"	Percentage of youth ministers who responded "strongly disagree"
1. I feel respected by the members of my congregation.	36	46	14	3	1	0
2. I feel valued and loved by the parents of youth.	19	44	29	6	2	0
3. I feel satisfied with the opportunities I have to use my abilities.	26	47	18	7	2	0

Figure 10.11—Percent agreeing to congregation's personal support

As is often the case, youth ministers with the largest youth groups experience the joys of service more often than those with fewer youth, this time in the form of congregational respect. Those with more than 100 students rate their level of support higher than those who average 40 or fewer young people. Ministers with 41 to 100 young people perceive their congregational support to be higher than those with fewer youth. There is a tendency, unfortunately, to associate professionalism with large numbers. It is easy for congregants to look upon the role of the youth minister as babysitting or merely "hanging out" if the group is small. When large numbers of teenagers participate in a ministry, adults begin to sit up and take notice. They develop a new respect for the ministers based on their own perceptions of teens. Adults tend to—

think disparagingly about teenagers in general, not just their own offspring. Probably every parent and teacher—not to mention every pastor and police officer—has muttered about the peculiar attitudes or misguided actions of youths. Part of this reaction undoubtedly results from personal experience. All adults know what they were like in the years between kidhood and adulthood. Hindsight should breed patience, but it rarely does. And patience is certainly valuable in dealings with teens, since it seems that youth is a step toward maturity that cannot be rushed.[10]

Even if these attitudes are unfortunate, they can yield greater respect and appreciation for youth ministers, simply because they can spend so much time with teenagers on a regular basis and actually survive! (See figure 10.12 below.)

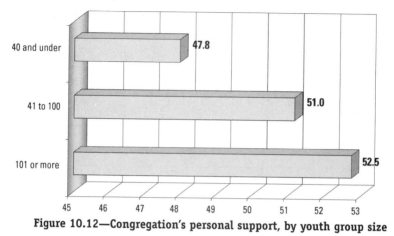

Figure 10.12—Congregation's personal support, by youth group size

Experience is also positively related to congregational support. (Highly significant differences occur between ministers who have served 16 or more years and those with four years of experience or less.) It is not hard to imagine that the most experienced youth ministers, who also report feeling more competent in their job performance and more confident in their abilities to lead (see chapter 9) would also enjoy greater attitudes of respect from their congregations. They have had more opportunities to gain the trust of the adults in their churches and organizations, thereby establishing themselves as credible ministers, worthy of their support. (See figure 10.13 below.)

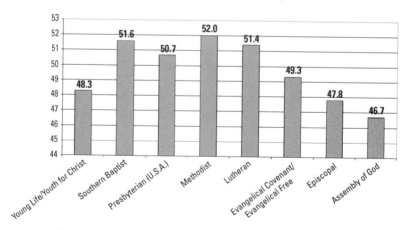

Figure 10.13—Congregation's personal support, by tenure

— youth ministry that transforms
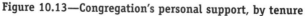

What can a youth minister do to earn greater support and respect from the congregation?

- Conduct yourself in a professional manner, and refrain from acting like a teenager.
- Always act with integrity and honesty; be a good steward of God's resources.
- Be vulnerable and open; admit your failures and ask forgiveness when appropriate.
- Be dependable. Do what you say you will do, when you say you will do it.
- Keep the lines of communication open; keep the congregation informed about what you are doing in your ministry.
- Live within your budget.
- Treat parents with respect; involve them in the ministry.
- Refrain from gossiping or complaining about other staff members, volunteers, youth, or their parents.
- Involve your youth in the life of the congregation.
- Look for opportunities to serve in other ministries in the church; participate in the life of the congregation.
- Fulfill the duties of a minister.
- Pray for the members of the congregation and let them know that you are lifting them up in prayer.
- Affirm and encourage others in tangible ways.

CLUSTER
Roadblocks to ministry

The best efforts of the youth minister will most likely appear ineffective if they are conducted in an atmosphere of hostility, competitiveness, or confusion. Conflict and tension, in effect, are roadblocks to successful ministry. This cluster consists of four items which represent ministry impediments; therefore, reverse scoring is used to identify which youth ministers experience the least amount of ministry roadblocks. It received the lowest overall grade on our organizational report card. It should be pointed out, however, that two of the items in the cluster refer to aspects of support for which the youth minister should assume higher degrees of personal responsibility than items in the other clusters: "Most of the people assisting in our youth ministry seem unclear as to the goals of our program" (item 3) and "Conflicts with coworkers hinder my ministry"(item 4). Responses to each of the items in this cluster are shown here:

Survey Item	Percentage of youth ministers who responded "strongly agree"	Percentage of youth ministers who responded "agree"	Percentage of youth ministers who responded "mildly agree"	Percentage of youth ministers who responded "mildly disagree"	Percentage of youth ministers who responded "disagree"	Percentage of youth ministers who responded "strongly disagree"
1. Considerable tension exists in our ministry.	4	9	19	21	33	14
2. Too much time and energy is spent getting things approved.	6	13	22	19	31	9
3. Most of the people assisting in our youth ministry seem unclear about our program goals.	3	8	20	26	34	9
4. Conflicts with coworkers hinder my ministry.	4	9	14	11	32	30

Figure 10.14—Percent experiencing ministry roadblocks

When 31 percent of the youth ministers are able to agree, even mildly, that their volunteers are not clear as to their ministry goals (item 3), it suggests that the minister has not taken the time to either involve them in the goal-setting process or adequately train them for their positions of leadership. Ministry is hampered when volunteer leaders don't understand its purpose. Doug Fields, in his book *Purpose-Driven Youth Ministry*, explains why this is so important.

> **Knowing why your youth ministry exists and having an articulated purpose statement will be of little value if you aren't communicating, driving, and supporting your purpose. The more people understand and rally behind your purpose, the healthier your ministry will become. This is where the true test of leadership will be played out...You must take on three responsibilities to make God's purposes known within your youth ministry: communicate the purposes, repeat the purposes, and make sure that key people memorize the purpose statement. Your purpose cannot become a common purpose until people know it. Until then you will be trying to build a ministry with misinformed, confused, and uncommitted players.[11]**

Youth ministers could significantly reduce their frustrations if they took the time to clearly communicate with their volunteer leaders.

These ministry frustrations are not unique to younger or more inexperienced youth ministers. In fact, the only significant group differences discovered from the data are between denominations or organizations—which should no longer be surprising!

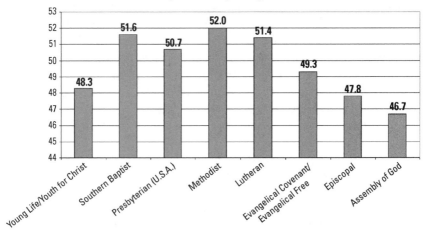

Figure 10.15—Roadblocks to ministry, by denomination/organization

Methodist youth ministers experience the most roadblocks to their ministry, significantly more than those in Episcopal and Assembly of God churches. Southern Baptist youth ministers also report frustration more often than their peers in Assembly of God churches. To understand these denominational differences, it is useful to look at how each of these groups respond to item 2, the greatest roadblock to ministry effectiveness: "Too much time and energy is spent in getting things approved". Of all of the participants, 18 percent agree or strongly agree with this statement. Responses by denomination and organization are shown in figure 10.16 below.

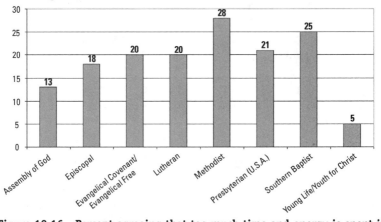

Figure 10.16—Percent agreeing that too much time and energy is spent in getting things approved, by denomination/organization

Church polity obviously determines how ministry decisions are made; the more red tape, the greater the frustration to the youth minister. Even though frustrating, it does not always have to be a negative, however. There is no way of knowing how many unwise decisions were short-circuited due to a procedural review required by a congregation. On the other hand, laborious systems of approval can be demotivating to a creative youth minister. Layers of approval, delays in decision-making, and obstacle courses of hoops and checkboxes can prevent timely action and keep youth ministers from being able to take advantage of some teachable moments. The Youth for Christ and Young Life organizations, due to the nature of their ministries, are able to act with much more spontaneity, free from some of these weighty constraints.

Conclusion

Youth ministers have historically received disparaging comments from the Christian community for a variety of reasons; you name the category, they have been negatively critiqued. Sometimes this criticism is justified and other times it isn't, but it can always be transformed into a positive experience. Consider the testimony of Mike Nygren, director of Student Leadership Ministries for Ginghamsburg Church in Tipp City, Ohio:

> **The position of youth leader is very visible, and many people keep a close eye on what we do. In the beginning I think I was intimidated by so many questions, by so many people questioning what we wanted to do "in the name of the Lord." I have now come to appreciate those people the most in the ministry. They have made the ministry stronger, they have made me stronger, they have encouraged me to do my homework more thoroughly, and they have caused me to "dream even bigger dreams of linking our teens with the needs of the world as seen through the eyes of Jesus.[12]**

In the same spirit of inquiry, it is time for the inquisitor's accusing finger to be pointed back at itself. According to this research, it is clear that the churches and organizations in which these ministries exist are in need of greater scrutiny and revitalization; while pointing out the specks of imperfection in the youth ministries, they have failed to notice their own lumbering faults.

The efforts of youth ministers will forever be stifled unless the Church comes to grip with its own negligence in being able to love as God loves. If the Christian community views youth ministry as an imperative, then new avenues of cooperation need to be constructed upon which youth ministers, their supervisors, congregations, denominations, and organizations can travel together toward common destinations.

THINK IT OVER, TALK IT THROUGH

1. Reflect on the organizational climate you have participated in that was most positive and stimulating. What factors seemed to contribute to this climate?

2. How do you think your ministry effectiveness been either strengthened or hindered as a result of the climate or support (or lack of it) in which you have worked?

3. If you could only choose one of the three positive conditions described in this chapter (positive organizational climate, personally supportive supervisor, personally supportive congregation) in which to work, which would you choose? Why?

4. What roadblocks to ministry have you experienced? How have they influenced your sense of support?

5. How can denominational/organizational cultures (vs. local church/ministry cultures) contribute to a sense of support or the lack thereof?

6. What sort of Youth Ministry Climate of Support Grade Card would you give the denomination or organization you know best?

Notes 10

1. Merton P. Strommen, *Five Shaping Forces: Using Organizational Dynamics to Do More with Less* (Minneapolis: Search Institute, 1980), 1.1-1.5.

2. To arrive at these letter grades, the following five-point grading scale was used: strongly agree—5 points (A); agree—4 points (B); mildly agree/mildly disagree—3 points (C); disagree—2 points (D); strongly disagree—1 point (F). For the item cluster "Ministry Roadblocks" the scale was reversed, and the grade reflects the degree to which ministers are free from these roadblocks in their churches and organizations.

3. Results of Search Institute study on "Effective Christian Education" reported by Peter L. Benson and Carolyn H. Eklin, cited in Merton P. Strommen and Richard A. Hardel, *Passing on the Faith: A Radical New Model for Youth and Family Ministry* (Winona, Minnesota: Saint Mary's Press, 2000), p. 158.

4. See Matthew 7:24-27 for Jesus' story of the wise and foolish builders.

5. Strommen1,4.

6. The Great Commission is found in Matthew 28:18-20 and the Great Commandment in Matthew 22:36-40.

7. Christian A. Schwarz, *Natural Church Development: A Guide to Eight Essential Qualities of Healthy Churches* (Carol Stream, Illinois: ChurchSmart Resources, USA edition,1996), 36.

8. Roland Martinson, "Getting to All God's Kids," *At-Risk Youth, At-Risk Church: What Jesus Christ and American Teenagers are Saying to the Mainline Church,* The 1997 Princeton Lectures on Youth, Church, and Culture (Princeton, New Jersey: Institute of Youth Ministry, Princeton Theological Seminary), 29-30.

9. Mike Nygren, *Missions and Youth Ministry, the Necessary Love Affair,* (self-published, Tipp City, Ohio: Ginghamsburg United Methodist Church), 56.

10. Quentin J. Schultze (project coordinator), Roy M. Anker (project editor), and others, *Dancing in the Dark: Youth Popular Culture and the Electronic Media* (Grand Rapids, Michigan: William B. Eerdman's publishing, 1991), 1.

11. Doug Fields, *Purpose-Driven Youth Ministry: 9 Essential Foundations for Healthy Growth* (El Cajon, California: Youth Specialties, 1998), 71.

12. Nygren, 57.

Gaining Broad Support

Chapter 11

Gaining Broad Support: Shared Ownership
Dave Rahn

In chapter 10 and now again in this chapter we are considering the broad support base that is essential for youth ministers to be fulfilled and their ministries to be effective. In our conceptual model of Transformational Youth Ministry, gaining broad support is an advanced—but necessary—value. The truth is that any approach to youth ministry that does not seek to cultivate support from significant stakeholders is destined to be short-lived.

If we step back from the research findings reviewed so far and simply ask the question, "Whose responsibility is it to minister to the young people in this community?" we will quickly conclude that the church must own this task. We will also agree that parents have been charged before the Lord with raising their kids to fear and honor God. With a little thought we may also realize that Christian teens don't simply want to watch youth ministry being done to them; they also want to step into their roles as co-ministers in the lives of their peers.

We designed one of the sections from our research survey to help youth ministers reflect upon items that may or may not be important to them. As a result we have learned that helping significant others share in the ownership of youth ministry is a pretty high value for many youth ministers. More specifically, attaining congregational support, helping parents minister to their teens, and giving young people ownership of the ministry are all important for youth ministers in America. Taken together these three imperatives testify to the practical wisdom of men and women who practice youth ministry. They recognize that they cannot bring about real transformation by simply executing youth ministry programs efficiently. There is no mechanical guarantee in youth work. In fact, if it takes a village to raise a child, youth ministers can identify the villagers who need to be on board with them if youth ministry is going to be at all effective. The entire church *must* be supportive. Parents *must* be involved. And young people themselves *must* agree that the youth ministry is worth their own investment.

Ripple effect
Perhaps more importantly, these three imperatives also signal a critical awareness of an underlying theological truth that needs to be operative

in any ministry. Ministry is never to be done in isolation, without regard for the consequences upon other people. The interdependent nature of the body of Christ has guaranteed that there is a ripple effect in ministry. What is done in the seemingly isolated environment of the church's teen room impacts the rest of the congregation and its family in direct and indirect ways. In fact, theological realities rather than empirical research are most likely to get our attention as imperatives of the church. After all, *must* is pretty strong language.

I know I didn't always understand this truth. Well-motivated and armed with a passion to conquer the world in Jesus' name, I savored my first full-time assignment with Youth for Christ after I graduated from college. I remembered praying that, if there were no one else committed to the task of youth evangelism, God and I would still form a majority partnership that couldn't be stopped. My dedication was sincere, but my theology was wrong-headed. In my desire to become a cowboy for Jesus I had unwittingly neglected others in the body of Christ who also need-ed to be involved in this great youth ministry calling. I acted as if I could actually do what God wanted me to do without church support, parental involvement, or even the partnership of young people them-selves. No wonder I began to burn out after four years of that pace. God never intended us to approach youth ministry—or any ministry—with such a Lone Ranger mentality.

It's comforting to know that so many of my youth ministry col-leagues seem to appreciate the importance of shared ownership in youth ministry. In this chapter we'll explore some of the findings that emerged from the portion of our survey labeled "evaluating their youth min-istry." In this section, youth ministers rated the relative importance of 21 statements by choosing from five response categories ranging from "extremely important" to "not important." Then they rated the degree of achievement they experience for each item by checking response options ranging from "extremely well" to "not at all."

It is from this section of the study that we have been able to learn how important it is to professional youth ministers that their youth ministries are broadly owned by others. Three different clusters from among these 21 items emerged from our first factor analysis to supply us with insights about the importance and achievement of congrega-tional support, the importance of helping parents minister to their teens, and the importance of giving youth ownership of the ministry. As we examine these findings in more detail, we'll also learn more about which youth ministers value this type of shared ownership the most, and which have not yet learned its importance.

CLUSTER
The Importance of Congregational Support

Three items in our survey cluster together to supply a reliable measure of the importance of congregational support to one's youth ministry.[1] As can be observed in the first response column below (see figure 11.1), three out of four youth ministers feel that this shared ownership of their youth ministries is at least "very" important—if not "extremely" important—to them. In fact, the second response column helps us understand that for only about one in ten youth ministers is shared ownership only "somewhat" important.

Survey Item	Percent indicating that this was either "extremely" or "very" important	Percent indicating that this was either "not" or "somewhat" important.	Percent indicating that this was being achieved either "extremely" or "very" well.	Percent indicating that this was being achieved either "not at all" or "somewhat" well.
1. Gaining church support for youth activities.	77	7	54	19
2. Helping youth feel loved and respected by their congregation.	72	11	39	30
3. Leading the congregation to place a high priority on youth ministry.	76	9	43	28

Figure 11.1—Importance and achievement of congregational support

This finding regarding declared importance suggests that the field of youth ministry is indeed maturing as youth ministers recognize the value of being tied into the larger body of Christ. Even parachurch organizations recognize the importance of increased connection to congregations. When Youth for Christ transitioned out of their rally focus in the 1950s to concentrate their efforts on teen clubs, the role of the professional staff person demanded that they become youth experts. These youth ministers poured their energy into direct ministry with teens, encouraging them and training them in all sorts of creative ways. Today's Youth for Christ staff person values building healthy partnerships with churches, so that the mission of evangelism among teens in the community is mutually shared. Years of operating as isolated experts have taught them that the task is too large to tackle on their own. Unless churches share in the ownership of the ministry there is little likelihood that Youth for Christ's mission will be accomplished.

Given the wide support for the importance of congregational support in youth ministry, how well is it realized? Not very well, according to the third and fourth columns in the above table.

From looking at this table, we can see that though congregational support is clearly important for the majority of youth ministers, not as many feel that they are realizing this support. About one of every four feels that this support is at best being realized only "somewhat" in their ministries.

What do we know about those youth ministers for whom this is either not as important, or for whom congregational support is not as readily achieved?

For one thing, we have learned that a youth minister's denominational background accounts for a lot of the differences observed in this matter of congregational support (see figure 11.1). We have come to expect that small, even significant differences between youth ministers from different organizational backgrounds aren't surprising. But the standard score variation between Presbyterian youth ministers and those from the Assembly of God represents a difference of more than 40 percent between their respective mean scores! These two groups are certainly unlike one another in their form of governance, and that may account for much of the difference between responses. For instance, it may be that youth ministry within the Presbyterian and United Methodist traditions depends on more formal congregational approval to operate than does that from an Assembly of God background.

Historical emphases within denominational families could also contribute to creating a culture where congregational support may be explicitly valued. In Wyckoff's early discussion of the role of objectives in Christian education (see chapter 5), the Presbyterians, Methodists, and Episcopalians all seem to embrace a vision of Christian education that is owned by the entire community of believers. Knowing that this 40-year old analysis did not address all participating groups in our study doesn't diminish the observation that historically held values may help us to understand the reason for some of the differences youth ministers express with regard to the importance of congregational support in their ministry.[2] For now it is noteworthy to observe that youth ministers from an Assembly of God background will likely value the importance of congregational support less than do other youth workers.

Perhaps we can understand these denominational distinctions by studying the significant difference that exists between youth ministers with different theological orientations (see figure 11.2 on page 289). Those who are theologically liberal indicated that congregational support is more important to them than did those who are theologically moderate. Moderates, in turn, considered this matter significantly more important than did theological conservatives. The standard score difference between theological liberals and conservatives on this matter represents about a 15 percent variation between their respective mean scores.

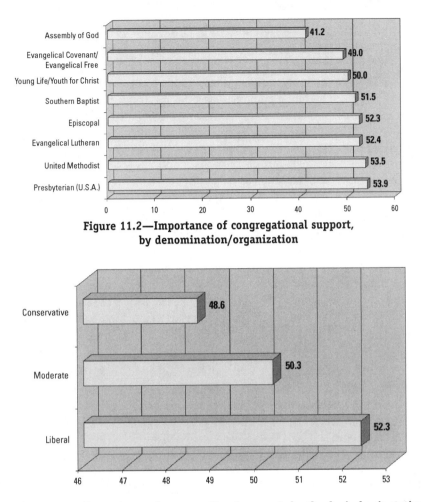

Figure 11.2—Importance of congregational support,
by denomination/organization

Figure 11.3—Importance of congregational support, by theological orientation

How should we interpret these findings? It is not hard to imagine that youth ministers of more conservative theological persuasion, like those from an Assembly of God background, may feel generally content with the call and support they experience personally from the Lord and his Word. Two features of evangelical conservatism include the very high view of Scripture and the insistence that each person must enter into a personal relationship with Jesus Christ for salvation. The practice of personal disciplines such as Bible reading and prayer—while observed by many in mainline denominations—may reflect the more private and personalized approach of conservatives as they experience their relationship with God. If such people feel personally led by God into their role as a youth minister, congregational support may be esteemed as desirable but unnecessary.

The fact that these differences of importance with regard to congregational support split along theological lines suggests that there is more at stake here than merely the practical (funding?) benefits of having one's youth ministry program supported. Does a conservative theological orientation place so much emphasis on one's personal relationship with God that our corporate interdependence is undervalued? Or, to frame the question in the reverse light, does a liberal theological orientation emphasize our collective identity in Christ, perhaps to the neglect of one's personal relationship with God? No doubt readers from each theological orientation will frame the question as it suits them, but the fact that we all must reckon with—and interpret—is that those with a more liberal theological orientation place a higher value on, and realize a higher degree of, congregational support than do those with more conservative convictions.

Of course a personally meaningful faith, where a relationship with God is practiced and valued daily, does not necessarily have to result in a privatized expression of that faith and ministry. In fact, faith is both an individualized practice and a communal exercise. Bonhoeffer's observation that "the last independent act I committed was when I became a Christian" testifies to this reality.[3] But if some youth pastors are certain that God has called them into youth ministry, then cultivating congregational support may be perceived by them as a wearisome burden rather than an essential ministry requisite. To further continue this line of reasoning, such youth ministers may feel—given the certainty of their call from God—that it is also more important that they spend their time in direct ministry with young people, helping *them* to enter into this same essential relationship with God, then it is to build complicated bridges of support with the congregation.

On the other side of the continuum it is reasonable to assume that in a more liberal theological tradition the call to youth ministry is experienced through the very practical expression of congregational support. In fact, this support may have the effect of *validating* your ministry if you are a youth minister tipping towards a more liberal theological orientation. Without the emphasis of more private experiences with God to depend upon, congregational support may be viewed as an essential condition for one's ministry.

There is yet another explanation worth exploring as we try to understand why congregational support might be more important to some youth ministers than it is to others. Churches that emphasize intergenerational approaches—including family ministry strategies—are likely to view congregational support as a necessity rather than a worthy option. Is it a coincidence that many of the earliest writers about family-based youth ministry have been from more mainline denominational backgrounds?[4]

The responses of those who thought congregational support was important to their youth ministries significantly correlated ($r = .56$) with those in our research who also identified the importance of helping parents minister to their young people.[5] Helping parents is a natural expectation where there is general congregational support for youth ministry. This cluster of items will be considered in the next section; it, too, falls under the "shared ownership" umbrella that collected together as a result of our second factor analysis.

CLUSTER
The Importance of Parental Involvement

Youth ministers have been challenged in recent years to consider how to reckon with the reality of family influence in their ministry to young people. Some versions of this ministry still put the burden of teen influence upon the youth ministry professionals, while other approaches feel that parents have this main role and it ought not be usurped.[6] Mark DeVries' *Family-Based Youth Ministry* calls youth ministers to two priority strategies: empowering parents, and equipping the church for the role of extended family.[7] Ben Freudenberg described the church's role as "equippers of families" in calling youth ministers to rethink youth and family ministry.[8] And more recently, Mert Strommen and Dick Hardel have published a plan for "a radical new model of youth and family ministry" that includes as one of its key features the need for congregations to strengthen family relationships. Drawing on an impressive and extensive body of research, this facet of the model identifies four strategies for strengthening family relationships and four strategies to help foster close relationships to God within the family. All eight of these strategies are identified below:

Strengthening Family Relationships
- parental harmony
- effective communication
- wise parental control
- parental nurturing

Fostering Close Relationships with God within the Family
- becoming Gospel-oriented parents
- communicating moral values
- being involved in service activities
- sharing faith at home[9]

How effective have these voices been at convincing youth ministers that equipping families for ministry is something they ought to be doing? Our research draws upon a highly reliable cluster of eight different items to measure the importance that youth ministers felt about helping parents minister to their own kids.[10]

Imperative of Parental Involvement

Survey Item How important is the following to your youth ministry?	Percent of respondents who indicated that this was "extremely important"	Percent of respondents who indicated that this was "very important"	Percent of respondents who indicated that this was "quite important"	Percent of respondents who indicated that this was "somewhat important"	Percent of respondents who indicated that this was "not important"
1. Helping parents become more involved in the lives of their children.	36	34	17	11	2
2. Providing opportunities for teens and parents to interact.	16	32	26	21	6
3. Strengthening family relationships.	38	35	18	7	1
4. Helping parents recognize and adopt wise methods of discipline.	14	26	24	25	10
5. Encouraging families to teach service as a way of life through their involvement in helping activities.	23	33	24	15	6
6. Gaining parental involvement in the ministry.	32	35	20	11	1
7. Giving special assistance to parents coping with non-traditional family issues.	11	28	32	23	7
8. Helping youth and their parents deal with conflict.	19	40	29	11	1

Figure 11.4—Imperative of parental involvement

It is clear from the preceding table that there seems to be more support among youth ministers for helping parents *generally* than there is for *specific* parent-training strategies. For each of three broad items ("helping parents become more involved in the lives of their children," "strengthening family relationships," and "gaining parental involvement in the ministry"), approximately seven out of every ten youth ministers could agree that the item was at least "very important" to their youth ministry.

On the other hand, when behaviors increased in specificity, youth ministers expressed that it was not as important to them. Two items describing more particular behaviors—"helping parents recognize and adopt wise methods of discipline" and "giving special assistance to parents coping with nontraditional family issues"—received less widespread support. Only four of ten indicated that these statements reflected something that was at least very important to their youth ministry. In fact, approximately one of every three youth ministers indicated that these items were only *somewhat important* to them, if they were important at all.

This observation makes one single item fascinating to scrutinize. Over half (56 percent) of all those surveyed indicated that it was at least very important to their youth ministry that they "encourage families to teach service as a way of life through their involvement in helping activities." While one out of every five youth ministers didn't feel that this was as important to their ministry, the specificity of this item and strength of support suggests that this is a high value worthy of further exploration. Youth ministers' intuition about the value of such activity upon a family seems well-founded. In their discussion of this element of youth and family ministry, Strommen and Hardel cite the results of Search Institute's "Effective Christian Education" study to make the point that involvement in service to others is a very significant predictor of faith maturity, contributing more than Sunday school, Bible studies, or worship services.[11]

How should these findings be represented? Youth ministers are largely supportive of the idea of helping parents minister to their youths. Indeed, if they registered opposition to such a goal it may be like voting against motherhood itself! But the framework of such support is still under construction, so that it's not as easy to conclude that every particular approach to helping parents may be deemed important by youth ministers.

It is time for some clear thinking about what parents are both entrusted and equipped to do in the faith formation of their children. Moses' instruction to Israel's moms and dads supply a compelling standard for us all:

> **Hear, O Israel: The Lord our God, the Lord is one. Love the Lord your God with all your heart and with all your soul and with all your strength. These commandments that I give you today are to be upon your hearts. Impress them on your children. Talk about them when you sit at home and when you walk along the road, when you lie down and when you get up. Tie them as symbols on your hands and bind them on your foreheads. Write them on the doorframes of your houses and on your gates.[12]**

If our kids are going to let their faith in Jesus become the central operational filter of their lives, they must see evidence of its all-of-life relevance. There are very few settings that can address this agenda more effectively than a Christian home dedicated to helping each family member follow Jesus with passion. The call by Moses to live faith with integrity and openness is a call for parents to participate in strategic ministry.

It's possible that youth ministers are unaware of some of the research that can inform specific ways of helping parents minister to their teens. For example, many youth ministers may not know that parents who are active in sharing their faith openly among family members have been over 30 percent more effective (on average) in helping their teens display ten desirable characteristics of committed youths.[13] And even though a regular dialogue with a teen's father has been shown to be directly related to mature faith, only 5 percent of Protestant youths currently experience this interaction.[14] Informed youth ministers can help parents understand what sort of efforts will be most effective as parents minister with their teens. The resources are certainly available today. And it ought to be clear that if youth ministers are genuinely interested in helping young people experience Christ-centered life transformation they must enter into meaningful partnerships with parents. It is a sign of health and hope that so many youth ministers already seem to appreciate this fact.

As with the earlier related cluster of congregational support, this issue involving shared ownership of parents also reveals some differences between youth ministers from different denominational backgrounds (see figure 11.5). Southern Baptists are significantly more interested in helping parents minister to their youths than are Presbyterians, youth ministers from evangelical and fundamentalist churches, Episcopalians, and those from the Assembly of God. In order to make sense of the standard scores reported below, it may be helpful to note that the difference in mean scores between Southern Baptists and Episcopalians represents nearly 25 percent; the difference between Southern Baptists and Assembly of God represents nearly 38 percent; and the difference between Episcopalians and Assembly of God youth ministers is about 18 percent. As was true for the matter of congregational support, Assembly of God youth ministers indicate that helping parents minister to their youths is significantly less important to them than it is for their colleagues from other denominations.

This relatively diminished sense of importance that Assembly of God youth ministers have for helping parents minister to their youths is consistent with their ranking with regard to the importance of congregational support. But this consistency does not make it a less puzzling finding. In fact, when I asked Monty Hipp, former national director of youth ministries for the Assembly of God, to help me understand this finding, he was also perplexed:

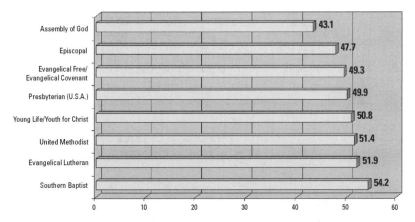

Figure 11.5—Importance of parental involvement, by
denomination/organization

**I am not sure as to why. It could be that the senti-
ment in the youth world in the AG is often a bit
negative towards families. The reason is that they
run into parents that are not in church and who
have some concerns as to the programs they run in
the youth circle. But to see the dramatic difference
is a surprise. I am concerned at your findings.[15]**

Monty's insight provides us a clue for interpreting this finding. We
know that no youth ministers report that "nurturing spiritual development" is either more important (chapter 4) or being achieved better
(chapter 5) than do those from an Assembly of God background. As
should be recalled from those earlier discussions, this cluster includes
statements such as "helping youths make a commitment to Jesus
Christ." If these youth ministers routinely encounter opposition from
non-Assembly parents as a result of their evangelistic zeal, it may help
us to understand why parental partnership is not as high a value for
them.

CLUSTER
The Importance of Youth Ownership

Protestant youth ministers in America have a nearly universal conviction that youths need to have ownership of the ministry. We come to
that conclusion on the basis of responses to the two different items
clustering to measure the importance that youth ministers attach to
helping youths' own ministry.[16]

Survey Item	Percent of respondents who indicated that this was "extremely important"	Percent of respondents who indicated that this was "very important"	Percent of respondents who indicated that this was "quite important"	Percent of respondents who indicated that this was "somewhat important"	Percent of respondents who indicated that this was "not important"
1. Giving ownership of our ministry to the youth.	42	36	15	6	1
2. Enabling youth to be involved in ministry.	51	37	10	2	0.1

Figure 11.6—Imperative of youth ownership

Veteran youth ministers have long appreciated how enthusiastic young people are in their patterns of attendance and participation when they feel like they own the ministry. "Those who care will be there." Ownership is the process of helping persons feel a stake in the outcome.

I remember the year I learned this lesson. I had decided that, rather than following my own plans for a fall kick-off, I would enlist a team of students to make all of the major decisions. They figured out where we should host our hamburger feed. They set attendance goals, determined the date and time, and made recommendations about what kind of program we should have. When there was a need for publicity, they were effective promoters. Because our goal was to expose as many new kids as we could to the ministry of Campus Life, they prayed deliberately and specifically. Then they invited those they prayed for. Their excitement ensured that the event would be successful. When it came time to actually have our great feast, they were deeply invested. If it fell short of our goals, they would feel the pain as much as—if not more than—me. After we realized that we had met our goals their celebration was genuine; they had earned the right to be proud of their efforts.

I have since seen the pattern of ownership dynamics repeat itself in countless untold ways. When the kids who are a part of a small group feel ownership they work to make it the best group possible. If they're coming out of a sense of obligation to the youth minister they won't attend long. When kids catch a vision for the potential of a trip or retreat, their enthusiastic support practically guarantees that the activity will be a winner. When teens decide that it would be a great thing for a bunch of them to find creative ways to serve the elderly in their community, their ownership will ensure that leaves get raked and walks get shoveled.

This principle of ownership is seen everywhere. Years ago, writing for those in business management, Maier represented the dynamic components in a formula. Only slightly adapted from that original form, it suggests that the *effectiveness* of any decision (goal, plan, etc.) is ultimately related to the *quality* of the decision times the *ownership* of those stakeholders who will be required to carry out the decision.[17] This adapted formula is represented below:

$$E_d = Q_d \; X \; O_s$$

Youth ministers seem to appreciate the fact that they cannot expect to be ultimately effective without the ownership of teens. This is true even if their ministry efforts represent the highest quality. The reason is clearly embedded in the formula above. If the participation of youth who are legitimate stakeholders in the ministry is necessary for the youth ministry to be truly effective, then their ownership is critical.

While the matter of giving youth ownership of the ministry is widely held as very important, it is nonetheless significantly *less* important to the oldest youth ministers than it is to all others (see figure 11.7). The standard scores below represent a difference of nearly 14 percent between the mean scores of the youngest and oldest youth ministers.

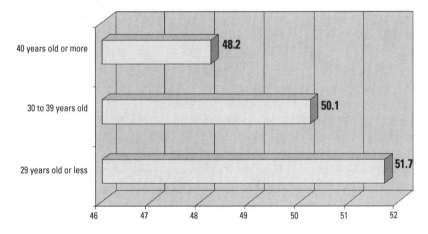

Figure 11.7—Importance of youth ownership, by age

Statistically significant differences of a less practical significance are also found between three other groups of youth ministers. The fact that youth ministers with the greatest experience value youth ownership significantly less than all others parallels the age-related distinctions that we have just discussed. Apparently the importance of youth ministry ownership is also more widely held by those with post-collegiate—including seminary—education, than it is by those who are only college educated. Given the fact that seminary-related training for youth ministers is a relatively recent development, it may be fair to describe the segment of youth ministers least likely to value youth ownership of the ministry as experienced, over 40 years old, and without seminary training.

I can offer a limited perspective that may shed some light on this age-tenure-training distinction. While I began my direct ministry with young people in the early '70s, it wasn't until a decade later that I began to appreciate and cultivate youth ownership of the Youth for Christ ministry I was leading. Not coincidentally, this value was born in graduate-level classes where I had a chance to develop more fully the theological foundations of my ministry. I am also suggesting that—at least in my segment of the youth ministry world—the idea of helping youths own ministry got popular attention in the early '80s. Perhaps the importance of youth ownership in ministry is a "given" for all of those who have entered the profession of youth ministry since; it certainly seems to be a high value for those on the scene today.

As many practical reasons as there are for cultivating young people's ownership of the ministry, there are also important theological issues at stake. All of us who are members of the body of Christ must grow into the responsibility of assuming our God-given role to minister to one another. There is nothing in God's word to suggest that teens should be excluded from this privilege because of their age. Rather they should be nurtured in the faith so that they can assume their responsibilities; this is the path for all of us in the Church. Teens can fairly be expected to embrace the ownership, not just of delivering their friends to youth meetings, but of exercising a ministry of influence in the name of Jesus Christ.[18] In so doing they will be equipped to assume meaningful leadership roles in the church.

Summary

Youth ministers in America want their congregations to be invested in their ministry to young people. They also want to help parents be successful with their teens, and want teens to demonstrate that this ministry is not something that happens *to* them, but rather something that happens *with* them. The fact that there are three clusters of items in our survey that collected together into a larger cluster suggests that each of these themes have a unifying thread that ties them all together. It is this thread that we have chosen to label "shared ownership."

Protestant youth ministers have matured. They have come of age. They recognize that building a youth ministry around charismatic personalities and fun programming is inadequate to accomplish what is really important. Instead, these youth ministers seek to build coalitions and partnerships with congregations, parents, and the young people themselves. There is no need to convince most youth ministers about the importance of these multiple stakeholders feeling a real ownership of the ministry. They recognize it for what it is: an imperative of the Church.

But that doesn't mean that they couldn't use a little help in bringing these important outcomes to realization.

1. In the last chapter we looked at the importance of personal support from the congregation. In this chapter we examined the importance of congregational support for youth ministry. How do you see the differences, and which is most important to you?

2. What are the difficulties we may encounter when we try to gain parental involvement in youth ministry?

3. Measures of *importance* are never black and white, yes or no considerations. Do you think it's likely that for some youth ministers, parental involvement simply isn't important *enough* for them to overcome the difficulties they encounter when they make an effort? How do such matters grow in importance for youth ministers?

4. Create a descriptive profile of a youth ministry where the young people have very little sense of ownership and compare it with a descriptive profile where the opposite is true.

5. Imagine that you are leading the youth ministry in one of the denominatons or parachurch organizations where measures of importance were not as high as you'd like. How could you bring about change in this value?

1. r = .77.

2. D.C.Wyckoff, *Theory and Design of Christian Education Curriculum* (Philadelphia: West minster Press, 1961), 72-75.

3. Dietrich Bonhoeffer, *Life Together* (San Francisco: Harper & Row, 1954).

4. See Mark DeVries, *Family-Based Youth Ministry* (Downers Grove, Illinois: InterVarsity Press, 1994) and Merton P. Strommen & Richard A. Hardel, *Passing on the Faith: A Radical New Model for Youth and Family Ministry* (Winona, Minnesota: Saint Mary's Press, 2000) for the genealogies of such approaches to youth ministry.

5. r = .56.

6. Dave Rahn, "Parafamily Youth Ministry," *Group* (May/June, 22:4, 1996): 36-39.

7. DeVries.

8. Rick Lawrence, "Why Youth Ministry Should Be Abolished," *Group* (July/August, 21: 5, 1995).

9. See chapters 2 and 3 of Merton P. Strommen and Richard A. Hardel, *Passing on the Faith: A Radical New Model for Youth and Family Ministry* (Winona, Minnesota: Saint Mary's Press, 2000).

10. r = .89.

11. Strommen and Hardel, 94-96.

12. Deuteronomy 6:4-9.

13. Strommen and Hardel, 98-99.

14. Peter L. Benson and Carolyn H. Eklin, *Effective Christian Education: A National Study of Protestant Congregations* (Minneapolis: Search Institute, 1990), 57.

15. Monty Hipp in an email response to Dave Rahn on April 14, 2000.

16. r = .78

17. Adapted from Norman Maier, *Problem-Solving Discussions and Conferences: Leadership Methods and Skills* (New York: McGraw-Hill, 1963), 3-9.

18. Dave Rahn and Terry Linhart, *Contagious Faith: Empowering Student Leadership in Youth Evangelism* (Loveland, Colorado: Group, 2000), 14-24.

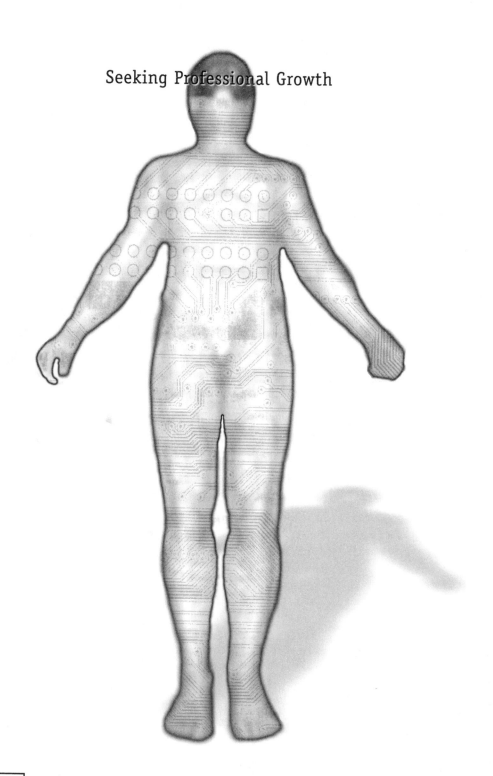

Seeking Professional Growth

Chapter 12

Seeking Professional Growth: Desired Training
Dave Rahn

It is time to cap off our conceptual model of *Transformational Youth Ministry*. The focus of this chapter ought to lead denominational and parachurch youth ministry leaders, pastors, educators, and congregational leaders to a research-based blueprint for training youth ministers.

It was in the spring of 1994 that I began to appreciate the fact that youth ministry training was becoming more complicated than ever before. That was the year that Sonlife—an organization dedicated to providing church-based ministry training to champion the Great Commission—convened a summit of the various youth ministry professors within their network. Some of those gathered had asked Sonlife for permission to teach some of their seminars in the context of their academic classes in youth ministry. This request left Sonlife's leadership scratching their heads. If college and seminary profs were going to teach the Sonlife Strategy Seminar, what role should Sonlife play in the training of youth ministers?

A mushrooming number of training organizations
Given the way that youth ministry has developed, this question is not insignificant. A great deal of youth ministry training that has taken place during the last quarter of the twentieth century has been delivered through organizations that have been largely created for this purpose.

Youth Specialties provides their yearly National Youth Workers' Conventions for thousands of full-time and volunteer youth ministers. They also conduct day-long resource seminars that tour the country, helping to equip approximately 20,000 youth workers annually. Add to all of this their vast historical publishing of books, magazines, and curricular resources, and it's not hard to agree that they have played a major role in youth ministry training.

Sonlife ranges in a bit of a different direction, having entered into semi-formal "endorsing denomination" relationships that tend to make their training officially approved by some denominations. The Evangelical Free Church and Evangelical Covenant Church—both participating in this research project—have had such an affiliation with Sonlife. The scope of Sonlife's multi-level training moves from philosophy overview to more focused leadership training, all with a view toward helping youth ministries become more purposeful.

Reach Out Ministries (Barry St. Clair) and *National Institute of Youth Ministry* (Jim Burns) have also been long-time participants in youth ministry training. And there have been robust training efforts that have emerged from mainline backgrounds, including *Center for Youth Ministry* (Paul Hill), the *Youth and Family Institute* (Augsburg College), *Youth Ministry Forum* (Princeton Theological Seminary), and *Joshua Force* (Fr. Chuck Reischman of the Episcopal Church).

Group Publishing has emerged as a significant contributor in the last few years, providing a national ministry convention and service-oriented workcamps in addition to their book and magazine publications. *National Network of Youth Ministries* has promoted the strategic value of working together in local communities. In fact, there are more and more groups dedicated to delivering specialized training to youth ministers. *Dare to Share* will help youth ministers train their teens in verbal witnessing skills. Youth ministers wanting to improve their speaking skills may choose to invest in Ken Davis' *Dynamic Communicators Workshop*. *Adventures in Missions* is but one of a number of organizations that help serve youth ministers who want to take their teens on short-term mission projects.

Each of these organizations contributes something to the youth ministry training smorgasboard. But they don't begin to tell the whole story. There has been a tremendously influential scope of resource training that parachurch youth ministries (Youth for Christ, Young Life, Campus Crusade for Christ, Fellowship of Christian Athletes, Youth With a Mission, etc.) have contributed. And, in various degrees, denominations have often promoted their own development courses for their youth ministers. Some of this training has been routed through denominationally approved seminaries and colleges; some has taken the form of continuing education and networking.

It doesn't take a rocket scientist to come to the following conclusion: Youth ministry training is a de-regulated industry with a free-enterprise approach that has spawned a richness of available options for youth ministers. While this environment may create some occasional confusion about *who* should provide *what* type of training to *whom*, the saturation level certainly ensures that youth ministers can get all of the training they need, right?

That's the sort of question we want to answer in this final chapter.

Difficulties of getting training in a new profession

There is a complexity to youth ministry that is reflected in the kind of professional growth desired by those who work with young people. Some of the variation stems from confusion that is the natural consequence of a discipline that is relatively new and still evolving. As Kenda Dean has pointed out, there have been many resources to help those who see their task as "doing youth ministry" but training is less available for those who wish to "pastor youth."[1]

Another explanation for the differences in desired training among youth ministers may be that there is a hierarchy to the skills that must be developed for long-term youth ministry effectiveness. Just when a youth minister in her mid-twenties starts to get comfortable with the family of relational skills she needs for the job, her group's numerical growth demands that she become skilled in programming. After a few years it becomes clear that she must also find ways to multiply her leadership through other people. These three skills alone—relational, programming, and multiplication—are not naturally related to one another. This means that transitions between the different phases of youth ministry may be bumpy indeed. Sounds plausible, doesn't it?

"May be," "could be," "what if"... this language is all too common in making youth ministry assertions. What do we really know about the kind of professional development resources that youth ministers in America want?

The youth ministers in our study were asked to identify how much each of 40 different items would contribute to their professional growth or to their greater effectiveness. Our survey used the following three different headings to divide items: "training that equips me to:", "greater knowledge or understanding of:", and "opportunities for me to:". After performing our original factor analysis we found that the items in this section of our study had formed eight different clusters that, when taken together, help us understand something about the nature of the training desired by persons in professional youth ministry:

Eight clusters: Explicitly identified professional development needs
- Communicating Biblical Truth
- Understanding Adolescent Development and Counseling
- Effective Ministry Strategies
- Biblical Knowledge and Pastoral Ministry Skills
- Knowledge of Family Development and Parental Training Skills
- Training in Administration and Management
- Opportunities to Gain New Ideas
- Opportunities for Peer Mentoring Relationships

In the bulk of this chapter we will explore the findings represented by these eight different clusters. They represent the *explicitly identified professional development needs* of youth ministers in America, and a great place to begin when formulating a training curriculum.

We will then draw upon the insights from earlier chapters to discuss how those *implicitly identified professional development needs* for American youth ministers inform our professional development plan. As a result, we will design an outline of the most clearly reasoned map for youth ministry professional development that has ever been available.

Training Need 1
Communicating Biblical Truth

Youth ministers recognize that their task exceeds their own capabilities. They must do more than offer attractive meetings, build winsome relationships, and design comprehensive programs. They must help bridge the gap between students who seldom read and the truth of Scripture. In fact, they must learn how to be skilled and reliable in their own handling of "the word of truth" (2 Timothy 2:15) so that they can communicate it to teens and let the Holy Spirit use it in the transformational process. The life change we seek in youth ministry can only be brought about as God works through various means toward his purposes. Like the psalmist, youth ministers understand that "unless the LORD builds the house, its builders labor in vain..." (Psalm 127:1a).

Six items in our survey clustered together around the idea of training that would assist the youth minister in handling biblical truth.[2] As can be observed from figure 12.1, a majority of youth ministers indicate a desire for training that will help them with some aspect of this task.

Survey Item I want training that equips me to:	Would contribute to my professional growth or effectiveness "very much"	Would contribute to my professional growth or effectiveness "quite a bit"	Would contribute to my professional growth or effectiveness "somewhat"	Would contribute to my professional growth or effectiveness "very little"	Would contribute to my professional growth or effectiveness "not at all"
1. Communicate the gospel.	34	32	24	9	1
2. Lead groups more effectively (discussions, Bible studies, planning).	24	36	27	11	2
3. Create meaningful Bible studies and educational experiences.	29	40	23	7	1
4. Think theologically when facing ministry issues.	21	33	31	12	3
5. Communicate clearly in speaking and writing.	23	29	29	14	5
6. Nurture youths' spiritual walk.	35	43	19	3	.3

Figure 12.1—Desired training in communicating biblical truth

Developing Adult Volunteers

Notice that while there are two items in this cluster that are explicitly related to communication skills (items 1 and 5), there is a difference in how youth ministers register their desire for each training. This gap may provide the key for interpreting the findings of this cluster. Communicating the gospel is a more complex task than clear communication. It is also more directly related to the matter of spiritual development.

As was identified earlier in the book, nurturing the spiritual development of young people is one of the top priorities of Protestant youth ministers in America. And, though it is also the outcome that is being achieved to the greatest degree, it appears that there is a hunger for improvement with regard to this task.

At any rate, when approximately 78 percent (see item 6, figure 12.1 on page 306) of youth ministers indicate that they strongly desire training for nurturing youth's spiritual walk they are likely testifying to the imprecision of the work that is most important to them. Youth ministry is—at a practical level—more of an art than a science. Christian growth in someone's life is as much a wonder to behold as it is an explainable result of deliberate behaviors. To return to the original question, we are more able to describe the dynamics of effective communication in general than the mysterious process whereby the gospel takes hold in a young person's life.

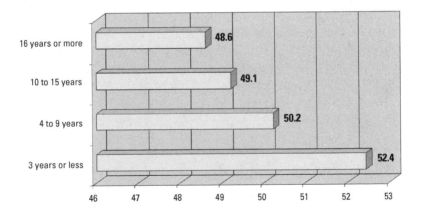

Figure 12.2—Training interest in communicating biblical truth, by tenure

While there is a strong general desire for training that helps youth ministers communicate biblical truth, we are also able to identify some particular groups who identify this need more prominently than others. The most significant difference can be observed between youth workers according to their level of youth ministry experience. Those with a youth ministry tenure of three years or less are much more likely to identify a desire to be trained in skills of biblical communication and nurture than are those at all other levels of experience (see figure 12.2). It is noteworthy to observe that the gap between the highest and lowest standard scores as recorded below represents aabout a 15 percent difference between the mean scores of those youth workers with the least experience and those with the most experience in youth ministry.

What else do we know about those who desire training that will help them communicate biblical truth in life-changing ways? According to the correlations from our research, a significant number also want to be trained in the basics of pastoral ministry, desire additional knowledge in adolescent development and counseling, and they want to be able to implement effective ministry strategies.[3]

Training Need 2
Understanding Adolescent Development and Counseling

A mother calls in tears. "Can you help me with my son? He's just learned that his father has been involved in homosexual activity and that's what led to our divorce. I'm afraid that Andy isn't handling his anger and confusion very well."

Youth ministers are not unaware of the developmental complexities facing the young people with whom they minister, but that doesn't mean that a phone call like the one above won't take their breath away. Chances are pretty good that their own memories of navigating through the turbulence of mental, social, moral, and physical development as teens aren't hard to recollect, but there are some encounters our experiences don't come close to preparing us for.

After the years of exposure that the writings of major theorists have been given, youth ministers have no reason to be unaware of the fundamental contributions of some common names with respect to adolescent development.

- Piaget located the all-important transition from concrete operational thinking to formal operational thinking at the beginning of adolescence.[4]
- Eriksen theorized that the most meaningful developmental task for teens is their search for personal identity[5], a task imaginatively captured by Sabatelli in the word "individuation."[6]
- Elkind described the "the imaginary audience" as a factor guiding teen social behavior.[7]
- Kohlberg connected moral reasoning skills to thinking skills in general, but didn't offer much help in understanding the connections between thinking morally and acting morally.[8]

And our own observation confirms another reality: physical changes that take place at the onslaught of puberty are significant enough in themselves to declare this time of life legitimately chaotic.

Aren't there more recent contributions to shed light on adolescent development?

There were three items in our survey that formed a sub-cluster describing this knowledge and training need among youth ministers.[9] The table below reveals the relative strength of this desire for each of the items.

Desired Training in Understanding Adolescent Development and Counseling

What is it that youth ministers really want when they indicate a desire for increased knowledge and understanding of adolescent development? Are they unfamiliar with the nearly common knowledge of the theorists described above? Or do they find that they need to do better at integrating such knowledge into practically helpful insights for their jobs?

Survey Item I want training that equips me to/or gives me greater knowledge of:	Would contribute to my professional growth or effectiveness "very much"	Would contribute to my professional growth or effectiveness "quite a bit"	Would contribute to my professional growth or effectiveness "somewhat"	Would contribute to my professional growth or effectiveness "very little"	Would contribute to my professional growth or effectiveness "not at all"
1. Counsel both youths and parents.	26	38	27	7	1
2. Moral development and factors that make for morally responsible living.	21	38	30	9	1
3. Child and adolescent development and the issues to be faced in addressing developmental goals.	12	30	40	15	3

Figure 12.3—Desired training in understanding adolescent development and counseling

Support for this latter interpretation comes from the fact that desired understanding of adolescents also correlated with an expressed need for training in counseling skills. Youth ministers have no doubt learned from their experience with teens to appreciate the wonders and mysteries of human development, especially as so many important transitions seem to converge during the second decade of life. As is true with so many issues in the urgency-driven, pragmatic world of youth ministers, the *So what?* question supplies the compelling reason for needing to learn more. Why should youth ministers learn more about adolescent development and moral decision-making? In order to better coach, counsel, and assist young people and their parents as they encounter some of the frustrations that accompany such growth. When knowledge can be put to use in our immediate context, it is considered a premium value. So, for example, to access the commonly presented notion of *adolescent egocentrism* so that it's actually helpful in the midst of a conversation with a teen is a more ambitious desire than simply wanting to understand adolescent development facts.[10]

Which youth ministers are most interested in this type of training and/or understanding? Those who have been on the job for three years or less. They expressed their desire for understanding the developmental issues of adolescents significantly more than those who have had the most experience in youth ministry. In fact, the difference between standard scores represents about a 13 percent margin between the desire of those with the least experience and those with the greatest in this area of professional development:

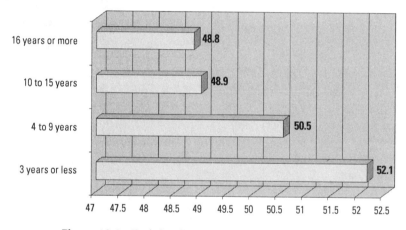

Figure 12.4—Training interest in adolescent development and counseling, by tenure

It should come as no surprise that those with the least experience may often register the greatest desire for professional growth. There's a lot to learn in the field of youth ministry, and the varied expertise required to do the job well is not quickly attainable.

Training Need 3
Effective Ministry Strategies

There are a number of tasks that compete for the attention of youth ministers. Besides building relationships with teens, they must cultivate adult relationships, plan and administrate effectively, develop teams of volunteers, speak, teach, counsel, train, write, program, budget...and much more! As youth ministers engage in these various activities they are often guided by a philosophical model, a template that helps them figure out how much emphasis to put into these various tasks. As we have already seen from chapter 4, this sense of direction was identified as the top priority for the youth ministers in our study.

Certain youth ministry models are explicitly identified and promoted aggressively in some youth ministry circles. Included among these are: purpose-driven youth ministry, Sonlife, student-led cell groups, campus clubs, youth churches, and family-driven youth ministry. Whatever strategy youth ministers are committed to helps them understand how they can balance the competing demands for their time. Models are constantly being developed by innovative youth ministers who are compelled, not just by the limitations of their time, but by the desire to maximize the effectiveness of their efforts.

Models and their making

How does this work? Consider briefly the task of youth evangelism. Someone committed to following Doug Fields' model will most certainly understand youth evangelism in relation to the concentric circles of different types of young people needing attention. Those Christians in the innermost circles, the core students, are to reach out to those who are in the outermost circles, those who are part of the crowd.[11] Sonlife-trained youth ministers may come to a similar conclusion, but they use a pyramid structure to help explain the different types of kids they work with, and they describe a process whereby growth-level teens might become ministry-level teens who are then equipped to reach out to their non-Christian friends.[12]

By way of contrast, those committed to student-led cell groups will develop their entire outreach strategy around small-group structures. Adults will play a more active role in such groups than those where kids are helped to establish Christian campus clubs as a basis for reaching out to friends.[13]

Pete Ward labels each of the above models as Inside-Out, insofar as they typically begin with Christian students and try to help these teens evangelize outside of their natural circle of friends. Some of his advocacy for youth churches is due to the natural consequence of an alternative model—one he labels as Outside-In. He would argue that youth evangelism must seek to go into subcultures where the gospel has not been established, to essentially plant churches. This requires an initiative of incarnational investment by adults among teens.[14]

There's a lot at stake for youth ministers as they decide what strategies will guide their efforts. Will their philosophy be coherent, that is, will it be logically defensible? Will their model satisfy their need to be faithful to biblical values? Can they make it work in a way that's doable by persons without the Superman emblem across their chest?

Our research reveals a cluster of four items that, when taken together, forms a highly reliable measure[15] of youth ministers' desire to grow in their understanding of a balanced ministry. Each of the four items contributing to this cluster, and the strength of the responses made, is represented here:

Desired Training in Effective Ministry Strategies

As can be readily observed in items 1 and 2, the practical, how-to dimension of youth ministry is the greater felt need of the youth ministers in our study. Over 60 percent of youth ministers value this type of knowledge (at least "quite a bit")—making it more desirable than a conceptual understanding of youth ministry models. No wonder we see so many how-to book titles promoted in youth ministry!

Survey Item Greater knowledge or understanding of:	Would contribute to my professional growth or effectiveness "very much"	Would contribute to my professional growth or effectiveness "quite a bit"	Would contribute to my professional growth or effectiveness "somewhat"	Would contribute to my professional growth or effectiveness "very little"	Would contribute to my professional growth or effectiveness "not at all"
1. How to plan a balanced youth ministry.	25	35	30	9	1
2. How to train youth in peer ministry.	23	43	26	6	1
3. Various youth ministry models.	16	33	36	13	2
4. Myself and my ministry.	19	32	34	13	2

Figure 12.5—Desired training in effective ministry strategies

In recent years, student-to-student ministry models have received considerable attention, and the significant support for training in peer ministry confirms that youth ministers' interest remains high for such help. Teens today are asked to lead worship teams among their friends, plan and lead campus Bible clubs and prayer groups, lead cell groups, and take greater responsibility for peer evangelism. Youth ministers would like help equipping their teens for such tasks.

One of the four components to Strommen & Hardel's youth and family ministry model is to intentionally establish a Christian youth subculture. Peer to peer ministry is at the heart of their strategy.[16] Based upon an earlier research project I have promoted student leadership as a ministry of influence.[17] Both of these recent publications point to the interest youth ministers have in incorporating peer ministry strategies within their overall approaches. It is not surprising that youth ministers in our study want to understand how to best train students for these various roles.

Who expresses the greatest training interest in effective ministry strategies? As has been true for desired training throughout this section, those with the least experience in youth ministry are hungriest for this kind of understanding; the differences between those with 3 years or less and all others are significant. In fact, the difference between those with 4-9 years of experience and those with 10 or more years in youth ministry is also significant, as can be seen in figure 12.3. The standard scores of 53.4 and 47.5 represent more than a 22 percent difference in the mean scores of those youth ministers with the least and most experience.

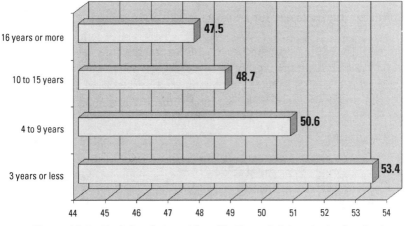

Figure 12.6—Training interest in effective ministry strategies, by tenure

A significant difference is also seen between respondents who work in either Youth for Christ or Young Life and those whose ministry is through the Assembly of God. Those from Youth for Christ/Young Life express a significantly greater desire for training in effective ministry strategies than fellow youth ministers from the Assembly of God. The standard scores of 52.4 and 48.3 represent a 16 percent difference in these two groups' mean scores. Is this greater desire reflective of the nature of para-church groups whose focus on evangelistic mission has them constantly wondering how to accomplish their task more effectively?

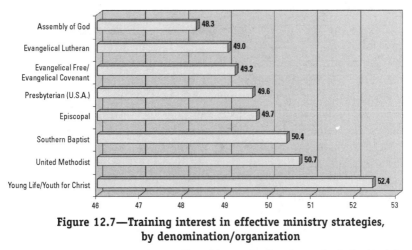

Figure 12.7—Training interest in effective ministry strategies, by denomination/organization

Additional factors showing statistically significant differences are found among youth ministers' who desire additional training in effective ministry strategies. While the practical implications of these differences may not be great, they seem to support the profile we have of those most interested in arriving at effective and personally fulfilling ministry strategies. A summary of the differences between groups is listed below.

Groups differing in desire for training in effective ministry strategies

Apparently education helps lessen the expressed need of youth ministers for training in effective ministry strategies. Why? Education creates space for students to explore personal and professional matters, so they can intelligently commit to a ministry direction that works *for them*.

These groups...	...indicated greater desire for this training...	...than these groups
theological conservatives & moderates		theological liberals
without seminary training		with seminary training
high school education or less		college education or more
college education		post-collegiate education
working in rural or town settings		working in large or inner cities

Look at the specific response items that form this effective ministry strategy training cluster (see figure 12.5 on page 312). How much youth ministry interest in the training described by item 1 can be attributed to the concept of "balance"? Item 4 supports the notion that an effective ministry strategy is a personal matter. Our planned approach *to* youth ministry affects our personal fulfillment *in* youth ministry. No wonder a having clear sense of direction is a top priority for youth ministers (see chapter 4). My personal life and ministry strategies meet together in *me*—they *must* complement one another if I am to be truly effective. Good education will strengthen this professional and personal integration.

Training Need 4
Biblical Knowledge and Pastoral Ministry Skills

For many youth ministers, both the means and desired ends of ministry are derived from the Bible. A lot of the counseling they do is not seen so much as a set of psychologically-informed listening skills as it is the ability to offer theological insights that help youth negotiate the demands of modern adolescent life. Pastoral skills are often connected to knowledge of the Bible. Even those formal pastoral functions in which youth ministers occasionally participate—such as weddings, funerals and baptisms—require some ability to draw on theological understanding and administer scriptural insights.

Three items in our survey formed a sub-cluster with a high degree of measurement reliability.[18] They address the overlap between the need to understand theology and biblical content and the need to employ basic pastoral skills—including counseling—in ministry. The fact that these three items correlated significantly with one another to form this sub-cluster helps us to understand that youth ministers feel the need to put their biblical insights to work in their jobs. The relative degree of this felt need for each of the items is reflected in the figure 12.8 below.

Survey Item Greater knowledge or understanding of:	Would contribute to my professional growth or effectiveness "very much"	Would contribute to my professional growth or effectiveness "quite a bit"	Would contribute to my professional growth or effectiveness "somewhat"	Would contribute to my professional growth or effectiveness "very little"	Would contribute to my professional growth or effectiveness "not at all"
1. Theology	21	31	33	13	2
2. The Old and/or New Testaments	27	31	28	12	2
3. Counseling and the basic skills related to a pastoral ministry	23	39	28	9	1

Figure 12.8—Training interest in biblical knowledge and pastoral ministry skills

Those persons with three years or less in ministry expressed a significantly greater desire for this kind of training than did those with more tenure in youth ministry. When examining these results in figure 12.9 note that the difference in standard scores between the least experienced and the most experienced represents an 18 percent difference between their mean scores.

Those with college degrees (standard score, 51.6) express a 14 percent greater desire for this type of training than do those at post-college education levels (standard score, 48.0). While not all post-graduate education is of the seminary variety, it is very likely that this difference is also reflected in the distinction between those without seminary training (standard score, 50.7) and those with seminary training (standard score, 49.0). After all, much seminary training focuses on just this type of biblically informed pastoral ministry.

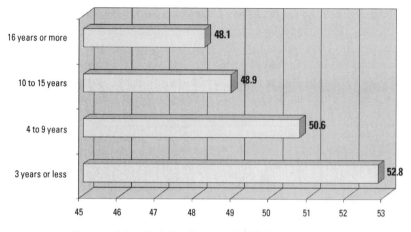

Figure 12.9—Training interest in biblical knowledge and pastoral ministry skills, by tenure

Training Need 5
Knowledge of Family Development and Parental Training Skills

Youth ministers find themselves facing greater challenges as the American family continues to experience erosion with regard to its role as the central building block of our society. Families used to be able to draw upon their own healthy and successful past as resources for current dilemmas; many families today have no experience of health upon which they can build. Where can they turn for their needed help?

Many youth ministers are beginning to appreciate the potential role they may play in this crucial arena of ministry. When they reckon with the powerful learning environment of the family they rightly conclude that cooperation and partnership is needed on behalf of teens. More and more help is becoming available. Among the most useful is Mert Strommen and Dick Hardel's new book, *Passing on the Faith: A Radical New Model for Youth and Family Ministry*. In this work the authors seek to explore the interactive effect of the family, the congregation, the community and culture upon ten desired outcomes in the faith formation of teens. By drawing upon the best research available, this model offers extensive hope to the youth minister who wants to learn more about how to help parents in their family development responsibilities.

Does this type of help represent a felt need in the professional development of youth ministers? Do youth ministers agree that the stakes are sufficiently high for them to think expansively about how the scope of their ministry must include more meaningful intervention with families? Frequency of responses to the three items forming this cluster indicate substantial interest from over 50 percent of those in our research for this type of greater training (see figure 12.10 below).[19]

Survey Item Opportunities for me to:	Would contribute to my professional growth or effectiveness "very much"	Would contribute to my professional growth or effectiveness "quite a bit"	Would contribute to my professional growth or effectiveness "somewhat"	Would contribute to my professional growth or effectiveness "very little"	Would contribute to my professional growth or effectiveness "not at all"
1. Family development, the dynamics of which characterize various family systems and their ministry needs.	44	39	15	2	.5
2. Training parents in parenting	29	38	25	7	1
3. How to train adults for mentoring.	14	27	38	18	3

Figure 12.10—Desired training in family development knowledge and parental training

Southern Baptists, Youth for Christ and Young Life staff persons, and United Methodists all express a greater desire (over 16 percent) for this type of understanding and expertise than youth pastors from the Assembly of God (see figure 12.11 on page 318). Given a similar finding reported in chapter 11, we recognize that more youth ministers within the Assembly of God tradition may limit their role to a direct ministry with young people.

Training Need 6
Administration and Management

As the profession of youth ministry grows, as churches have become more complex in their operations, as numbers of students involved in youth ministry increase, the expectations upon many youth ministers intensify. Today's youth ministers must recruit, screen, and train volunteers, delegate tasks effectively, and multiply their ministry through others. Even the job interests that have been expressed so far in this chapter can complicate a ministry focus. Their variety leads to a desire for increased training in the kind of administrative and management skills that will help them to meet many difficult—but worthy—expectations.

Six items formed a cluster that describes the expressed need for this kind of training among the youth ministers in our study.[20] How intense was the expression of this need? figure 12.12 identifies the strength of the responses for each item in this professional development cluster.

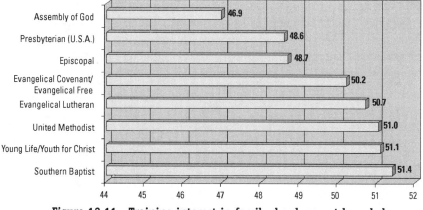

Figure 12.11—Training interest in family development knowledge
and parental training, by denomination/organization

Survey Item Training that equips me to/or gives me greater knowledge of:	Would contribute to my professional growth or effectiveness "very much"	Would contribute to my professional growth or effectiveness "quite a bit"	Would contribute to my professional growth or effectiveness "somewhat"	Would contribute to my professional growth or effectiveness "very little"	Would contribute to my professional growth or effectiveness "not at all"
1. Become a better administrator.	19	28	35	14	4
2. More effectively manage my time.	25	29	30	13	3
3. Make use of computer technology for ministry.	26	33	28	11	3
4. How to delegate job tasks, roles, and responsibilities.	24	35	30	10	2
5. How to use a small group of peers or friends to meet my needs for accountability.	15	32	33	16	3
6. How to use interns effectively.	18	32	29	14	7

Figure 12.12—Desired training in administration and management

At first glance it seems fair to observe that about half of youth ministers feel the need for the kind of training that will help them with practical tasks of management and administration. Simple enough to see, now it's time to move on, right? Yet there may be an indicator of the health of youth ministers contained in one of the item's responses. Better than one out of five respondents feel little or no need to receive training in "how to use interns effectively" (item 6). While it is not surprising that so many youth ministers do not experience this advanced opportunity to multiply themselves as a felt need, it is interesting that half of those surveyed expressed interest in this kind of professional development. We'd like to suggest that such an expression is not likely to come from youth ministers who are so overwhelmed by the tyranny of their normally undone tasks that they cannot lift up their eyes to the expansive vision connected with using interns. In this case, the expression of the desire to learn how to use interns effectively may be a wonderful sign of health and maturity for the youth ministry profession.

Who is the most interested in receiving professional development assistance in management and administration? It should come as no surprise that it is those youth ministers working in the largest congregations (see figure 12.13). Greater numbers often require systems and policies to ensure that communication is accurately transmitted across the board. Advanced budget preparation, forecasting, long-range planning, recruitment strategies, computer networking, work requisitions, and countless other details often accompany the day-to-day operations within large churches. Such an environment necessitates advanced skills in administration and management. The difference between the standard scores of youth ministers working in congregations greater than 1000 and those working in congregations less than 500 represents a 14 percent variation between scores.

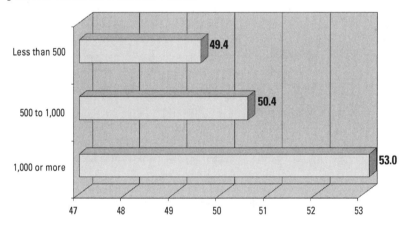

Figure 12.13—Training interest in administration and management, by congregation size

It makes sense—as it has for every expression of professional development—that youth ministers who are youngest are the ones most interested in management and administration resource help. As they "learn the ropes" they soon recognize the limitations of working without help.

As motivated as I was in my earliest years of ministry, I could not do all that was required of me when the ministry experienced fruitful growth. It became clear that I could not personally provide personal relational influence to all of the young people who were hungry for such interaction. Every answer to this crisis pointed to my need to find and develop new people who could join me in my mission. As soon as those people became a part of my ministry team, I discovered I needed to adjust my personal planning patterns to accommodate their need to be prepared. I needed to redouble my communication efforts so that we could operate effectively and without confusion. My volunteers needed resources that I didn't need, training and opportunities that I had long before received. I found that I had to invest myself in efforts that were not immediately and clearly connected to my direct ministry with kids. My youthfulness may have temporarily masked my awareness of my administrative deficiencies, but I became alert to my needs soon enough, well before I was 29 years old.

Similarly, the youngest youth ministers in our study express a greater desire for training in management and administration than those who are the oldest; the standard score differences between these two groups represents an 11 percent gap (see figure 12.14).

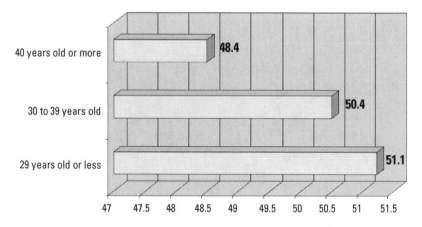

Figure 12.14—Training interest in administration and management, by age

Three other sources of variation in desire for this type of training by youth ministers are not as naturally explained. The standard score variation between youth ministers working in Youth for Christ/Young Life and those working in the Evangelical Lutheran Church in America represents a difference of 28 percentiles (see figure 12.15). The gap between those identifying themselves as theologically conservative and those theologically liberal represents a difference of 20 percentiles (see figure 12.16). And the standard score distinction between men's and women's desire for assistance in administration and management repre-sents a 14 percent difference (see figure 12.17).

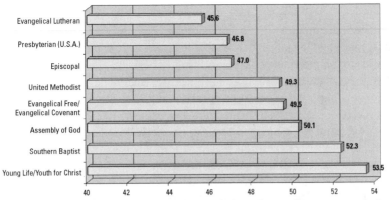

Figure 12.15—Training interest in administration and management, by denomination/organization

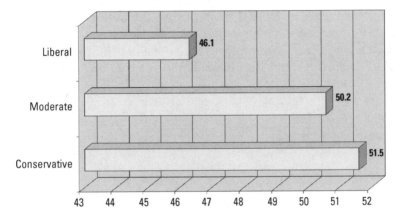

Figure 12.16—Training interest in administration and management, by theological orientation

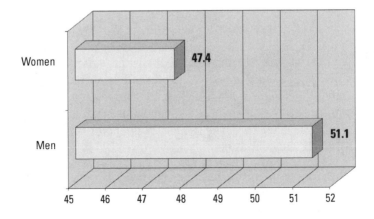

Figure 12.17—Training interest in administration and management, by gender

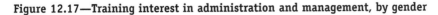

Is there a common thread between these groups that can help us understand why these differences fall in the way that they do? Can it be a bias toward a programmatic orientation, where "success" is an important value and measured in no small way by observable indicators? Those who work with such an orientation may want skills that multiply their effectiveness through other persons.

At this point we employed the Automatic Interaction Detection analysis to help us understand which of the above variables were most significant in accounting for the different levels of interest expressed between groups with regard for administration and management training. By doing so, we learned that the key factor in explaining the differences had to do with gender.

Subsequent breakouts in this sophisticated computer analysis helps us to understand the rest of the story. While the standard score for all women in their desire for administration and management training is 47.4 (see figure 12.18), the score drops to 46.9 for those women working in congregations less than 1000. But it jumps to 52.7 for those women working in congregations greater than 1000. This variation between women according to congregation size represents a 22 percent difference in their expressed desire for this sort of training.

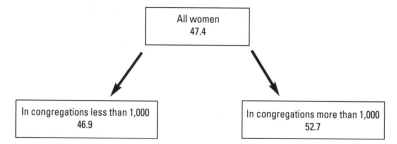

Figure 12.18—Women's desire for administration and management training

So what factors are the greatest predictors of variation for male youth ministers in their desire for this sort of professional development? Unfortunately, the answers are a little more complicated for men. The most significant factor for them is the denominational affiliation in which they work. After that, the secondary predictor varies from denomination to denomination.

For example, in figure 12.19 below, we can see that while men working as youth ministers in the Assembly of God register a standard score of 53.7, it goes to 55.4 for those 29 years old or less. For the youngest youth ministers in the Assembly of God who happen to work in large cities or their suburbs it increases to 58.7.

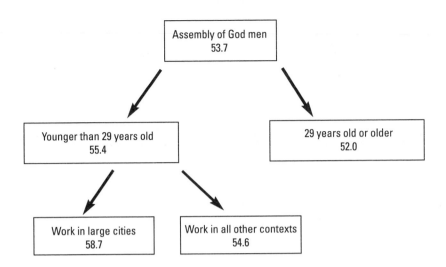

Figure 12.19—Assembly of God men's desire for administration and management training

Figures 12.20, 12.21, and 12.22 trace similar breakdowns for youth ministry men who are Southern Baptist, Evangelical Lutheran, and a collapsed group of United Methodist, Young Life and Youth for Christ men. As can be seen, the key factor for Southern Baptists is the length of time the men have served in ministry. For each of the other groups the critical issue is the average number of youth participating in the ministry.

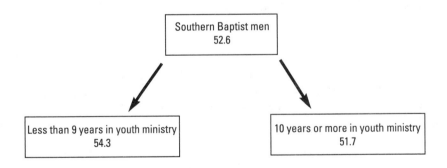

Figure 12.20—Southern Baptist men's desire for administration and management training

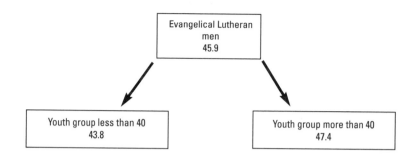

Figure 12.21—Evangelical Lutheran men's desire for administration and management training

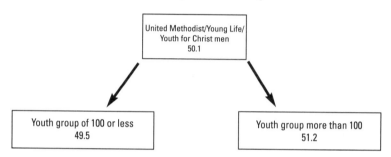

Figure 12.22—United Methodist, Young Life, and Youth for Christ men's desire for administration and management training

This information is a marketer's dream! If I wanted to design a seminar that would assist youth ministers with their administration and marketing skills, it is now clear who would be most receptive to my training pitch. Women working in congregations over 1000, young men who are Assembly of God urbanites, and Southern Baptist men who have been on the job for nine years or less could all be prime candidates for this particular professional development opportunity. On the other hand, don't bother calling on Evangelical Lutheran Church in America men with small size youth groups—it doesn't seem that administration and management holds much interest for them.

Training Need 7
Opportunities to Gain New Ideas

Under the wide heading of professional growth and development many youth ministers attend conferences, workshops, and purchase resource material for the express purpose of filling their creative reservoirs. In 1999 Youth Specialties' two National Youth Workers' Conventions hosted more than 10,000 volunteer and professional youth workers. This same organization began when their founders collected youth ministry ideas from experienced youth workers, collated them, and published them in an easily accessible form. Volumes of *Ideas* continue to be solid sellers for Youth Specialties, and even express as a formalized outcome one of the tangible benefits of professional networking.

Three items from our research survey clustered together to help us understand the degree to which youth ministers desire more of these idea-gathering opportunities.[21] The response frequencies to each of the items (see figure 12.23) reveal the strength of this resource and networking need.

Survey Item Opportunities for me to:	Would contribute to my professional growth or effectiveness "very much"	Would contribute to my professional growth or effectiveness "quite a bit"	Would contribute to my professional growth or effectiveness "somewhat"	Would contribute to my professional growth or effectiveness "very little"	Would contribute to my professional growth or effectiveness "not at all"
1. Gain new ideas.	44	39	15	2	.5
2. Network with other youth ministers.	29	38	25	7	1
3. Review and purchase resource materials.	14	27	38	18	3

Figure 12.23—Training interest in opportunities to gain new ideas

There is not much doubt about the fact that youth ministers universally feel the need for new ideas. Their ministry demands constantly tax their creative energies. The burden is not just to come up with meetings each week that hold the interest of kids. Sometimes youth ministers want a change of pace for their own soul. And why not? The median tenure of the youth ministers in our study is about 8 years. If they average 50 preparations a year (they likely have more responsibilities than that) by the time they're into their 8th year of ministry they have invested themselves in at least 400 different meetings or activities, each one involving young people whose tolerance for radio talk instead of music compels them to switch stations in an instant. This MTV crowd is a tough bunch. No wonder 83 percent of youth ministers could use some new ideas.

It also is clear that more youth ministers feel a greater need to expand their professional networking (perhaps as a means to getting these new ideas) than to purchase additional resource materials. Perhaps this desire to purchase new resources is tempered by the concern over limited money. After all, 44 percent of youth ministers are at least "somewhat concerned" that their youth ministry programs do not receive enough funding. One out of five youth ministers feel very little need for additional resources provided by publishers, etc.

The fact that those with the least amount of youth ministry experience express the need for idea-gathering opportunities to a significantly greater degree than do their more seasoned colleagues suggests that the need is not the result of Idea Burnout. In fact, it's more likely that less experienced youth ministers simply need to learn some of the "tricks of the trade." The variation in mean scores between those with 3 years or less on the job and those with 16 years or more is 14 percent (see figure 12.24).

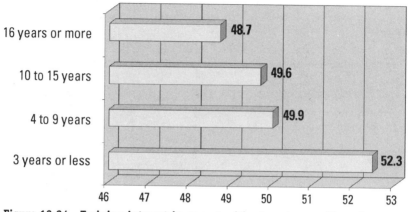

Figure 12.24—Training interest in opportunities to gain new ideas, by tenure

Women also express a desire for these opportunities in their ministry 10 percent more often than do men (standard scores, 51.7 versus 49.4). This may reflect the sense that many of the current opportunities for networking and idea-exchange have yet to fully address women's particular needs within the profession. Diane Elliot has suggested that one of the issues facing women in ministry is that there are few resources available that specifically target women in youth ministry.[22]

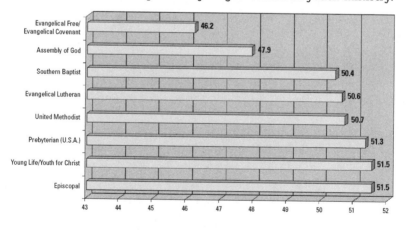

Figure 12.25—Training interest in opportunities to gain new ideas, by denomination/organization

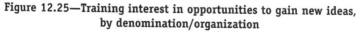

The youth ministers who are part of the Evangelical Free Church and the Evangelical Covenant Church express significantly *less* desire for these type of opportunities than do most of their colleagues (see figure 12.25). Given what we know of these groups and the samples contributing to this research, there is a good likelihood that this is less of a felt need forall of the right reasons. That is, Evangelical Free and Evangelical Covenant churches have managed to create within their relatively small denominations a very strong youth ministry network, one supportive of training, development, and—by extension—the exchange of ideas.

Less robust but still statistically significant are the differences among youth ministers according to their education levels. Those with high school diplomas or less want these opportunities more than those whose educational level is beyond college and seminary training. Those *without seminary training* express a greater desire for these opportunities. It is very likely that one of the side benefits of higher education is that one's creative resources—including ideas, relationships, and ways of thinking—are significantly expanded.

Training Need 8
Opportunities for Peer Mentoring Relationships

In the Great Commandment Jesus admonishes his followers to make disciples (Matthew 28: 19-20). The apostle Paul writes to his young protegé, Timothy, to encourage him to entrust the gospel to reliable men who will, themselves, do the same (2 Timothy 2: 2). Paul himself benefited from such a mentoring relationship with Barnabas. There is something important about training people for ministry that is better "caught" in the context of close relationships than it is taught in formal educational settings. Values are transmitted, commitments inspired. In addition, the individual interaction and teacher responsiveness of any tutorial relationship is hard to improve upon when it comes to addressing one's particular and specific concerns for growth.

The final cluster in this section on youth ministers' desired training measures the expressed need of respondents for opportunities to mentor and be mentored by professional colleagues and peers. Three items constitute this cluster[23] (see Figure 12.26).

While reciprocal mentoring opportunities are a strongly held desire for many youth ministers, the need for healthy, growth-nurturing staff relationships is articulated by nearly three out of every four youth ministers. Does this reflect an unmet desire or a non-negotiable value? Our findings in an earlier chapter (see chapter 11 on *Support*) suggest that youth ministers widely experience positive personal support from their supervisors. This expressed desire for reciprocal mentoring relationships has become a standard expectation among youth ministers.

Survey Item Opportunities for me to:	Would contribute to my professional growth or effectiveness "very much"	Would contribute to my professional growth or effectiveness "quite a bit"	Would contribute to my professional growth or effectiveness "somewhat"	Would contribute to my professional growth or effectiveness "very little"	Would contribute to my professional growth or effectiveness "not at all"
1. Be a mentor to another youth minister.	17	30	36	14	3
2. Be mentored by someone outside of my ministry.	27	32	26	12	3
3. Have close staff relationships that develop and challenge me professionally.	36	37	21	5	2

Figure 12.26—Desire for opportunities for peer mentoring relationships

We know that those who are youngest want these opportunities more (13 percent) than do their older colleagues (see figure 12.27). We also know that those who are theologically conservative and moderate express a greater desire for opportunities to develop these relationships (12 percent) than do those whose self-described theological orientation is liberal (see figure 12.28). And we know that those whose work affiliation is in Youth for Christ/Young Life express a significantly greater desire (17 percent) for such opportunities than those working in the Presbyterian Church (see figure 12.29).

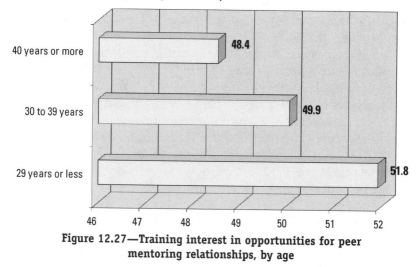

Figure 12.27—Training interest in opportunities for peer mentoring relationships, by age

Our data also shows that youth ministers with less experience, in larger congregations, and with no more than high school diplomas all want opportunities for mentoring relationships with their peers more than do their respective counterparts. It makes sense that the greater the pressures—for any of the reasons above—the greater the need for relationships that nurture one's professional development. Many youth ministers move through seasons where the need is high for someone to come alongside of them.

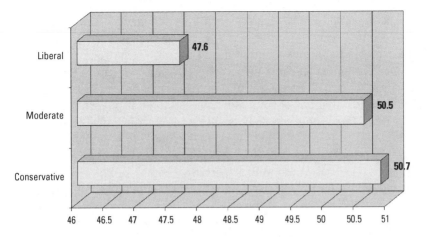

Figure 12.28—Training interest in opportunities for peer relationships, by theological orientation

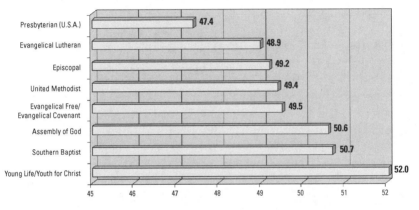

Figure 12.29—Training interest in opportunities for peer relationships, by denomination/organization

Conclusions about Explicitly Desired Professional Development Needs

The data presented so far in this chapter reveals some important insights about the expressed professional development needs of youth ministers.

First, it seems clear that immediately practical training is more highly valued than knowledge or understanding that answers the question of "why?" In virtually every case where the items within a cluster are both practical and conceptual one sees the greater desire for that kind of training.

Second, persons most hungry for professional growth are those with least experience and least education. More specifically, those with less than three years of experience in youth ministry can feel overwhelmed as the complexity of the task rushes at them. Those with only a high school education or less express greater development needs. This makes perfect sense when one considers the role of education in one's personal and professional development.

Finally, the three most universally agreed-upon training needs highlight the diversity of expectations youth ministers must try to meet. Better than three out of four youth ministers want opportunities to gain new ideas. The same number seek training that will help them nurture young people in their spiritual walk. And nearly as many want to enjoy close, nurturing, and professionally challenging staff relationships. If youth ministers were to participate in close-knit teams that are committed to ministry problem-solving, resource development and continuous improvement, that may go a long way toward meeting the deepest of their explicitly identified needs for professional development.

Now the question to explore is, "How do implicitly identified professional development needs either enrich or add to our understanding of the type of training that would be most beneficial to Protestant youth ministers in America?"

Formulating a Professional Development Plan

Throughout this book we have explored youth ministers' concerns, their priorities, the type of outcomes that are important to them, assessments of their professional ministry effectiveness, their sense of support, and the degree to which they want to broaden the base of ownership for their ministry. The insights from these collective chapters suggest the presence of youth ministers' professional development needs that may not have been explicitly addressed in the previous section. These implicitly identified needs add detail to the understanding we have about the shape of a plan for the professional development of youth ministers. It would be a mistake to neglect this important information in designing any comprehensive training curriculum.

As can be observed from the outline below, the eight professional development clusters we have just examined have been restructured to form the backbone of a map for the professional growth of youth ministers. Those explicitly identified needs have been designated with a dark bullet (•) preceding them. Those elements of the plan with a hollow bullet (°) preceding them represent major insights from our study of Protestant youth ministers in America. All have been collected under meaningful headings that describe the outcome objectives that training for youth ministers should seek to bring about. We believe that youth ministers' professional development ought to **ENABLE** them to—

Establish personal vision
Nurture teenage faith
Accommodate developmental realities
Build meaningful support
Locate effectiveness indicators
Expand ministry partnerships

Further, we believe that if youth ministry training is concentrated in these six areas the expressed concerns, hopes, and expectations of professional youth ministers can be addressed in a meaningful way. In the Youth Minister's Professional Development Map below, these issues have been aligned as sub-points (a reduced font size and indentation should help the reader recognize them) wherever it seems that they may be meaningfully addressed in a curriculum.

Youth Minister's Professional Development Map

Establish Personal Vision
- *Arriving at effective and personally fulfilling ministry strategies*
  - Addressing the expectation that there should be competent job performance

- *The priority of a clear sense of direction*
  - Addressing the expectation that there should be confident leadership

Nurture Teenage Faith
- *Communicating biblical & life-changing truth*
  - Addressing the expectation that there should be creative responsiveness to youth culture

- *Biblical knowledge & basic pastoral ministry skills*
  - Addressing the expectation that youth ministers should be theologically grounded

- *The priority of the spiritual development of youth*
  - Addressing the concern that youth are disinterested and apathetic
  - Addressing the hope that youth display joyous attitudes of respect & love
  - Addressing the hope that youth serve the church & community
  - Addressing the hope that youth are active in public witness & ministry
  - Addressing the hope that youth (ultimately) own the ministry

Accommodate Developmental Realities
- *Understanding adolescent development leading to effective counseling*
  - Addressing the concern that youth are disinterested and apathetic
  - Addressing the hope that family relationships are strengthened
  - Addressing the expectation that there should be creative responsiveness to youth culture

- *Knowledge of family development and parental training skills*
  - Addressing the hope that family relationships are strengthened
  - Addressing the expectation that there should be positive relationships with parents

Build Meaningful Support
- Opportunities to gain new ideas

- Opportunities for mentoring relationships with peers
  - Addressing the concern of a lack of personal support in ministry

- Positive organizational climate

- Congregation's personal support
  - Addressing the concern over inadequate finances
  - Addressing the concern of a time conflict between job & personal life
  - Addressing the concern of a lack of personal support in ministry
  - Addressing the concern of feelings of personal inadequacy
  - Addressing the concern of a lack of self-confidence
  - Addressing the concern that youth ministers may feel unqualified or job
  - Addressing the concern that youth ministers experience strained family relations
  - Addressing the concern that youth ministers may experience burnout

- Supervisor's personal support
  - Addressing the concern of a time conflict between job & personal life
  - Addressing the concern of a lack of personal support in ministry
  - Addressing the concern of feelings of personal inadequacy
  - Addressing the concern of a lack of self-confidence
  - Addressing the concern that youth ministers may feel unqualified for job
  - Addressing the concern that youth ministers experience strained family relations
  - Addressing the concern that youth ministers may experience burnout

Locate Effectiveness Indicators
- Competent job performance
  - Addressing the concern of a time conflict between job & personal life
  - Addressing the concern of a time conflict between administration & youth relationships
  - Addressing the concern that youth ministers may feel unqualified for job
  - Addressing the concern that youth ministers feel personally disorganized

- Confident leadership
  - Addressing the concern of feelings of personal inadequacy
  - Addressing the concern of a lack of self-confidence
  - Addressing the concern that youth ministers may feel unqualified for job

- Motivation derived from God's call
  - Addressing the concern of feelings of personal inadequacy
  - Addressing the concern of a lack of self-confidence
  - Addressing the concern that youth ministers may feel unqualified for job

- Theological grounding

- Commitment to specialized youth ministry training
  - Addressing the concern that youth ministers may feel unqualified for job

- Effective youth relationships
  - Addressing the concern of a time conflict between administration & youth relationships

- Positive relationships with parents & adults

- Creative responsiveness to youth culture

- Ability to develop adult volunteers

- Personal peer involvement in ministry

Expand Ministry Partnerships
- Training in administration & management
  - Addressing the concern of a time conflict between administration & youth relationships

- Addressing the concern that youth ministers feel personally disorganized

• The priority of volunteer recruitment & training
  - Addressing the expectation that adult volunteers are developed

• Congregational ownership
  - Addressing the concern that youth & church are disconnected
  - Addressing the expectation that one's peers are involved in ministry

• Helping parents minister to their teens
  - Addressing the hope that family relationships are strengthened
  - Addressing the expectation that there are positive relationships with parents & adults

• Giving teens ownership of ministry
  - Addressing the concern that youth are disinterested and apathetic
  - Addressing the hope that youth own the ministry
  - Addressing the hope that youth display joyous attitudes of respect & love
  - Addressing the hope that youth serve the church & community
  - Addressing the hope that youth are active in public witness & ministry
  - Addressing the expectation that there are effective youth relationships

While the six headings have been supplied to offer a meaningful organizational scheme, the content of this training plan has been supplied exclusively from the research discussed in this book. Are there other sources that can or should be drawn upon in order to enrich this map for professional development? What other elements "ought to" be included in youth ministry training?

This question goes to the fundamental assumptions behind curriculum design. Whenever we are sure that certain values must be transmitted accurately to students we exercise a strategy of *control* with regard to curriculum. We begin with the desired end in mind and try to create an educational plan that will ensure that youth ministers will arrive at the designated outcome. Alert to the fact that not all values are equally—or passionately—held by youth ministry experts, consensus has not been easily arrived at. For years an organization of youth ministry professors (*Youth Ministry Educators* began in 1994) has considered the merits of creating a more uniform set of standards with regard to the educational preparation of youth ministers. At times the members got hung up over the details of control and oversight, and whether sanctioning one's youth ministry training is a universally desirable outcome. In the fall of 1999, the most ambitious attempt yet was made to advance this agenda. A team of youth ministry professors, led by Dr. Steve Gerali of Judson College, proposed that *Youth Ministry Educators* might adopt a commitment to the following outcomes and processes. By doing so, the advocates of the proposal hoped to ensure that uniform minimum standards would be in place, establishing a target for the growing number of educational institutions seeking to equip students for the practice of youth ministry.

1999 YME Proposal for Common Curriculum Standards

I. Youth Minister's Maturity

Does the school have a small group and/or mentoring and/or accountability structure in place?

There may be a variety of adult/student relational structures to attain a minimum faculty-student ratio of 1/30, including adjuncts, grad assistants, and outside ministers.

How do each of the following get accomplished in an institution's program, and how are assessment conclusions drawn?
- spiritual formation
- ethics
- life management

II. Youth Ministry Understanding

Theological/biblical literacy: equivalent of 15 semester hours of biblical/theological content.

Foundational literacy: equivalent of 3 semester hours, that supplies an overview of the youth ministry field (e.g., current paradigms, youth ministry models, history of youth ministry)

Sociological/psychological literacy: equivalent of 6 semester hours in adolescent psychology and sociology with emphasis in adolescent development, and cultural assessment

III. Youth Ministry Competencies

Internship/practicum: hands-on youth ministry field experience with supervision and evaluation (minimum equivalent of 2 semesters part time or 1 semester full time)

How do each of the following get accomplished in an institution's program, and how are assessment conclusions drawn?
- communication and teaching skills
- administration and organization skills
- programming skills

- counseling/helping skills
- leadership development skills
- research skills

These three headings were derived from a modest proposal and discussion I had facilitated with parachurch youth ministry trainers Lynn Ziegenfuss (Youth for Christ), Dave Garda (Sonlife), Kevin Harlan (Fellowship of Christian Athletes), and Dan Webster (formerly of Willow Creek, then involved with Authentic Leadership).[24] The thrust of that article was to suggest that there were at least three educational warehouses that needed to be established to "store" the training objectives for youth ministers, and the notion was benign enough that there wasn't much for the training experts to disagree with.

That wasn't the case with the now-expanded proposal that was deliberated by the nearly 80 youth ministry educators gathered in San Diego for their fall meeting in 1999. It wasn't easy to get discussion about the *content* of the standards being proposed. Members tripped over both the idea and the practical implementation of control. The proposal was dismissed.

I've found myself disagreeing with professional colleagues in the past over the topic of youth ministry training. When I wrote a review of the "best youth ministry training available" in 1995 persons I respect very much suggested that my standards for excellence in youth ministry training didn't match their values.[25] I have come to appreciate the fact that good people may often disagree about what is most important.

Moving ahead

The contribution of this research project may help us acknowledge a new baseline for cooperation in youth ministry training. The study of Protestant youth ministers in America has helped us to hear from the *real* experts. May we shape our professional development strategies to help these faithful men and women address their concerns and realize the hopes and expectations to which God has called them.

It is our prayer that this book signals an important new standard for youth ministry's knowledge base. By reporting on youth ministers' concerns, priorities, achievements, goals, and experience of support we have helped to establish a clear picture of the state of the profession of youth ministry at the turn of the century. We have had a chance to identify factors that predict both fulfillment and frustration. When we began this study we expected that the "cries" of youth ministers would dominate this book. It's a joy to celebrate a healthier professional reality than we had hypothesized.

In fact, it's a joy to be able to draw upon more than our collective educated guesses in framing this portrait of American Protestant youth ministers. Let's continue to move forward as we build upon the certainty of what we now know to be true.

THINK IT OVER, TALK IT THROUGH

1. If you had the chance to attend a professional development seminar, or class, or networking meeting where you could have any one of the eight training needs described in this chapter met, which one would you attend?

2. Imagine you have been granted scholarship money for the youth ministers you know in your local community to attend the same sort of professional growth experience described in question #1. Which one would you send them to? Why?

3. What would be the best professional development investment your denomination or parachurch organization could make?

4. Examine the *ENABLE* **Youth Ministry Professional Development Map** and determine what you think *ought* to be included that's not currently in this plan. Then identify what values have led you to such a conviction about the professional development you might obligate other youth ministers to go through.

1. Kenda Creasy Dean and Ron Foster, *The Godbearing Life: The Art of Soul Tending for Youth Ministry* (Nashville: Upper Room Books, 1998), 16.

2. The reliability measure for this cluster is .86.

3. Correlations are r = .67 for pastoral ministry training; r = .64 for training in adolescent development and counseling; and r = .63 for training in effective ministry strategies.

4. Rolf E. Muss, "Jean Piaget's Cognitive Theory of Adolescence," in *Theories of Adolescence* (New York: Random House, 1962-1988), 176-189.

5. Erik H. Erikson, *Identity: Youth and Crisis* (New York: Norton, 1968).

6. Ronald M. Sabatelli and Aviva Mazor, "Differentiation, Individuation, and Identity Formation: The Integration of Family System and Individual Developmental Perspectives," *Adolescence* 20, 79 (1985), 620-21.

7. David Elkind, *All Grown Up and No Place to Go* (Reading, Maine: Addison-Wesley, 1984), 33-36.

8. I arrived at these conclusions after submitting a review, "Kohlberg in the 1980s," for a Purdue graduate class in 1990.

9. The reliability measure for this sub-cluster is .70.

10. Elkind, 33-36.

11. Doug Fields, *Purpose-Driven Youth Ministry* (Grand Rapids, Michigan: Zondervan/Youth Specialties, 1998), 83-97.

12. As taught in Sonlife Strategy Seminars and other training events sponsored by this organization, based in Elburn, Illinois. Their annual report in 1998 indicated that they had trained 49,420 youth leaders through these Strategy Seminars since 1980, and another 41,012 volunteer youth workers through their Foundations Trainers since 1989.

13. Many First Priority campus club strategies can be described in this way.

14. Pete Ward, *God at the Mall* (Peabody, Maine: Hendrickson Publishers, 1999).

15. The reliability measure for this cluster is .80.

16. Merton P. Strommen and Richard A. Hardel, *Passing on the Faith: A Radical New Model for Youth and Family Ministry* (Winona, Minnesota: Saint Mary's Press, 2000), chapter 6.

17. Dave Rahn and Terry Linhart, *Contagious Faith: Empowering Student Leadership in Youth Evangelism* (Loveland, Colorado: Group Publishing, 2000).

18. The reliability measure for this sub-cluster is .81.

19. The reliability measure for this cluster is .71.

20. The reliability measure for this cluster is .74.

21. The reliability measure for this cluster is .71.

22. Diane Elliot, "What Are the Issues Women Face in Youth Ministry?" in Richard R. Dunn and Mark H. Senter III (eds.), *Reaching a Generation for Christ* (Chicago: Moody Press, 1997), 285.

23. The reliability measure for this cluster is .69.

24. Dave Rahn, "What kind of education do youth ministers need?" unpublished paper.

25. Dave Rahn, "The Best in Youth Ministry Training," *Group* 22, 1 (November/December, 1995), 32-35.

Appendix

How the Study Was Conducted
Mark J. Brekke and Milo L. Brekke, Brekke Associates, Inc.

Study design

The *Study of Protestant Youth Ministers in America* began as the brain-child of Mark Lamport of Link Institute for Faithful and Effective Youth Ministry, a department of Huntington College of Huntington, Indiana. In 1996, sensing a chasm in knowledge about those in the profession in which Link Institute specializes, the Institute, under Lamport's leadership, conceived of a research study with the following objectives:

- Provide a research base for the profession of youth ministry.
- Develop a data-based conceptual model of youth ministers and youth ministry as it exists today.
- Provide a basic text that supplies needed guidelines for successful youth ministry.
- Provide information for the development of more effective and relevant curricula for the training of youth ministers.

A research team was formed, including Mark Lamport, David Rahn, and Karen Jones (all of Link Institute), and Merton Strommen, arguably the premier researcher on youth and family ministry in Protestantism today. During the instrument-development phase of the study, the team enlisted the services of Mark Brekke and Milo Brekke of Brekke Associates, Inc., in Minneapolis. Both Brekkes had worked extensively with Strommen on many studies at Search Institute during the 1970s and 1980s, and they were able to add necessary scientific and analytic expertise to the team.

Together the research team designed a study that followed the same research methodology as used for Strommen's successful earlier studies of youths and family, *Five Cries of Youth* and *Five Cries of Parents*.[1] In brief form, the design included the following steps:

Instrument development
- Definition of the domain of study through collection and analysis of open-ended questions of professional youth ministers.
- Development of items to quantifiably measure the domain of issues,

concerns, and needs.
- Pretesting and analysis of the questionnaire.
- Revision to final form.

Sample selection
- Acquisition of mailing lists of full-time youth ministers from a wide range of Protestant denominations and parachurch youth groups.
- Random sampling from mailing lists.

Data collection
- Survey by mail following the methods of Dillman.[2]

Analysis
- Empirical identification of internally consistent item clusters, each describing a particular facet of youth ministry.
    Data preparation
    Combining denominations into families and weighting
    Searching for structure
    Identification of item clusters
- Computation of cluster scores for each survey respondent.
- Empirical identification of families of clusters, providing a framework for interpreting the data.
    Identification of second-order cluster families
    Summary of search for structure
- Analyses of averages and ranges of cluster scores for the total sample.
- Computation of *standardized* cluster scores for each survey respondent.
- Analyses of group differences using standardized cluster scores.
- Analyses to sort out the relative relationship of multiple demographic variables.

Limitations of the study
- Sampling frame
- Response rate
- Cluster reliability
- Group differences
- Summary regarding limitations of the study

The remainder of this Appendix describes, in detail, each of the above steps.

Definition of the domain of study

In 1996 a total of 7,500 youth ministers from all over the United States assembled at the Georgia Dome in Atlanta for the largest gathering of youth ministers to date. A sample of 2,130 of those youth ministers was secured, representing full-time youth ministers from dozens of denominations and parachurch organizations. They additionally reflected a wide range of age, geographic location, and experience.

The sample of youth ministers was asked to respond to a 20-question, open-ended questionnaire that asked, in a variety of ways, for them to tell—
• What they liked best about youth ministry.
• Their biggest obstacle to an effective youth ministry.
• Their biggest concern today in youth ministry.
• What especially pleased them in their work with youth.
• What they find most encouraging or discouraging.

The research team performed a content analysis of the responses to the questionnaire, identifying 16 areas of issues, concerns, and needs of youth ministers—areas that defined the domain of study for the project:
1. Use of time: Balancing job and personal life.
2. Need to prioritize: Where to spend time and energy.
3. Personal concern: Feeling adequate.
4. Sources of satisfaction: Working with youths.
5. Involving parents: Gaining their cooperation.
6. In-service training: Being equipped to train.
7. In-service training: Areas of special interest.
8. Congregational obstacle: Respect for youth ministry.
9. Desired outcome: Teen ownership.
10. Ultimate outcomes: Long-term commitments.
11. Sources of regret: Disappointing outcomes.
12. Money: A troubling issue.
13. Sources of satisfaction: Supportive people.
14. Call to ministry: Motivating factors.
15. Youth ministry: Perceiving the task.
16. Sense of mission: Purpose of youth ministry.

Development of items

Although that open-ended survey of youth ministers had qualitatively identified the boundaries and general areas of study, in order to achieve the study objectives it was essential to more precisely map the domain and quantify levels of concern and need within the domain. Accordingly, the research team developed 256 discrete, single-thought items that

covered the domain, approaching each of the 16 domain areas from a variety of angles or perspectives. In an initial pretest questionnaire, the items were organized into four broad sections:
- Degree of Concern
- Extent of Perceived Disparities
- Personal Evaluation
- Desired In-service Training

Each section used fixed, ordered-response possibilities that had been used successfully in previous studies of youths and families. Demographic and personal descriptive items were also included in the pretest questionnaire.

Pretest and analysis of items

The pretest questionnaire was administered to approximately 75 United Methodist youth ministers in Dallas in January 1998. In addition to answering each item, the respondents were asked to evaluate the quality of the item:
- Item okay.
- Item is hard to understand, unclear.
- Item can have more than one meaning.
- Item uses words that I do not understand.
- Item is repetitious.

Respondents were also asked to underline problem words or phrases, and were asked several open-ended questions regarding ways to improve the survey.

Revision to final form

The research team carefully analyzed the responses to the pretest questionnaire—both item responses and item evaluations. Items identified by the respondents as problematic were revised or thrown out. Items with poor distributions of response (i.e., that did not discriminate well) were discarded. A few additional items were added when it became clear that an item could have multiple meanings, or if new perspectives regarding the domain area were identified. After several weeks of such analysis, the instrument took final form as a paper-and-pencil questionnaire called "A Study of Protestant Youth Ministers in America", containing 243 items in six sections, each with a fixed set of response possibilities and containing 17 demographic or personally descriptive items interspersed through the questionnaire, as seen in Table A.1:

Table A.1

Questionnaire Content

Section	Number of items	Response stem, response possibilities, and values given to response possiblities for cluster scores	Number and content of demographic/descriptive items
Section 1: Youth Ministry Concerns	70	Read each statement, determine if it is true for you, and select the appropriate response: [item] • 1 = Not true for me, and not applicable/ never true for me • 2 = Not true for me, and was once true/ no longer is true • 3 = True for me now, and concerns me very much • 4 = True for me now, and concerns me quite a bit • 5 = True for me now, and concerns me somewhat • 6 = True for me now, and concerns me very little	8 • Age • Race • Gender • Marital status • Tenure (years in youth ministry) • Children at home • Ever terminated from a youth ministry position • Denomination/group now serving
Section 2: Evaluating Your Youth	20	Looking at my ministry, I see youth who are... [item] • 4 = Often true • 3 = Sometimes true • 2 = Rarely true • 1 = Never true	4 • Type of education in youth ministry • Rural/suburban/urban youth ministry location • Region • Highest education level achieved
Section 3a: Evaluating Your Youth Ministry: Importance (Note: The items in sections 3a and 3b are the same. Respondents were asked to answer regarding both Importance and Achievement.)	21	How important are the following statements to your youth ministry: [item] • 5 = Extremely important • 4 = Very important • 3 = Quite important • 2 = Somewhat important • 1 = Not important	0
Section 3b: Evaluating Your Youth Ministry: Achievement (Note: The items in sections 3a and 3b are the same. Respondents were asked to answer regarding both Importance and Achievement.)	21	In your opinion, how well is this aspect of your youth ministry being achieved or realized: [item] • 5 = Extremely well • 4 = Very well • 3 = Quite well • 2 = Somewhat well • 1 = Not well	0

Sample selection

Acquisition of mailing lists

The research team made the decision to sample full-time youth ministers only. Part-time youth ministers were not sampled for the study,
principally because the study focus was on youth ministry as a *profession*. In addition, the research team felt that they would encounter

greater difficulty and get relatively less information from part-time youth ministers because of their relatively limited experience, probable shorter tenure, and probable higher transience.

Mailing lists for currently employed, full-time youth ministers, as well as support and permission for the study, were requested and obtained from 10 Protestant denominational offices and three para-church youth ministry groups (see table A.2, page 347). It should be noted that formation of such lists was not without a certain degree of difficulty, especially in some of the mainline denominations. In fact, the study helped some groups refine their own youth minister databases. (Though it was never tested scientifically, upon reflection it might be said that the ease of getting a complete and accurate mailing list was a reasonably good predictor of the denomination's or group's relative ranking on a number of the eventual cluster scores.)

Random sampling from mailing lists

The denomination/parachurch contacts working with the research team provided estimates of the total number of full-time youth ministers working in their organizations. As the mailing lists were acquired, however, it soon became evident to both the research team and the contacts that those estimates were very much in error. Consequently, the research team concluded that the mailing lists themselves were the best representation of the proportion of full-time youth ministers employed in each denomination/parachurch group. A random sample of 5,017 youth ministers was drawn from the mailing lists (see table A.2, page 347). The sample generally matched the denomination/parachurch proportions represented by the mailing list, oversampled groups with small mailing lists so that the expected returns would be enough for the comparison of that group with the others, undersampled groups with very large mailing lists since a proportional number was not necessary for the intended analyses, and was expected to yield approximately 3,000 returns, based upon a target return rate of 60 percent—a number sufficient to perform the designed analyses.

Data Collection and Preparation

Survey by mail

The data collection was performed following the methods of Dillman.[4] the surveying process was done in two waves. Each wave included three mailings: a cover letter with questionnaire and return envelope; a post-card reminder one week later; and a second postcard reminder after two more weeks. The first wave of 5,017 questionnaires was mailed in April

1998. Very quickly, approximately 600 were returned as undeliverable (bad address, no forwarding address, died, etc.). Of those 600, approximately 500 were replaced and mailed to by randomly sampling from the remaining youth ministers in the mailing lists. (Not all could be replaced due to the limited numbers on the mailing lists.)

The first wave yielded 1852 returns. During the summer of 1998, the denomination/parachurch youth ministry contacts sent a letter to their constituents, encouraging them, if they had not completed and returned the questionnaire, to do so if they still had it, or to do so using a duplicate questionnaire that would be mailed to all nonrespondents in a second wave. The second wave of 3,165 questionnaires was mailed in December 1998, having been delayed due to a shortage of funds. The number that was returned as undeliverable in the second wave was not replaced, again due to financial limitations. This reduced the number of youth ministers who had the opportunity to respond to the survey (i.e., according to the Postal Service, they received the survey) to 4,689 (5,017 minus a total of 328). There were 564 returns from the second wave, making a total of 2,416 completed questionnaires. The return rate, therefore, was 2,416 of 4,689, or 51.5 percent. Table A.2 shows the counts mailed and returned by denomination/parachurch group.

Table A.2

Sampling, mailing, and return counts and percentages by denomination/parachurch group

Denomination or parachurch group	Mailing list count	Percentage group list if of total	Number randomly sampled and mailed	Percentage group sample is of total sample	Number who received questionaire	Number of completed questionaires returned	Response rate (completed/ received)	Percentage group response is of total response
Assembly of God	823	7.6	551	11	539	249	46.2	10.3
Episcopal	152	1.4	127	2.5	122	73	59.8	3.0
Evangelical Covenant	200	1.9	139	2.8	128	68	53.1	2.8
Evangelical Free	697	6.5	150	3.0	125	50	40.0	2.1
Evangelical Lutheran	1,197	11.1	500	10.0	484	234	48.3	9.7
Independant Fundamentalist Churches of America	55	0.5	55	1.1	39	16	41.0	0.7
National Baptist Convention (USA)	88	0.8	81	1.6	69	12	17.4	0.5
Presbyterian (U.S.A.)	599	5.6	501	10.0	443	224	50.6	9.3
Southern Baptist	4,603	42.7	1,551	30.9	1,453	531	36.5	22.0
United Methodist	805	7.5	597	11.9	573	331	57.8	13.7
Young Life	960	8.9	391	7.8	368	243	66.0	10.1
Youth for Christ	538	5.0	308	6.1	299	189	63.2	7.8
Youth With A Mission	66	0.6	66	1.3	47	19	40.4	0.8
Unknown (survey participants who failed to respond or did so incorrectly)						177		7.3
TOTAL	10,783	100.0	5,017	100.0	4,689	2,416	51.5	100.0

Data capture

The questionnaire booklet was printed as a mark-sense, machine-scannable form. The returned booklets were scanned by Link Institute and reviewed for accuracy by members of the research team. A total of 2,416 non-blank returns were captured and subsequently used for analysis.

Analysis

Empirical identification of internally consistent item clusters

Data preparation

Once scanned into an electronic file and verified by Link Institute, the file of 2,416 returns was turned over to Brekke Associates, Inc. for analysis. The file was converted to a SAS® (version 6.12) dataset, with full variable and value labels. Univariate statistics and frequency distributions were run and compared to those generated by Link Institute to ensure that the translation was accurate, and they were examined to confirm that the item distributions were reasonable and that there were no items with extreme numbers of missing data. The data passed all such tests. Item values were assigned as indicated in table A.1 above. Missing and multiple marks were given missing data values which excluded the values, but not the respondents, from statistical procedures. Unless otherwise indicated, all analyses were performed using SAS.

Combining denominations into families and weighting

It had been hoped that there would be enough surveys returned from each denomination/parachurch group that each group could be compared on its own to the others, and so that the returns from each group could be randomly split into two groups for "random-half" development of item clusters. Unfortunately, there were not enough returns for several groups to make this possible. Consequently, the research team organized the 13 original groups into eight "denominational families," based upon similarity of belief and culture. Families empirically identified in *Ministry in America* were also used as a basis and model for combining groups.[5] In particular, the following groups were combined into single families:
• Evangelical Covenant, Evangelical Free, and Independent Fundamental Churches of America into "Evangelical A" family.
• Assembly of God and Youth With a Mission into "Evangelical B" family.
• Presbyterian Church (U.S.A.) and National Baptist Convention (U.S.A.) into "Presbyterian-Reformed" family.

• Young Life and Youth for Christ into "Christian Churches (not Disciples)" family.

All other denominations were left uncombined, each representing its own family.

For the development of item clusters, it was desirable that each denominational family be equally represented. The research team did not want particular families to dominate the search for structure (described below) simply because they had a greater number of survey returns (e.g., Southern Baptists). Thus, the respondents in each denominational family were assigned weights so that, in the statistical analyses, they would be equal. Weights were assigned so that the weighted total for each of the eight families was 292.375. (292.375 equals 1/8 of 2339, the number of respondents who identified the denomination/group they were currently serving.) The 177 respondents who did not identify their denomination/group were each given a weight of 1.0, so their weighted total was 177.0. Their total weight was lower than those of the denominational families: a compromise between excluding them from the analysis and giving them equal input into the analysis. The weights were used only for the development of item clusters. All other analyses were performed unweighted.

Searching for structure

When the American public considers results of a survey, it most often thinks of polls, which consist of just a few items, asked of a carefully selected sample of people. We are used to hearing the results of political polls, Gallup polls on a variety of issues, and exit polls during elections that report the percent of voters answering a question a certain way (often "yes" or "no," or "which candidate"), with a margin of error of typically 3 to 4 percent.

While those types of surveys are very useful, they are also very limited. They answer single questions, but do not capture either the breadth of context and reasoning of the respondents, or the depth of meaning which underlies the respondents' answers. They are also unable to reveal anything about the way in which people *structure* their thinking on the issue. That is, typical polls do not capture the *cognitive constructs* (dimensions, compartments, facets, areas of concern, etc.) that often subconsciously underlie the answers.

This study of youth ministers and youth ministry was designed to do what the typical poll does not: to map and study the domain of youth ministry as it is lived, felt, perceived, and conceived by youth ministers today. There are several advantages to this kind of research. The primary one is that past research has shown that, once the domain is mapped, the boundaries and landmarks (the conceptual structure) remain consistent both for a broad group of people (in this case, youth ministers across many denominations and parachurch groups), and over a long period of time (often 20 years or more). For example, when Merton Strommen carried out trend analyses on the structure identified in his book, *Five Cries of Youth*, he found no change after 15 years in four of the five constructs, and only slight change in the fifth. This kind of consistency and persistence of structure allows researchers to study trends over long periods of time, make decisions with lasting impact, and to develop tools, materials, and curricula that have broad and continuing value.

One key feature of this more expansive and persistent research is the identification of what we call *item clusters*. An item cluster is a set of interrelated items in which each item asks a slightly different question having to do with the same topic, issue, or cognitive construct, but asks it from a different angle or in a different way. A good item cluster is one that is *internally consistent* (which is a measure of reliability)—that is, people who give a high rating to one item in a scattered set of perhaps five or six items tend to give a high rating to *all* of the items in the set. Simultaneously, those who give a low rating to one item also tend to give a low rating to the other items of the set.

A second feature of this research is that the item clusters are identified *by the respondents themselves* by the way they answer the full questionnaire, not by the researchers beforehand. Item clusters are developed using the data collected with the questionnaire. The researchers do not presuppose that certain items are related to certain others. Granted, they have developed the questionnaire with questions they think are probably related. But beyond this, they developed the questionnaire hoping to include items that covered the entire domain of study. The respondents' answers to the items are then analyzed using techniques that identify which items are more tightly interrelated with each other than with the rest of the items in the questionnaire (more on the techniques below). The analysis is done blind to the content of the items—that is, when interrelated sets of items are identified, they are formed without any attention to the content of the questions. Only the *consistency* of the respondents' answers is taken into account.

After each item set is found, the researchers then look at the content of the items in each set and identify and name the larger concept that each item set is describing. What results are item *clusters*, each describing a discrete concept more accurately than any single item can, and together providing a map of the field of study.

What exactly are "clusters"?
An example might be helpful. Say that a researcher is interested in foods people like and dislike. So the researcher develops a questionnaire

that asks how much a person likes or dislikes different foods. The researcher puts items regarding virtually every type of food they can think of into the questionnaire. After surveying a few thousand people, the researcher applies the techniques to search for the structure of food likes and dislikes that underlie people's answers.

Let's say that many interrelated item sets are identified, but let's examine a set that contains brownies, Hershey bar, Fudgesickle, Cocoa Puffs, and Nestle Quik. The researcher examines this set and quickly realizes that the concept being described is "preference for chocolateness." That is, people who like one type of chocolate-flavored food tend to like others. By using this set of items to measure how much people like chocolate-flavored foods, the researcher gets a much more reliable answer than if only one of the items were used. By using item clusters such as this, the researcher also gets the advantage of being able to study a smaller set of concepts, but a set of concepts more thoroughly defined and manageable, as opposed to studying each individual item. Finally, since researchers have identified a conceptual area with each item cluster, they are in a much better position to use the information to develop new materials that will be accepted, or that meet the needs of a group of people.

For example, suppose the researcher found that people tended to like chocolate-flavored foods more than lime-flavored foods. The researcher could then reasonably predict that, all else being equal, a new chocolate desert would sell better than a new lime dessert.

Item clusters based on the original questionnaire items are often called *first-order clusters*. It is also possible to search for structure among the first-order clusters, using the same process as described above. This, then, yields a *second-order* structure, or *cluster families*, that further defines the domain of study.

Imagine a map of the world. The entire map is the *domain of study*. To know more about the domain, one might study individual people as *items*. Those people group into cities, or *first-order clusters*. Finally, the cities group into countries, or *second-order cluster families*. Now one can begin to make sense of the domain, because the map now has delineated areas and landmarks.

When doing this type of research, it is important to understand that though the *structure* that one finds is generally stable and persistent over time, the *level* of each conceptual construct in the structure can vary dramatically between groups and over time. In the chocolate example, the level or degree of liking chocolate-flavored foods might differ significantly between men and women, children and adults, different ethnic groups, or regions of the country. Or it might change in one group over time (if, say, chocolate was found to be a carcinogen). The beauty of highly reliable item clusters is that one can be much more confident that observed differences or changes are real, because a cluster measures the construct more precisely and consistently than does a single item.

This study of youth ministers, then, used the process of searching for structure (i.e., building reliable item clusters) in order to—
• Map and better describe the domain of youth ministry as experienced by youth ministers.
• Provide a framework for thinking about youth ministry.
• Compare groups on measures related to youth ministry.

Identification of item clusters

The original study design called for developing item clusters using three mathematical methods:
• Principal component (factor) analysis, with varimax rotation (using PROC FACTOR in SAS version 6.12).
• Principal factor analysis, with varimax rotation (using PROC FACTOR in SAS version 6.12).
• Homogeneous keying (using software developed by Brekke Associates, Inc., based upon the work of Loevinger, et al.[6]).

Each of these methods is blind to content, not informed by any preconceived categories, and designed to identify distinct, interrelated sets of items. Several test analyses were run to compare the results of the two factor analysis methods. Results were very similar, with the principal component method tending to identify a few more sets than did the principal factor method. Consequently, in the interest of efficiency and cost, only the principal component factor analysis and homogeneous keying methods were analyzed to develop the first-order item clusters.

Each of the two mathematical methods was used to analyze the items from the questionnaire. Items were grouped for independent analyses by the type and number of response possibilities for the items. In addition, each analysis was performed on three groups of respondents: the total group of respondents, and each of a randomly selected split-half sample, stratified by denominational family. So each of the sections of the questionnaire was analyzed six times (2 methods x 3 groups = 6 analyses). Each analysis was weighted using the denominational family weights as described above.

For each questionnaire section, the results of the six analyses were compared, and item sets were identified. In order to become a named cluster for further use in the study, a set of items had to meet the following criteria:
• Identified by both methods.
• Identified in four of the six analyses.

- Internal consistency reliability (as estimated using Cronbach's alpha) of at least 0.55.
- Contains items that each have a factor loading of 0.35 or greater in the principal components analysis. (A factor loading is the correlation of the item with the component, i.e., the factor.)
- Contains no items that *cross-load* (i.e., that have a factor loading of 0.35 or greater on multiple factors).

The item sets meeting these criteria were identified by one member of the analytic team. Once identified, each cluster was passed to a second member who created a table that included the exact text of each item, factor loads, and the estimate of reliability. Each set was then passed to a third member of the analytic team who carefully examined the content of all of the items in the cluster, identified the concept that served to "skewer" the set, and gave the cluster a title and sentence description. That member also evaluated the fit of *borderline items* (i.e., items with relatively low factor loads) to the rest of the cluster, and decided whether the item would remain in the cluster.

This process of analyzing the 243 questionnaire items yielded 48 first-order item clusters. Each cluster table, including its name and sentence description, was passed to the authors, who made a final review of cluster content. The 48 clusters were determined in this review to be clear, discrete, and eminently sensible. Therefore, the clusters as determined by the three analysts were accepted without modification. The final cluster tables may be further reviewed at the Huntington College Link Institute Web site (www.linkinstitute.com).

Computation of cluster scores

For each respondent, a score for each cluster was assigned by computing the mean of the respondent's answers to the cluster items. The respondent must have answered at least two-thirds of the cluster's items to be given a valid score. If not, the score was set to a missing value that excluded the score, but not the respondent, from statistical analyses.

Identification of second-order cluster families

The 48 cluster scores were analyzed to determine whether a second-order structure existed. A total of six analyses were performed: principal components and principal factor analyses for each of the three analysis groups (total and each split-half sample). Homogeneous keying was not used. The authors compared and evaluated the analyses, finding, again, very similar, consistent, and sensible results across all six. The authors decided to settle on the results of the total group principal factor analysis, which grouped the 48 clusters into seven cluster families. In general, the cluster families grouped clusters along the lines of the sections of the original questionnaire, although this pattern was not absolute. The authors analyzed the meaning of each cluster family and used the families to determine the chapters of the book. Again, these cluster families can be examined at www.linkinstitute.com.

Summary of search for structure

In brief, the search for structure took the following path:
• Thousands of open-ended responses to 20 questions posed to 2,130 youth ministers, which were analyzed and organized into...
• A questionnaire containing 243 items answered by 2,416 youth ministers, which organized into...
• 48 item clusters, which organized into...
• Seven cluster families, which became the chapters of...
• This book.

Univariate analyses of cluster scores.

The mean, standard deviation, and range of scores were computed for each cluster. The authors analyzed the statistics to understand and report overall levels and ranges of scores.

Computation of standard scores

As indicated in table A.1 (page 345), each section of the questionnaire had its own set of item responses and item values. In addition, the distributions of cluster scores, even from the same section of the questionnaire, varied considerably in shape, range, and central tendency. Consequently, the cluster scores had different theoretical ranges, actual ranges, means, standard deviations, and skew characteristics, all of which made comparisons between cluster scores extremely difficult.

To address this problem, the research team decided to convert the cluster scores to standard scores with mean = 50.0, and standard deviation = 10.0. Standard scores make comparisons much easier, since a change of 1.0 is always the same amount, in terms of the standard deviation from the mean, no matter where on the distribution one is working. E.g., the difference between 56 and 60 is the same amount as the difference between 41 and 45. In addition, relative rankings of groups can be more easily compared between clusters, since a certain standard score is the same distance from the mean for each of the standardized clusters.

Analyses of group differences

One of the goals of the study was to understand whether and how groups of youth ministers and congregations differed significantly in their judgments regarding aspects of youth ministry. To determine this, a series of unweighted, one-way analyses of variance (ANOVA) were performed. In these analyses, the average cluster scores for subgroups of respondents are compared (e.g., male versus female), and the probability is calculated for that difference in averages occurring purely by chance in our sample. For each cluster, a set of ANOVAs was run in which the cluster score was the dependent variable, and each of 12 demographic/descriptive variables was used as the independent variable.

The 12 demographic/descriptive variables were selected from among the 17 that were included in the questionnaire based upon their: having a good distribution of responses; having subgroup sizes adequate for comparisons; and being variables over which a youth minister or congregation might have influence. For several of the variables, response categories were combined to satisfy the first condition. The 12 variables finally used as independent variables in the individual one-way ANOVAs were:
- Age
- Gender
- Tenure
- Denominational family
- Whether youth minister had seminary training
- Population and rural/suburban/urban characteristic of where the youth ministry program is based
- Region of the country
- Highest education level
- Theological orientation
- Size of congregation (as indicated by average Sunday morning worship attendance)
- Size of youth group
- Approach to youth ministry (see Niebuhr[7])

In general, given the number of respondents in the study, a difference between subgroups of two points in any cluster standard score was *statistically* significant ($p < 0.05$, i.e., less than 5 percent probability of occurring by chance). The authors felt that a difference of three was the threshold of *practical* significance, however, so only differences of three or more are reported in the book.

Analyses to sort out the relative influence of multiple variables

The number of respondents was not sufficient to perform thorough multivariate analyses of variance or multivariate regression analyses. In light of the study objectives, this was not of huge consequence, however, since the objectives were primarily to describe the domain and current of youth ministry and youth ministers rather than build a predictive model of youth ministers' and congregations' behavior or performance regarding youth ministry.

Nevertheless, in a few instances it was helpful to begin to untangle the web of relationships of the demographic/descriptive variables relative to particular clusters. For this work, the research team used a method known as Automatic Interaction Detection, or AID—a method first developed by Sonquist, which essentially emulates a researcher using one-way ANOVAs to progressively identify combinations of demographic groups that have the widest difference of average scores on a particular variable.[8] As an exploratory technique, and as a way to determine the relative influence of independent variables to a dependent variable, it has become a standard, well-accepted tool among statistical analysts. For this study, we used AnswerTree® from SPSS, Inc. to perform the AID analyses.

AID results are frequently represented as a large tree diagram, where every *node* splits the group into two *branches*, based upon the independent variable (in our case, demographic/descriptive variable) that produced the greatest difference in the dependent variable (cluster) at that node. As you might imagine, with 12 independent variables, the resulting tree diagram for each AID analysis in our study covered an entire wall. Consequently, the AID results printed in the book have been simplified to show only the paths producing differences of greatest practical significance.

Limitations of the study

Every research study has limitations. In fact, it has been said that the mark of a good researcher, especially in the social sciences, is the ability to make sound, well-reasoned compromises. Our study was no different from any other in that respect. Though many of the limitations and compromises have already been mentioned, this section discusses them in greater depth.

Sampling frame

As indicated above, the identification of full-time youth ministers by the denominational and parachurch groups was, for many of the groups, quite difficult. In many cases, the initial estimate by the denominational office of their count of full-time youth ministers was extremely inaccurate. This study provided the impetus for several offices to update their mailing lists. Are we certain that we got a complete and accurate list of the full-time youth ministers in any of the denominational or parachurch bodies from which to draw our sample? No. Are we certain that the numbers sampled from those lists are precisely representative or proportional to the distribution of youth ministers in the country? No. Was it the best list available at the time without an extraordinary expenditure of time and money? Yes.

The sampling frame might also be critiqued as not having included the full breadth of Protestant denominations in the United States. It is true that many individual denominations were not represented. However, of the 14 U.S. Protestant denominational families empirically identified in *Ministry in America,* the original sampling frame of this study contained representatives from 11 of them (only Disciples of Christ, Free Church, and United Church of Christ were not represented). It is unfortunate that the small number of returns from some groups necessitated combining into only eight families, but it still can be argued that the core of Protestantism in the U.S. was well represented.

One might also argue that limiting the study to full-time youth ministers excludes a host of youth ministers and youth ministries. This is, in fact, true. But, as previously stated, this was a study of the *profession,* not avocation, of youth ministry. Furthermore, given the difficulties encountered in reaching full-time youth ministers with our survey, it is hard to imagine that a representative study of part-time youth ministers could be done at any reasonable cost.

Response rate

Ideally, the response rate to the study would have been 80 percent, and we had hoped for 60 percent. We used Dillman's methods of surveying precisely because they were designed, and have been demonstrated to achieve, those levels of response. The response rate to our questionnaire was somewhat less: 52 percent. This is not a small issue, in that we really don't know anything about nearly half of our sample. Had money and time permitted, we would have done a nonrespondent phone follow-up, but those resources were not available to us. So we must concede that this is a weakness of the study.

Sadly, our observation over the past 20 years indicates that response rates to most surveys began to drop severely in the mid-1990s. The survey industry is well aware of this growing problem, and the cause is fairly clear: with the explosion of customer satisfaction surveys, marketing surveys, and direct mail and phone marketing over the past dozen or so years, the American public is saturated with requests for information. Increasingly, many people are viewing any kind of survey as an invasion of their privacy and time, and they are simply saying, "No!" Our recent experience has been that even with multiple follow-up mailings that include updating undeliverable addresses with available information from both the U.S. Postal Service and multiple credit bureau databases, it is very frequently difficult to exceed 50 percent return rate in scientific studies within single organizations. From that perspective, a 52 percent return from such a wide range of organizations and settings is quite remarkable, and is indicative of the dedication of youth ministers today.

Also indicative of that dedication is the fact that the data formed such tight, meaningful item clusters. Formation of meaningful clusters *at all* provides significant evidence that the questionnaire was answered thoughtfully and carefully; otherwise there would have been random, nonsensical relationships among item responses. So although the response rate was somewhat less than we had hoped, it is clear that the persons who did respond took the survey very seriously and provided us with excellent data.

A further goal we had regarding response rate was to secure eight to ten respondents per questionnaire item. This is usually the minimum necessary to identify item clusters using the process we designed into this study (and used successfully in many past studies). The 2,416 respondents to the 243 items is almost exactly 10 respondents per item. In that respect, the response rate met our goal.

Cluster reliability

The usual target for the development of an item cluster is an internal consistency reliability (Cronbach's alpha) of 0.70 or greater. In this study, both the mean and median reliability across the 48 clusters was 0.76. The range was from 0.58 to 0.89, with 79.2 percent of the clusters having a reliability of 0.70 or greater, and 58.3 percent having a reliability of 0.75 or greater. These are excellent numbers. Rarely, in our over 30 years of experience, have clusters formed so cleanly, meaningfully, and tightly. The results "hang together," an important benchmark for studies of this type. We do not believe the cluster reliabilities to be a weakness or limitation of the study.

Group differences

The authors selected a difference of 3.0 or greater between groups on standardized cluster scores (mean = 50.0, standard deviation = 10.0) to be of practical significance for discussion in the book. In general, a difference of only 2.0 was large enough with this sample to be of statistical significance ($p < 0.05$). Clearly, selecting 3.0 is an arbitrary judgment, and one might argue for a different threshold, either higher or lower. Again, however, the group differences identified with that threshold were very consistent and made extremely good sense. From that perspective, we are comfortable with our decision.

Summary regarding limitations of the study

Finally, one must ask whether the limitations in the study affected the results and their generalizability. In any scientific discipline, the answer to that question ultimately depends upon other studies that attempt to replicate or use the results. In our case, this study was the first of its type in the field of youth ministry, so we cannot answer with certainty. We can, however, make some observations regarding the question, based upon our collective professional experience and knowledge.

In our judgment, the greatest weakness of the study is the response rate. We really do not know what effect the other 48 percent of the sample would have had on the results. However, the general level of cohesiveness of the clusters, as represented by the reliability estimates, indicates that the empirically derived conceptual *structure* applies generally across all the kinds of youth ministers in the respondent group. If the nonrespondents included, in large numbers, kinds of youth ministers that were not included among the respondents, then the structure we found might have been different if the return rate were significantly higher. We believe that it is highly unlikely that the nonrespondent group is that different. Therefore, in our opinion, the conceptual structure—the map of the domain of youth ministry—is quite likely generalizable to all full-time Protestant youth ministers.

The relative *level* of item and cluster scores, however, is another matter. The level of scores could be affected quite dramatically by the low response rate, depending upon the proportionality of kinds of youth ministers among the respondents versus the non-respondents. It is easy to hypothesize, for example, that the nonrespondent group included a greater proportion of overworked, inexperienced, harried youth ministers who simply did not have the time to complete the survey. If that were the case, then the level of item and cluster scores would have been quite different with a higher return. Whether the group comparisons would have changed as a result is unknown.

All things considered, we believe that this study was successful. The original objectives were achieved: a research base for the profession of youth ministry has been established; a strong conceptual model of youth ministers and youth ministry has been developed; we have been able to identify critical elements and issues which relate to successful youth ministry; and we have developed a data-based outline for curriculum for the training of youth ministers. We, the research team, are proud to present our work to the church.

1. Merton P. Strommen, *Five Cries of Youth* (San Francisco: HarperCollins, 1988); Merton P. Strommen and A. Irene Strommen, *Five Cries of Parents* (Minneapolis: Augsburg Youth and Family Institute, 1985).

2. Don A. Dillman, *Mail and Telephone Surveys: The Total Design Method* (New York: John Wiley & Sons, 1978).

3. H. Richard Niebuhr, *Christ in Culture* (New York: Harper & Row, 1951).

4. Dillman.

5. David S. Schuller, Merton P. Strommen, and Milo L. Brekke (eds.), *Ministry in America* (San Francisco: Harper & Row, 1980), 57-58.

6. J. Loevinger, "A Systematic Approach to the Construction and Evaluation of Tests of Ability," Psychological Monograph 61, 4 (1947), iii, 49; J. Loevinger, "The Technique of Homogeneous Tests Compared with Some Aspects of Scale Analysis and Factor Analysis," Psychological Bulletin 45 (1948), 507-529; P. DuBois, J. Loevinger, and G. Gleser, "The Construction of Homogeneous Keys for a Biographical Inventory," Research Bulletin 52, 18 (Lackland Air Force Base, San Antonio: U.S.A.F Human Resources Center, 1952).

7. Niebuhr.

8. J.A. Sonquist, *Multivariate Model Building* (Ann Arbor: University of Michigan, 1970).

Bibliography

Benson, Peter L., and Eugene C. Roehlkepartain. *Beyond Leaf Raking: Learning to Serve/Serving to Learn*. Nashville: Abingdon Press, 1993.

Benson, Peter L., and Carolyn H. Eklin. *Effective Christian Education: A National Study of Protestant Congregations*. Minneapolis: Search Institute, 1990.

Black, Wesley. *An Introduction to Youth Ministry*. Nashville: Broadman Press, 1991.

Boshers, Bo. *Student Ministry for the 21st Century*. Grand Rapids, Michigan: Zondervan Publishing House, 1997.

Cailliet, Emile. *Young Life*. New York: Harper and Row, 1963.

Chromey, Rick. *Youth Ministry in Small Churches*. Loveland, Colorado: Group Publishing, 1990.

Courtoy, Charles Webb. "A Historical Analysis of the Three Eras of Mainline Protestant Youth Work in America as a Basis for Clues for the Future of Youth Work." Dissertation. (Divinity School of Vanderbilt University: 1976.)

Covey, Stephen R. *The 7 Habits of Highly Effective People*. New York: Simon & Schuster, 1989.

Cressey, F.G. *The Church and Young Men*. Chicago: Fleming H. Revell, 1903.

Dausey, Gary (ed.). *The Youth Minister's Source Book*. Chicago: Moody Press, 1983.

Dean, Kenda Creasy, and Ron Foster. *The Godbearing Life: The Art of Soul Tending for Youth Ministry*. Nashville: Upper Room Books, 1998.

DeVries, Mark. *Family-Based Youth Ministry*. Downers Grove: Intervarsity Press, 1994.

Dunn, Richard R., and Mark Senter. *Reaching a Generation for Christ*. Chicago: Moody Press, 1997.

Edelwich, J. *Burnout: Stages of Disillusionment in the Caring Professions.* New York: Human Sciences Press, 1980.

Elkind, David. *All Grown Up and No Place to Go.* Reading, Massachusetts: Addison-Wesley, 1984.

Erikson, Erik H. *Identity: Youth and Crisis.* New York: Norton, 1968.

Faracas, Steve, and Jean Johnson. *Kids These Days: What Americans Really Think about the Next Generation.* New York: Public Agenda, 1997.

Fields, Doug. "The Power of God." *Youthworker,* July/August 14, 6 (1998).

Fields, Doug. *Purpose-Driven Youth Ministry.* Grand Rapids, Michigan: Zondervan Publishing House, 1998.

Hill, Paul. *Up the Creek with a Paddle.* Minneapolis: Augsburg Fortress, 1998.

Hill, Paul. "Youth Ministry Is Spelled A.D.U.L.T. R.E.N.E.W.A.L." Paper. (2000).

Holmen, Mark A. *How to Be an Effective Youth Leader.* Minneapolis: Augsburg Youth and Family Institute, 1996.

Jenny, Gerald (1928). *The Young People's Movement.* Augsburg Publishing House, Minneapolis, MN.

Jones, Karen Elaine. "A Study of the Difference Between Faith Maturity Scale and Multidimensional Self-Concept Scale Scores for Youth Participating in Two Denominational Ministry Projects." Dissertation. (Southern Baptist Theological Seminary: 1998.)

Jud, Gerald J., Edgar W. Mills, Genevieve Walters Burch, and Earl C. Brewer. *Ex-Pastors: Why Men Leave the Parish Ministry.* Boston, Massachusetts: Pilgrim Press, 1970.

Laliberte, Richard. "Men and Women Managing Conflict," *Relationships: An Open and Honest Guide to Healthy Connections.* New York: McGraw-Hill, 1989.

Lambert, Daniel. *Determining the Research Needs in North American Christian Youth Ministry: A Delphi Study.* Dissertation. (University of Cincinnati: 1999.)

Lamport, Mark A. "What Is the Status of Professional Youth Ministry?" in Richard Dunn and Mark Senter (eds.). *Reaching a Generation for Christ*. Chicago: Moody Press, 1997.

Lawrence, Rick. "Why Youth Ministry Should Be Abolished," *Group*, July/August 21, 5 (1995).

Lawrence, Rick. "The Money Game," *Group*, November/December 26, 1 (1999).

Martinson, Roland. *Effective Youth Ministry: A Congregational Approach*. Minneapolis: Augsburg Publishing House, 1988.

Martinson, Roland. "The Role of the Family in the Faith and Value Formation of Children," in *Leadership Manual*. Minneapolis: Youth and Family Institute, 1998.

Martinson, Roland. "Learning across Generations," in *Leadership Manual, The Child in Our Hands*. Minneapolis: Youth and Family Institute, 1998.

McCarty, Robert J. *Survival in Youth Ministry*. Winona, Minnesota: St. Mary's Press, 1994.

McGee, Robert S. "Our Search for Significance," in Les and Leslie Parrott (eds). *Relationships: An Open and Honest Guide to Healthy Connections*. New York: McGraw-Hill, Inc., 1993.

Murnion, Philip J. *Parish Ministers: Laity and Religious on Parish Staffs*. New York: National Pastoral Life Center, 1992.

Muss, Rolf E. *Theories of Adolescence*. New York: Random House, 1988.

Napier, Augustus Y., and Carl A. Whitaker. *The Family Crucible*. New York: Bantam books, 1978.

Niebuhr, H. Richard. *Christ in Culture*. New York: Harper & Row, 1951.

Otis, Frank. *The Development of the Young Peoples Movement*. Chicago: University of Chicago Press, 1917.

Parrott III, Les. *Helping the Struggling Adolescent: A Counseling Guide*. Grand Rapids: Zondervan Publishing House, 1993.

Laliberte, Richard. "Men and Women Managing Conflict," in Les and Leslie Parrott (eds.). *Relationships: An Open and Honest Guide to Healthy Connections*. New York: McGraw-Hill,Inc., 1993.

Peters, Clarence. *Developments of the Youth Programs of the Lutheran Churches in America*. Dissertation. (Concordia Seminary: 1951.)

Rahn, Dave. "The Best in Youth Ministry Training." *Group*, November/December 22, 1 (1995).

Rahn, Dave. "Parafamily Youth Ministry," *Group*, May/June 22, 4 (1996).

Rahn, Dave, and Terry Linhart. *Contagious Faith: Empowering Student Leadership in Youth Evangelism*. Loveland, Colorado: Group Publishing, 2000.

Rinehart, Mike. "W.O.L.F.: The Balanced Ministry Proverb," in *Up the Creek With a Paddle*. Minneapolis: Augsburg Fortress, 1998.

Roehlkepartain, Jolene L. *Youth Ministry: Its Impact on Church Growth*. Loveland, Colorado: Group Publishing, 1989.

Saint Clair, Barry. "How Can We Find and Support Volunteers?" in Richard R. Dunn and Mark Senter III (eds.). *Reaching a Generation for Christ*. Moody Press: Chicago, IL., 1997.

Schwarz, Christian A. *Natural Church Development: A Guide to Eight Essential Qualities of Healthy Churches*. Emmelsbull, Germany: C & P Publishing, 1998; Published in USA by Carol Stream, Illinois: ChurchSmart Resources, 1996.

Senter III, Mark. *The Coming Revolution in Youth Ministry: And Its Radical Impact on the Church*. Wheaton, Illinois: Victor Books, 1992.

Spaulding, Helen, and Olga Haley. *A Study of Youth Work in Protestant Churches*. Report. (Chicago: National Council of Churches in the U.S.A.: 1955.)

Strommen, Merton P. *Five Cries of Youth*. San Francisco: HarperCollins, 1988.

Strommen, Merton P. *A Study of Generations*. Minneapolis: Augsburg Publishing House, 1980.

Strommen, Merton P., and Shelby Andress. *Five Shaping Forces: Using Organizational Dynamics to Do More With Less.* Minneapolis: Search Institute, 1980.

Strommen, Merton P., and Richard Hardel. *Passing on the Faith: A Radical New Model for Youth and Family Ministry.* Winona: St. Marys Press, 2000.

Taylor, Bob R. *The Work of the Minister of Youth.* Nashville: Convention Press, 1982.

Thompson, Marjorie. *Family: The Forming Center.* Nashville: Upper Room Books, 1989.

Tierney, Hayes Taylor. *Making a Difference: An Impact Study of Big Brothers/Big Sisters.* Philadelphia: Public/Private Ventures, 1995.

Trabert, G.H. *Church History for the People.* Columbus: Lutheran Book Concern, 1923.

Volf, Miroslav. "Floating Along?" *The Christian Century.* 117, 11 (April 5, 2000).

Walker, Gary. "Meeting of the Funders of the Big Brothers-Big Sisters Study." November 15, 1995.

White, James. *Intergenerational Religious Education.* Birmingham, Alabama: Religious Education Press, 1988.

Wyckoff, C. Campbell, and Don Richter. *Religious Education Ministry with Youth,* Birmingham, Alabama: Religious Education Press, 1982.

Yaconelli, Mark. "Youth Ministry: A Contemplative Approach," *The Christian Century.* (April 21-28, 1999).

Yaconelli, Mark. "God Encounters: How Spiritual Exercises Can Change Your Kids," *Youthworker,* July/August (1999).

and change of philosophies, 122
and commitment to Christ, 132
and development of attitudes of respect and
   love, 184–185
discarding of youth organizations by, 146, 147
and disinterested and apathetic youth, 64–65
early professional youth group leaders, 30–31
early youth groups, 29
and family relations, 173
and female ministers, 163
and large youth groups, 65–66
minister age and experience, 233
minister training, 320
and mission statements, 123–124
and organizational climate, 266
and public witness and ministry among youth,
   192
and purpose-driven youth ministry, 71–72
and service-oriented youth, 188
and spiritual development of youth, 162
Walther League, 29, 147
and youth commitment to Christ, 158
and youth ownership, 167

M

Marriage and youth ministers, 91–95
Martinson, Roland, 122–123, 169–170,
   175–176, 272
Mather, Cotton, 27–28
McGee, Robert, 96–97
Mead, Margaret, 147
Men and Women Managing Conflict, 91–92
Methodist Church, 49, 68–69, 146, 158
   and denominational youth organizations,
      147, 150
   and development of attitudes of respect and
      love, 185
   and family relations, 173
   minister age and experience, 233
   and organizational climate, 266
   and public witness and ministry among
      youth, 192
   and service-oriented youth, 188
   and spiritual development of youth, 162
   and youth ownership, 167
Ministers
   . *See also* individual denominations; Volunteers;
   Youth ministry
   and administration and management skills,
      317–324
   and age and experience, 230–234
   approaches to family relations, 173–174
   and biblical knowledge, 315–316
   building confidence and self-esteem among,
      89–91, 98–100, 205–207, 236–238, 243–245
   building feelings of qualification for youth
      ministry among, 104–105

building organization skills among, 108–109
building stronger family relations among,
   94–95
burnout among, 75, 109–114
and change of philosophies, 121–122
and change through contemplation, 120–121
characteristics of, 163, 188–189
and congregational support, 274–277, 287–291
and creative response to youth culture,
   207–209
determining priorities for, 119–120
and disconnect between youth and church,
   53–60
discontent and turnover among, 34–37
and disinterested and apathetic youth, 60–72
dual kingdom approach to, 214–216
early youth, 29–34
and education and training, 238–241,
   303–306, 314
effective relationships between parents and,
   217–219, 231–234
and effective youth relationships, 216–217,
   236–238
and entertainment-based ministry, 67–72
and family relations, 168–176
feeling disorganized, 105–109
feeling unqualified for youth ministry, 100–105
and feelings of personal inadequacy, 86–91,
   95–100
female, 102–103, 108, 161, 162–163, 228–230,
   322–324, 326
and fringe benefits, 74
and inadequate finances for youth ministry,
   72–76
and interpersonal relationships, 212–219
and job performance, 203–205, 235–236,
   243–245
and job satisfaction, 36–37, 41–43
knowledge of family development and parental
   training skills, 316–317
lack of respect and personal support for youth,
   76–80
and large youth groups, 64–65, 78–79, 104,
   158–160
and lead teams, 52
loss of confidence among, 95–100
male, 162–163, 229–230, 322–324, 326
and ministry goals, 199–201
and motivation by God's calling, 214–216
and networking, 112, 221–222
and opportunities for peer mentoring relationships, 327–330
and opportunities to gain new ideas, 324–327
and organizational climate, 261–272
and parental involvement, 217–219, 291–295
and perceived importance of spiritual
   development, 133–135